The

DIGITAL SCRIBE

A WRITER'S GUIDE TO ELECTRONIC MEDIA

CD AT REAR

LIMITED WARRANTY AND DISCLAIMER OF LIABILITY

The DIGITAL SCRIBE

A WRITER'S GUIDE TO ELECTRONIC MEDIA

JAMES RAY MUSGRAVE

AP PROFESSIONAL
AP Professional is a division of Academic Press, Inc.

Boston   San Diego   New York
London   Syndey   Tokyo   Toronto

AP PROFESSIONAL
An Imprint of ACADEMIC PRESS, INC.
A Division of HARCOURT BRACE & COMPANY

ORDERS (USA and Canada): 1-800-3131-APP or APP@ACAD.COM
AP Professional Orders: 6277 Sea Harbor Dr., Orlando, FL 32821-9816

Europe/Middle East/Africa: 0-11-44 (0) 181-300-3322
Orders: AP Professional, 24–28 Oval Rd., London NW1 7DX

Japan/Korea: 03-3234-3911-5
Orders: Harcourt Brace Japan, Inc., Ichibancho Central Building 22-1, Ichibancho Chiyoda-ku, Tokyo 102

Australia: 02-517-8999
Orders: Harcourt Brace & Co. Australia, Locked Bag 16, Marrickville, NSW 2204, Australia

Other International: (407) 345-3800
AP Professional Orders: 6277 Sea Harbor Dr., Orlando, FL 32821-9816

Editorial: 1300 Boylston St., Chestnut Hill, MA 02167; (617) 232-0500

Web: http://www.apnet.com/

United Kingdom Edition published by
ACADEMIC PRESS LIMITED
24–28 Oval Road, London NW1 7DX

Library of Congress Cataloging-in-Publication Data
Musgrave, James Ray.
    The Digital Scribe: a writer's guide to electronic media / James
Ray Musgrave.
        p.   cm.
    Includes index.
    ISBN 0-12-512255-1 (alk. paper). —ISBN 0-12-512256-X (CD-Rom)
    1. Multimedia systems.   2. Technical writing.   I. Title
QA76.575.M88   1996
070.5'79--dc20   95-47341
                                                                      CIP

Printed in the United States of America
96 97 98 99 IP 9 8 7 6 5 4 3 2 1

Author's Biography

James Ray Musgrave is a college English teacher and writing consultant in San Diego who develops multimedia software for the San Diego and Imperial Counties Multimedia Consortium. He was a Communications Specialist in the United States Navy, and he is interested in seeing that his readers are able to profit from the cutting edge technology being developed today. He has worked as a writing consultant to business and industry for over fifteen years; for five years, Mr. Musgrave was the Supervisor, Management Development, at the Industrial Relations Center, California Institute of Technology. He has also been a marketing director, a sports writer, a TV newswriter, and a magazine editor. He is married to Ellen, also a college English instructor, and they live in San Carlos, California.

Contents

Preface

In a recent futuristic article by management guru Peter F. Drucker (*The Atlantic Monthly*, November 1994), the author coined the term *knowledge worker*, for those professionals in today's economy who have the expertise to become independent from both government and from their employers:

> [I]n the knowledge society the employees—that is, knowledge workers—own the tools of production. Marx's great insight was that the factory worker does not and cannot own the tools of production, and therefore is "alienated." Increasingly, the true investment in the knowledge society is not in machines and tools but in the knowledge of the knowledge worker. Without that knowledge the machines, no matter how advanced and sophisticated, are unproductive (Drucker, p. 71).

When I worked at Caltech's Industrial Relations Center back in the 1970s, Dr. Drucker was saying that business people were coming to a crossroads of information technology that would "put them back into the driver's seat." As usual, he was correct.

This book has developed because I, as a writer and teacher, could see that the new knowledge workers out there—the professionally independent entrepreneurs like you—need to be educated for the technology that has leapt ahead of them. The advent of the computer, the CD-ROM disc, the World Wide Web, the Internet, and multimedia paperless publishing all tell me there is a need to give knowledge workers the writing skills necessary to use these tools to their greatest advantage.

Spending over 15 years as a writing consultant and as a teacher of college students, I have attempted to train both audiences so they could own the skills to cope with the information bonanza that awaits them at the edge of the vast communications network called the *information highway*. I know from experience that unless they are equipped to write in the correct way, for the correct audience, they could figuratively drown in the communications tidal wave.

The days of the standard teaching of rhetorical modes have almost ended. Most modern schools are today equipping their students with computer composition tools like Intel Networks, PC-Chalkboards, Collaborative Writing Software, and a variety of other high-technology tools. The old rule of computer education applies—find the software you need to teach; then, find the hardware to use it.

I presently teach a composition class on a computer network. The next step, as I see it, is to remove the classroom (and the high administrative costs that go with it) and use the modem and the Internet to teach. Some schools have already done this, such as Oberlin College in Ohio, where each freshman is given his or her personal PC upon entrance to the university. They keep their entire four years of learning on their own laptop! New York University has also implemented instruction on-line, giving students who hate commuting into the city a chance at learning from home. We have certainly come a long way from the days of furiously scribbling notes in the back rows of dusty lecture halls. It is becoming—actually—a "plugged-in" generation of knowledge seekers, who can reach around the world for their information sources.

I can remember when it was "tune in, turn on, and drop out." Today, knowledge entrepreneurs have spun Timothy Leary's adage around: instead, they "drop out" of the public and private sectors to become independent, professional consultants. They "turn on" to the Internet and multimedia; they "tune in" to the world of almost instantaneous communication via the modem with multimedia dimensions. What a trip!

ACKNOWLEDGMENTS

I want to thank all my brothers and sisters out there in cyberspace for their encouragement and creative input. I especially want to thank Jenifer Niles, my editor at AP Professional, and her assistant, Jacquelyn Young, for their tireless effort going over my writing and giving superb suggestions and responses. My agents at Waterside Productions, Matthew Wagner and David Fugate, have been there on-line when I needed them, and they will be sending me my royalty payments as well! And my wife, Ellen Bernabei-Musgrave, or "the Bible Lady" (not to be confused with the Church Lady of SNL fame), who has been appropriately bugging me when I was lost in the Net browser or playing a CD game, when I should have been writing. She is my love and my real (not virtual) wife. Without her, I would probably not have kept at it. I also want to thank my stepson, Ari, who can be reached at our e-mail if you want original art designs for your home pages or for your home from a really talented young artist (musgrave@mail.sdsu.edu).

And thank you, my dear reader, who shall make me proud out there on the live wire, with your creative home pages, your exciting stories, and your fascinating research. Please send me your success stories and your suggestions, so I can make the next edition of this text even better. With computers, the technology is changing and improving so rapidly that you can blink and lose some innovations. You can be my "blinkers" out there. I guess that was what people meant when they talked about the "thousand points of light."

Introduction

If you are a writer who needs to see his or her name under a headline or see the hypertext or Web pages come alive with creative flair, then this book is for you. I have attempted to give a resource and a learning tool to the writing professional and the writing novice who are transitioning into the worlds of multimedia and the information superhighway.

In Part I, I will take you through a general overview of what opportunities are out there in cyberspace for writers, into a specific tutorial that covers the steps needed to produce the best writing for this medium. Included in this part of the book will be lessons aimed at training you to think with your senses and prewriting techniques that have proved successful in business writing courses and in college composition courses. I include a detailed exploration into hypertext and hypermedia and how these terms apply to electronic writing. I have also provided you with step-by-step lessons on creating digital video, storyboarding, and a special chapter on "How to Create Your Own Home Page on the Internet." There are sample responses at the end of some chapters for you to check your answers.

The next section (Part II) will explore how surveying your market is worth the time and effort. Many marketers on the Net forget this important step, and I will show you what you should do to make certain your market is out there. Whether you are a freelancer, a publisher, or a product entrepreneur, this section will assist you in your market research. This section will also show you the software that is out there and how you can get it. I will also evaluate the best software on the market for the digital scribe who takes writing seriously and who wants the least amount of technical hassle. The final part of this section will focus on new ideas for you to explore as a commercial venture. With the advent of Netscape Communication's plug-in applications like Hot Java, Shockwave for Director, and the new Netscape Navigator Gold, the writer on the Net has even more opportunities to cash in as a developer of commercial home pages and multimedia catalogs for businesses. See examples from my own Web site (http://www.geocities.com/Athens/1210) and follow me on a step-by-step description of how I set it up (Part I).

I will also cover the legalities that the digital scribe must know, in Part III. A complete governmental guide to copyright law and serial law will be covered in depth. You can set up your own magazine, newsletter, and bookstore with the information supplied in this section. This allows you to bypass the publisher and reap the profits for yourself.

Part IV will cover the journalistic opportunities out there for you. I will cover the varieties of writing that are particularly attractive in this new medium, and I will supply you with all the check-off sheets you need to get started on your way to fame and fortune. This section will cover self-help books, biographies, travel books, magazine articles, sports, current events, features, on-line fiction, and other types of Net writing you can do for fun and profit. The final part of my book will explore the ways you can submit your work in cyberspace. Besides the regular channels (electronic book publishers and e-zines), I will also show you how to set up your own cyberstation—and you do not have to own a computer to do it! Included in this section are mailing lists to subscribe to on the Net and the variety of electronic publishing services out there for you to use. In addition, I try to separate the good publications from the bad, so you don't have to find out the hard way.

Part

I

Prewriting

1

The Medium Is the Message

YOU ARE WHAT YOU WRITE

This chapter will cover the following:

- How to get others to sell your e-books
- Courses in multimedia authoring
- What creativity means

You must realize that when you are on-line, the medium becomes the message. You will discover that the sophisticated user and potential consumer on the network expects the latest technology. That means you must be able to write your message using multimedia "image enhancements."

If you want to compile and disseminate e-books yourself by working directly with an on-line virtual bookstore and fulfillment agency, try SoftLock, Inc., 144 Grubb Road, Malvern, PA 19355. Its Internet address is http://www.awa.com. With SoftLock, you receive monthly sales reports and payment (whatever you charge, subtract $1.50 and 20% of the purchase price for each copy sold). SoftLock also displays e-books you create on its Internet World Wide Web Server for a $10 registration fee. I will be discussing SoftLock later in this book, in the section on ways you can protect your sales documents from piracy and ensure a definitely happy customer.

 As a special service, I am including a sample multimedia educational product, Grammar Made Easy, Module One (for Windows). This project was developed under the auspices of the San Diego and Imperial Counties Community Colleges Association (SDICCA), of which I am a member. I am also including sample multimedia software on the CD, as well as preformatted mailing labels to reputable literary agents (no reading fees). Also on the CD are demos of HTML and VRML software—the latest applications to hit the Net. Note that you cannot use the Macromedia demo or the Asymetrix ToolBook applications without having these applications' run-time viewers on your computer already, but you may see the full demo of Q-Media, one of the best multimedia products for under $200 that I have ever seen (version 3.0 can even import Microsoft PowerPoint Presentations). I have also included some excellent shareware applications: SoftLock, Ares, E-pub, Dart, and Iris.

It may be of interest to you that there is a certificate program now in place at one of the colleges where I teach. Grossmont Community College, in El Cajon, California, now teaches "Multimedia Technology." It is one of the first courses in the nation to be offered to the community, and it shows how quickly this technology is taking off. If you need extensive training in this area, I highly recommend this type of course.

CREATIVITY DEFINED

However, before I get into the creative side of writing, I want to define *creativity* the way I see it. You see, we all possess creativity because creativity is nothing more than making playful connections in a logical and intelligent manner. The "playfulness" to which I am referring comes from the child within. You know, the fun-loving kid you left somewhere back in your past and promptly forgot about when you "matured" through the play-dooming experiences of high school and college, and then (gasp!) into a professional occupation of someone's choice (your child-self usually has little real say in this matter). This is the same creative kid who raised his hand vigorously in the third grade when the teacher asked if anyone could write poetry, but who looked down at his hands and mused to himself, "I wonder what kind of poet she really means—deconstructionist, absurdist, or the confession school?" when the college Literature 228 professor asked the same question in your sophomore class. By the time you reached college, you were drained of most of your creativity because the kid inside was sitting in the back seat of your brain bus, waiting to get off at the next playground, while you, the maturing adult, grew more and more responsible, orderly, and regimented in your thinking until you could no longer feel the thrill of almost peeing your pants at the thought of the brand new day spread out before you.

Now, instead of the excited type of creative awareness of the simple and brilliant wonder in life (what the Zen Buddhist people call *suchness*), you exile yourself to office politics, have a casual affair, or visit some adult playland (usually a bar, a New Year's or Christmas office party, or one of many other adult "games" out there), where you become "childish," rather than truly and creatively childlike.

Yes, but children are children, and adults are adults. What does creativity have to do with a child's state of mind? My definition of *creativity* says that you must first see life as a child would; in other words, you must be able to understand that life is, in fact, one big playground and that your writer's self simply uses that image to focus on, until you can use that playful attitude in your creative focus. Notice the word *focus*. This is the only element of reality from adulthood that can benefit the creative writer. Focus gets the job done. Focus gives you the necessary eye for organization and detail. Focus gets you moving and working hard toward that deadline. But focus will never—I repeat—never replace the creative spirit and vital energy of your childhood. However, the best writers are able to generate those creative energies and playful attitudes in their work, so that we the readers can luxuriously take a break from ourselves and learn what full enjoyment of existence really means!

Go ahead, I dare you. Watch a five- or six-year-old as he or she gets in touch with the universe. These children (and they are in us always!) instinctively trust in their higher powers (us) and promptly make their lives a fun-filled romp of interconnected bliss, where, if asked about what "love" means, these children will reply, "It means ya get shot by a arrow and walk around crazy all day." Or, when asked why engaged couples hold hands in the movies, they tell us, "So's their rings won't fall off. They paid too much money to lose them!" What adult could think of such creative answers? Not many that I know. But the child inside of you can think of a million snappy answers. This is the same child I will bring out in you in the following chapter.

I end this chapter with a note to you, the new digital scribe of the coming bold era in electronic communications: many multimedia software packages such as Macromedia's Author/Director and Asymetrix's Multimedia ToolBook are coming out with the technology that will enable you to create your own interactive publications and put them directly on the Internet to let the masses decide if you are a genius or not (see the chapter entitled "How to Create Your Own Home Page on the Net.") You will not have to worry about buying an agent a new car or giving away your rights to a publisher; you will be able to go directly to the buying public itself. This, in my estimation, will be the turning point for the digital scribe and

Drucker's knowledge worker. Your creativity will be the only ability keeping you from competing with the big boys. And creativity is what this book teaches you.

2

Techniques of Prewriting for Electronic Media

This chapter will cover the following:

- The Sign mind and the Design mind
- Clustering to access your Design mind
- The "trial-web shift"
- Unity through recurrence
- Using language rhythms
- Images and metaphors
- Creating tension
- Multimedia awareness development

Every writer, no matter what the experience level, has to face that same blank computer screen or white page each day. Prewriting is the process of coming to terms with that blankness and filling it with meaningful symbols. Those symbols, if you are a print media writer, are known as "words." However, if you are an electronic writer, a whole new world opens up to you, and you must also become familiar with how to prewrite for sound, touch, taste, and smell, in addition to the printed words.

I often use an unconventional paperback text in my Freshman Composition courses called *Writing the Natural Way*, written by Dr. Gabriele Lusser Rico. She subtitles this text *A Course in Enhancing Creativity and Writing Confidence.* I will be discussing the seven ways to release one's expressive powers that Rico says are necessary to the writer. If you can master the source of your inner creativity, then you can go on to produce documents that will blaze on the new electronic highways of technological opportunity.

THE SIGN MIND AND THE DESIGN MIND

Rico says that we produce different kinds of messages with the two halves or hemispheres of our brain: the Sign (left) mind and the Design (right) mind. In summary, the left hemisphere controls our sequential, one-at-a-time logic, or our linear thinking (Sign mind). It splits the world into identifiable, nameable bits and pieces. It also is controlled by rules and draws on preexisting fixed codes and accumulated, organized information. It further has the power of syntax, the grammatical stringing together of words. This side of our brain can remember complex motor sequences: it knows "how." It is expressive in words, but primarily words used as a sign: "A woman is a female human being."

In contrast, the Design mind (right hemisphere) is an all-at-once processor of information and looks at the whole: a face. It connects the world into related wholes rather than seeing individual parts. It is analogic: it sees correspondences and resemblances. It is receptive to qualitative, unbounded aspects of the world: feeling states. It charts the emotional nuances of thought rather than the informational. Thus, it produces imagistic thinking. It also uses transformative, open-ended ideation, drawing on unbounded qualitative patterns that are not organized into sequences but that cluster around images of crystallized feelings. It has limited verbal syntax but responds to words as images or sentences recalled as a single unit, such as the words of a song, a poem, or a jingle. It can remember complex images, but it is mute—it uses pictures, not words. It discovers "what." It is receptive to words as design: "wide warm woman, white-thighed. Wooed and wed. Wife . . . " (John Updike).

The corpus callosum serves as the connecting point between these two halves of our brain. It allows them to communicate with each other at the rate of thousands of impulses per second, but it can also inhibit this informational flow so we can focus our talents on a particular task requiring the use of one side. For example, the idea for this book came when I saw that the world of linear computers needed a boost from the right hemisphere world of imagination. I saw that I could write a book that would serve as a metaphorical corpus callosum for the two halves of the writing world: the left hemisphere–dominated world of business, engineering, and science and the right hemisphere–dominated world of literature, film, and art. I saw that many professionals in the left, or Sign, world needed to be able to think creatively and to *design* documents that affected the feeling side of their readers and users. Conversely, many right, or Design, world professionals needed to learn to think more logically and learn that unless ideas were planned out sequentially, no great vision would come to life. In other words, as Henry David Thoreau once said, "You may build your castles in the air, but then you must lay the foundations for them here on earth."

I saw that the media in the computer industry was replete with a tremendous number of creative linear "gadgets" that let you link up with just about everything but that very little content creativity was out there. The need remained to teach the basics of a new kind of writing, and this book addresses that new need.

CLUSTERING TO ACCESS YOUR DESIGN MIND

Clustering is the process that Rico says is a natural function of the brain's need to associate images to find meaning in pictures or images that come from our subconscious. The "clusters" are the random associations that spring to mind around a nucleus or core ideation, in the form of a word or a short phrase. Engineers and computer scientists can best associate the concept with the flow chart, but there is one basic difference: clustering is a totally free and uninhibited process of brainstorming, whereas a flow chart has a definite *linear progression* leading to an end goal. Both processes have a goal in mind, however, and both processes can be mapped out on paper or on a computer.

In fact, interactive game designers use a form of clustering when they plan their game ideas. In the book *Interactive Writer's Handbook* by Wimberley and Samsel, for example, the design structures and paths for gaming are given in a clustering type of relationship (pages 140–146). This is to interrelate all the paths so the user gets the feeling of an intrinsic harmony and organization to the overall structure.

As a result, clustering is a process of brainstorming ideas that is not without structure or meaning. However, I do want to emphasize that your mind must be unstructured and unfettered when you do the initial imagining to get the associations. This is extremely important for application in electronic media because the digital scribe is working with much more than just the written words as symbols of meaning. He or she must also visualize in a sensory and emotionally stimulating way, in the same way you will learn in the first part of this book.

I will now give you the chance to try your hand at clustering. I will choose the "nucleus" words and you will cluster the associations that come to mind. Place your clustering associations in small circles on a page around the word, visually similar to the way protons and electrons form around a molecule's nucleus or planets revolve around a star. See how natural this all is? The words you must find associations for are *digital scribe*. I chose this term because it is central to my book and its purpose. Place these two words in the center of a sheet of blank paper and draw a circle around them. Then, let your mind go free, and perhaps close your eyes. What pictures do you see that you can associate with this concept? Do not censor what at first you might think are crazy associations. You will discover that the right hemisphere of your brain will find connections that will amaze you! However, you must use your left hemisphere to give the pictures you imagine some definable meaning that can be expressed in one or, at most, a few words. Remember. Your Design mind is at work initially, picking up random messages from your past, bits of songs, bites of poetry, pictures from life. But once you have a picture, you must use your Sign mind to focus in and name that experience or feeling, so you can put it as a cluster on the page. You will see what you can do with all of this creative energy very shortly. I will include a sample response at the end of this chapter.

Now that you have a good selection of clusters around your nucleus concept, *digital scribe*, I want you to search for what Rico calls the "aha!" or "trial-web shift" experience. This is when you read over your clustered associations and "discover!" what you want to write. In other words, as the writer, you are the one responsible for determining the thesis or topic of your message. This trial-web concept means that you have connected the thoughts about your possible writing topic, and you are now ready to see how you can focus and write about those clusters that most intrigue you in some logical and "left hemisphere" fashion (the web shift experience). For example, here is an exercise for you to see how clustering leads to the trial-web shift.

Trial-Web Shift Exercise

Suppose you have clustered the following random details: fat man, airplane, woman, bathroom, emergency, pilot.

Try to come up with a story that can be created using these details. Write it out in script or story form to create associations (a story) out of random details.

If you had not done the clustering, then you could never have associated those people. And the trial-web shift was critical because it is the Design mind's way of associating and communicating the images in a meaningful and creative way. However, the Sign mind gave you the words to express the pictures, and it also supplied you with the step-by-step approach that led to the end of the story. Thus, the Sign and Design minds work in harmony to produce the best possible result.

You can think of the trial-web shift as the Design mind's way of coming up with the thesis or message you want to communicate, using the bits and pieces of your clusters that intrigue you the most. The clusters, therefore, serve as the parts you use in a creative way to communicate an interesting message, story, or a complete vision (as in visual art).

Now draw your own cluster around *digital scribe* and then write a one-paragraph vignette that communicates the interesting things you see from your collection of clusters, just as you wrote the story based on the above exercise's clusters. Your creation need not be a script or story, however, unless you are so inclined.

RECURRENCE: A WAY TO UNIFY YOUR WRITING

Rico mentions another technique that she terms *recurrence*. This has also been called the *natural rhythm of life*. We are able to capture this natural repetition of sounds, motion, and feeling very easily in our childhoods. You can probably recall the way you were always humming or singing some rhyme or sing-song ditty when you were small. This is our human ability to recognize the power of recurrence in our communications. Advertisers are also well aware of this phenomenon. In fact, many award-winning, highly creative ads do not sell their products because the creators of the ads forgot about the power of recurrence. But everybody remembers the recurring jingle that we can sing at a moment's notice, repeating the telephone number, address, and the name of the product or sales location as if we were little kids again.

Poetry is probably the foremost example of the power of recurrence in our communications. Pattern recognition is best demonstrated when the author has something musical and whimsical to say. When Shakespeare gives us, "It was a lover and his lass, With a hey, and a ho, and hey nonino, That o'er the green corn-field did pass, In spring time, the only pretty ring time, When birds do sing, hey ding a ding, ding, Sweet lovers love the spring" (*As You Like It*, Act V, Scene 3), we are hearing the master craftsman giving us a song that we will remember for the "spring time, the only pretty ring time," and "birds do sing, hey ding a ding, ding, Sweet lovers love the spring." The recurrence of those images and sounds makes us want to tap our toes or hum along, even without music. This is the power of properly placed recurrent sounds and words.

The digital scribe can learn from this. To communicate on the electronic superhighway, one must be ready to combine lyrical prose with music, and what better way than to use recurrence? We are seeing more VRML (virtual reality markup language) being used on the Internet, and soon our home pages will be nothing more than shopping malls, museums, and theme parks, where the user can browse, shop, and ride at leisure, taking in all the sights, sounds, and wonders that the scribes and developers can create. What better way to do this so that your visitor will remember the experience than by using recurrence to reinforce the poetry of the language you use?

Exercise

For your exercise, I want you to imagine you are creating a VRML world using Home Space Builder or Virtus WalkThrough, or some other VRML modeler. Your task is to write some poetic lyrics to go with pictures you will hang on the walls of your building. First, what type of building will the visitor view? Second, what picture will you hang for them to click on in order to hear your ditty or recurrent lyric? Some of you may also be musicians, and you can feel free to orchestrate your words as well with a little tune. However, it is not required. Write four or five lines of prose that use recurrent repetition to reinforce the image you are communicating. You may check the sample answer at the end of the chapter.   ■

LANGUAGE RHYTHMS: THE BEAT WORDS CAN DANCE TO

Robert Louis Stevenson referred to rhythms of sentences as "the pattern of sound in time." In the womb, we could hear the sound of our mother's voice as she sang, talked, and laughed. This feeling continued into our lives as we were rocked, sung to, talked to, and enchanted, until we were actually "bubbling over" with babbling enthusiasm and loquacious grins. Japanese women, in particular, believe that by playing classical music while pregnant they will influence the yet-to-be-born youngster to appreciate good music. This love for rhythm stays with us throughout our lives.

Jim Crosswhite of the Writing Program at the University of California, San Diego, claims that, contrary to popular belief, students are actually doing more than mastering the basics of English and are sophisticated in grasping the technical aspects of writing. He complains, however, that they rarely write authoritatively, honestly, or in their own voices. In the framework of this chapter, "voiceless" writing could be called Sign-mind (left hemisphere) writing in the extreme. The active participation of your Design mind in the writing process adds authenticity as you listen with your inner ear and see with your inner eye. When our Sign and Design minds learn to cooperate, our words take on the rhythm and resonance that Peter Elbow (father of "freewriting") insists are essential to voice: "Real voice is whatever yields resonance, whatever makes the words bore through" (Rico, page 136).

When I was an undergraduate, one professor gave us linguistics students an assignment that had us imitate the voice and style of a popular author of our choosing. We were told to use a common fable or story and then to retell that story using the "voice and rhythm" of our chosen author.

I chose John Steinbeck, and my piece to retell was the story of "The Three Little Pigs." Steinbeck's rhythm was very easy to copy, and I had no trouble duplicating the flowing nature images and long, metaphorical sentences that were the mark of this man's unique voice. Here is a short passage from that paper:

> And when it came time to go out into the country to vacation, the third little pig decided he would stay at home and build his house. He would let his two idle brothers drink rotgut whiskey, chase skirts, and generally play the fiddling grasshopper to his industrious ant. He was one old pig who believed in weighing a pound of prevention and staying out of the devil's workshop. You never knew when some lone wolf was going to try to take it all away from you, and he, for one, was going to be prepared!

Listen to the sounds and rhythms of one Will Shakespeare:

> Blow, winds, and crack your cheeks! rage! blow! You cataracts and hurricanoes, spout till you have drenched our steeples, drowned the cocks! Your sulphurous and thought-executing fires, vaunt-couriers to oak-cleaving thunderbolts, singe my white head! And thou, all-shaking thunder, smite flat the thick rotundity o' the world! Crack Nature's molds, all germens spill at once, that make ingrateful man! (*King Lear,* Act III, Scene 2).

If it amuses you to read this rhythmic chant, it may amuse you further to be "sworn a foul curse" in the style of Shakespeare. The Internet has a Shakespeare home page (http://www.yahoo.com/Arts/ Humanities/Literature/Authors/Shakespeare_William) where you can be cursed at in the bard's distinct style. You can even leave your own curse, as I did, and show that nocturnal scum what a really accursed wretch he is!

Parallel rhythms are some of the simplest and most powerful forms. The Sign-mind principle behind parallel rhythms is this: let words and phrases seek their own kind—noun to noun, verb to verb, and so forth. For example,

A *jug* of wine, a *loaf* of bread, and *thou* (nouns/pronoun)

Eat, drink and *be merry!* (verbs)

I came, I saw, I conquered! (clauses)

However, the appeal of parallel form for the patterning Design mind goes deeper still, into the emotional and aesthetic senses; the structure of parallel forms is not only explainable in terms of grammatical constructs but is also highly audible and memorable. This is very important to the digital scribe, who must always think about how words can be constructed so they can link up with the other senses. As I mentioned earlier, VRML and, to a lesser degree, HTML, pose unique challenges to the writer in electronic media. Unless one can understand the power of parallel structures and rhythms, one will have a difficult time communicating in the circumspect way needed for the greatest aesthetic and emotional appeal inside these rather geometric and isolating structures. But perhaps the most important thing to the digital scribe is the tremendous tearing hurry that most digital readers are in. You have 15 seconds (the duration of the short-term memory) before the reader clicks on a hyperlink looking for something more exciting. Attraction, retention, and communication of the message—in that order—are the key factors. By using the parallel forms suggested, you can provide the interest and the aesthetic appeal to keep the digital reader glued to your screen.

Therefore, not only can the writer repeat parallel nouns, verbs, and phrases to create interesting combinations and rhythmic effects, one can also combine feelings and emotions to gain powerful, linguistic balance and sensory meaning. Edgar Allan Poe is one of the best American writers of this kind of emotionally rhythmic language. Listen to the final stanza of "Annabel Lee":

> For the moon never beams without bringing me dreams
>   Of the beautiful Annabel Lee;
> And the stars never rise but I see the bright eyes
>   Of the beautiful Annabel Lee;
> And so, all the night-tide, I lie down by the side
> Of my darling, my darling, my life and my bride,
>   In her sepulchre there by the sea—
>   In her tomb by the side of the sea.

Note how Poe repeats the feelings of loneliness (moon never beams, stars never rise, I lie down by the side) and of recurrence (Of the beautiful Annabel Lee). He also uses his thesaurus and gives us two different, yet concretely resonant meanings for the feeling of death (sepulchre, tomb).

I hope you are getting the message. Your assignment for this writing technique is to copy the rhythm of Poe's "Annabel Lee," but instead of using his language, substitute your own words and phrases to capture the same emotional effect. It may be noteworthy to also understand that, if you choose another writer's work to imitate (especially if the writer's copyright has expired), it is not plagiarism to change the words and to keep the rhythms! Some of us have been born without much rhythm (remember the stereotype Richard Pryor gave his audiences of the tight-butted white man who just could not, for the life of him, boogie in time to the music?). Here is your chance to prove you indeed have rhythm!

IMAGES AND METAPHORS: AN INNER, CREATIVE ABILITY THAT SEPARATES HUMAN FROM BEAST

The ability of the human mind to capture the total picture of an experience makes us unique in the world. However, until we were able to convert those "picture stories" into words, we were locked into our tribes' traditions, rarely ever escaping out into the broader knowledge of the universe outside our primitive lives. But the need to share our experience in pictures was great. Thus, artistic expression was born, and at last humans had the ability to communicate knowledge without getting locked into tribal tradition.

I remember the brilliant metaphor my Hindu professor gave in our class, Quest for Self—East and West. Imagine that an elephant is God and is locked inside a dark room. Outside, three wise men are waiting to pay him a visit. Each one goes inside the pitch-dark room. The first takes hold of the elephant's trunk and exclaims, "Aha! God must be a long root of the banyan tree." The second wise man enters and grabs onto the elephant's (God's) tail and says, "I see. God is a snake." Finally, the last wise man enters and he walks right into the elephant's broad side. "God cannot be grasped!" he exclaims, and he runs out of the room. My professor said that each wise man represents (symbolizes) a different religion. Everyone believes differently about the essence of God, yet God remains unchanged.

Metaphors and images give us a way to communicate symbolically, so that our viewers and listeners can grasp the essence of our "picture" in one dazzling display. Electronic media is spectacular for this type of symbolic imagery because it offers so many options. But the digital scribe who cannot capture the pictorial essence of his or her message is not thinking metaphorically.

Images and metaphors arise spontaneously, intact and whole, from the roots of the psyche. This encapsulating phenomenon makes the experience vivid and memorable later in life. The easiest "capsules" to remember are those charged with human emotion: what you were doing when someone you loved or admired was killed; the location and circumstances of your first kiss; the setting of your first real date; your first lover and where you were when you met him or her. These are the easy ones to symbolize in your mind, so you can recall them pretty quickly by clustering the images the way you did earlier.

Rico says we gain our ability to image in childhood by imagining such creatures as monsters, witches, and fairy godmothers (Rico, p. 157). Even more grotesque and sometimes beautiful images come about when we are subject to highly emotional states: hunger, isolation, fear, nightmares, dreams. The images arise because it is our inner child's reaction to the emotional state brought about by experience in the outside world during the day.

For example, Shirley Jackson wrote the short story "The Lottery" at one sitting, "in a frenzied state of urgency," and she had it in the mail to the *New Yorker* that same afternoon. It became one of the most controversial and most responded to stories in the history of that literary magazine. Why? It is a metaphorical image of a childhood nightmare: that the world outside the family can murder you for no reason. The reason this story was received with such emotional passion was because Jackson (like Joyce Carol Oates, another of my favorite contemporary authors) has the ability to describe in vivid words the nightmares that scare us in our private, inner worlds. All the great horror writers do the same thing. They have the unique ability to conjure up particular images that are so packed with emotion that we must respond to them as readers.

Some psychiatrists say they can understand you in a special way by analyzing your dreams. Dreams are nothing more than imaging at its very best. However, the best digital scribes soon learn they must be able to dream sitting in front of the computer terminal, connected to a variety of software programs and manipulating keystrokes, icons, sounds, and graphics like a maniac. Without the ability to think metaphorically, the writer will remain mediocre.

Metaphor

A *metaphor* is a comparison between "things" from different classes. These "things" can be objects, ideas, processes, or anything else we use language to represent. The metaphor can be expressed in a straightforward fashion: "You are the sunshine in my life." It can be streamlined into a name, often a product name: Plymouth Sundance. It can be done with a verb or verb phrase: "He was lucky to skate away from that disaster." Think of a simile as a metaphor that includes the word *like* or *as*. Think of an analogy as a metaphor that has four parts: A is to B as C is to D. And don't worry about classifications. Worry about powerful, effective writing.

Metaphor is powerful because it is compact: "heart of stone." It involves the senses: "Don't rain on my parade." It explains one thing in terms of another: "Writing this paper is like wandering through a maze—I can't see where I'm going and I don't remember how I got here."

Some people use metaphor naturally. If you aren't one of them, you can still learn to write them. You can force a plant bulb to flower out of its normal season by changing the natural conditions—in effect, "fooling" the plant into blossoming in an unnatural season. In writing, you can force a metaphor into bloom by changing the natural conditions. Set out to write some, and you will. The following examples are one writer's attempts to explain an abstract process—his thinking. In "forcing" these metaphors, the student (Bobby Bascomb) discovered something about his own thought processes and explained his discoveries in a way anyone can understand.

Example: Forcing a Metaphor

1. My thinking is like a bath tub filled to the top, with the water still running, because it is just about to overflow.

2. My thinking is like a pack rat's home because I never forget anything.

3. My thinking is like a fun house mirror, because what I am thinking comes out completely distorted when I speak.

I give the following exercise to my Freshman Composition students each semester. I am going to give it to you as well. However, you must remember that thinking metaphorically is more complex if you want to be successful in the electronic writing world. Not only do you have to come up with the perfect metaphor to represent your game, your product, or your service, but you must also connect it to other enhancing sounds, animations, and even entire databases. The success of the interactive game *Myst*, for example, has come about because the creators knew users would respond to the fantastic inner, dreamlike world they created. It both scares and attracts the user, thus giving a sublime satisfaction to the inner child.

Exercise: Forcing a Metaphor

Begin with the object, subject, or topic that you wish to write about. Let's say "your written voice" is the subject. You need to find five things with which to compare your voice. A "thing" can be an object, person, process, idea, or anything else with definable characteristics. Set up your paper to look like this:

My voice is like

_____ (thing 1) because _____.
_____ (thing 2) because _____.
_____ (thing 3) because _____.

When you select things for comparison, look for the unusual and the outrageous. The purpose of the metaphor is not to show what is already known but to reveal a new way of looking at things. You should be as surprised at the discovery as any other reader.

To say your voice is "like a rasp because it's rough and raspy" is not very remarkable or new. Here is a simple rule to follow when listening to your writing for fresh language: If you've heard the phrase more than once or twice, it's probably a cliché.

After you've written five of these, drop the inessential words. Revise to make the verbs do the work. If you're determined to be raspy, "I rasp" is more forceful and direct than "my voice is like a rasp because it's raspy."

Strive for power and economy in the metaphors, and let the rest of the writing do the rest of the work. Select one or more of the metaphors and use them as a basis for further development (Purves, *Creating the Writing Portfolio,* pages 60–61). ■

At the end of this chapter I will give you an excellent response that came from one of my students. She was having a great deal of trouble with her grammar early in the semester, but after I explained that grammar was a logical, left-brained activity that is separate from her marvelous creativity, she responded to this exercise with a bursting bouquet of lovely images.

CREATING TENSION IN YOUR WRITING

My favorite quotation of all time comes from none other than that old alcoholic and Jazz-ager, F. Scott Fitzgerald: "An intelligent person is one who can understand both sides of a conflict or problem and still be able to function in the world." I find it quite interesting that great writers often come up with advice to others that they themselves find most difficult. Fitzgerald obviously had a problem functioning without a cushion of booze around his psyche, and this ultimately destroyed his perspective. However, no writer was better at establishing "creative tension."

Rico gives an excellent definition of *tension* when she says:

> 'Tension' does not refer to the anxiety you might feel when writing an essay exam or being interviewed for a job. The word comes from the Latin, *tensio*, meaning 'stretched,' as in 'extension,' a stretching out, a reaching for ways to join images, connect new patterns, reconcile opposites. Thus when I speak of creative tension, I mean the tensions you produce in your writing through oppositions, juxtapositions, and resolutions of seemingly contradictory ideas or feelings. The purpose of fostering creative tension is to evoke in your reader not only to lend intensity and surprise to natural writing but also to help you regard seemingly irreconcilable opposites in a new light. In so doing, you will avail yourself of the possibility of new and unexpected patterns by taking from each opposite what is useful and reconciling it in your writing (page 211).

Albert Rothenberg, a psychiatrist and student of the creative process, terms this process of creating tension *Janusian thinking*, after the Roman god Janus, whose two faces point in opposite directions. In Janusian thinking, two or more opposites are conceived simultaneously as equally operative and valid (Fitzgerald's quote). The study of physics shows us that, depending on how we look at it, light can appear sometimes as electromagnetic waves, sometimes as particles.

This paradox led to the formulation of quantum theory, the basis of modern physics. The apparent contradiction between particle and wave images was solved in a completely unexpected way, which called into question the very foundation of the traditional mechanistic worldview.

This technique is the mark of a great writer. The very soul of fiction is contained in the author's ability to create conflict that leads to satisfaction and a reconciliation or alienation of some kind. When you have mastered the art of creative tension, you are well on your way to being a true cyberspace writer. In natural writing, the tension between opposing forces becomes a creative principle because it stimulates fundamental and surprising innovations. Creative tension brings new lifeblood into seeing and writing, producing effective surprise and reflecting connectedness. To the Sign mind a polarity is the presence of two irreconcilable opposites. But to the Design mind a polarity represents the ends of a single, indivisible whole. Like Indra's net, which is the Hindu metaphor for the cosmos (the inner microcosm is a symbol of the outer macrocosm, just as the outer universe is a symbol of the inner imagination), the Design mind has a different focus, that's all, for it is the simultaneous recognition of opposites as equally valid.

Rico makes this clear when she says:

> The function of creative tension in writing is precisely to reflect the profound truth of the both/and, rather than only the either/or, nature of life. We can perceive both ways because we have two brains, which process the flux of the world in radically different ways. Our Sign mind tends to focus on the either/or, crisply and clearly cataloguing, making judgments, establishing rules. Our Design mind tends to focus on the both/and, with its ambiguities, its malleability, its flow. Again using the terminology of physics, we might say that our Sign mind thinks in terms of fission, the act or process of splitting into parts, while our Design mind thinks in terms of fusion, the act of liquefying or melting together by heat. Fission separates

out; fusion merges. Fission focuses on particles—a drop of energy; fusion, on waves—a sea of energy (page 213).

I use movies in my classes because image stories educate in a different, and in some ways, more satisfying way than books. That is (by the way) *exactly* why writing for electronic media is so exciting. The digital scribe can combine text and vision to create a perfect metaphor for human life! One movie I show my students is called *A Bronx Tale*, which is about a young boy growing up in the New York of the 1950s and 1960s. The creative tension is established because this boy learns from two very different fathers. One, his biological father, is an honest, hard-working bus driver, whose favorite saying is "The worst thing in life is wasted talent." The other is the neighborhood "tough guy," who takes a liking to the kid and who really does not want the boy to become what he has become. Thus, even though the tough father is a murderer, his internal nature is to prevent the boy from turning evil. This leads to his saving the boy's life later in the movie, and it even brings the boy closer to his own father in a paradoxical way. They are reconciled at the tough guy's funeral after he was gunned down by the son of a fellow gangster whom he killed many years before (bad karma). The karmic law is satisfied, and the viewer is left satisfied, but the satisfaction includes a paradoxical and creatively tense respect for a character who would be (in a less effective movie) a stereotyped villain.

Creative tension makes your reader or viewer think about how strange life can be sometimes. People who seem to be evil often do good deeds. Saints sometimes fall. Heroes lose, and sinners win. Thus, Juliet calls Romeo a "beautiful tyrant." And a little Italian boy growing up in the Bronx learns from a gangster about goodness.

My novel, *Russian Wolves*, has a climactic scene in the Bolshoi Ballet Theater, when my mad serial killer and assassin sees what he has become and recognizes the paradox of his inner world as it is juxtaposed against the insanity of the outer world of gangsterism and racism running amok in Moscow.

"Fellow Muscovites! I am the Wolf of Justice! Andrei Roma-
novich Chikatilo. My father was a traitor during the war. I am
also a traitor to you. I have killed many children—God forgive
me! But my mind has left me. I answered to my inner world
and it was wrong! Do you really understand? My inner world
was wrong! Please, you have seen that your outer world of
Communism was wrong. I looked, moments before, through
my rifle scope…"

There were gasps from the audience.

"… as the President's little girl watched the fantasy on the
stage, and my mind became clear for the very first time in my
life. I know this story. My mother told me this story. The wolf
is fooled because people learned to hide. Understand, my
countrymen! Understand *me!* I could *not* learn to hide!"

The story Chikatilo refers to is the children's fairytale "Peter and the
Wolf"; this insane man has warped that childish vision into an inner
and demonic defense against what he saw as an unjust world around
him.

Exercise

The exercise for this writing technique involves your ability to create
tension through similar word pairs. As always, you may cluster
around this word pair to discover your trial-web shift. But then I
want you to write about the opposing forces implied in your pair.
This will give you the necessary practice to be able to work on
creating tension in your own writing. The word pair nucleus you
will cluster is *taste/savor*. You may look up their literal definitions,
but be certain to use your Design mind to make the necessary
creatively tense connections between the two concepts. ∎

The other obvious way you can create tension in your writing is to purposely place opposing words, concepts, and feelings next to each other to see if they have some metaphorical or emotional connection. Remember, your Design mind makes the necessary links between these (at first glance) opposite forces. Just as the universe is circular, so is the human mind. Unless we can feel satisfied after we have read or experienced an electronic document, game or presentation, we will probably not be aesthetically renewed. There will be an empty feeling in the pit of our stomachs and we will feel uncomfortable with you, the digital scribe, whose sole responsibility is to make certain that your reader or observer or user keeps coming back for more!

RE-VISION: SEEING WITH NEW EYES

This technique lets you clean up your act, so to speak, by going over your work and the previous techniques you have been using, and making them sparkle. The focus must be clear; your recurrences must be meaningful; your images, sharp; your language, pleasingly rhythmic and evocative; and your tension, dynamic. In this final phase of your writing you must look at your writing more critically than you have done up to now, using the detail-oriented talents of the Sign mind yet at the same time checking the detail against the global vision of the Design mind, which ultimately dictates all major decisions. Thus true revision becomes an intensely cooperative process between the two hemispheres, a process of continual modification toward your envisioned whole.

This is where you lose your inner child, and the adult takes over. I tell my freshmen that they should imagine that they are sane people with multiple personalities and that one of their personalities is a little blue nun who teaches grammar. This sister is a strict grammarian who insists upon perfect sentence structure, proper punctuation, and flawless spelling. You must look over your work with a scathingly thorough eye. One great writer once said that you are not a true writer until you realize that a properly placed period can sound like a cannon going off. Until your re-vision eye can place cannon balls in strategic places, you have not finished.

However, "getting the words right" does not mean that your exclusive task is to correct your grammar, spelling, and punctuation errors. No, you must also check your words for their proper meaning (in relationship to your purpose or theme), and you must make certain your words have the right aesthetic quality for the audience you are addressing. Perhaps you can even get two or three people to go over your work and see if they can see it the way you see it. If they can't, then perhaps you need to clarify a few things. I tell my students to get at least three others to critically review their work. First, for content; next, for grammar, punctuation, and spelling.

Most writing teachers will tell you that you can lose adjectives and replace them with active verbs. I agree. Crisp, moving action and character-enhancing dialogue does more for the digital scribe than a whole cornucopia of flowery adjectives.

Another way you can revise is to recluster. This is a process whereby you take some vague word or concept in your piece and use it as a nucleus to cluster around. Usually, the passage is missing something. It is vague, it is obscure, it is not as precise and as magic as you want it to be. Reclustering will help you discover the best possible image or combination of words.

The following exercise will test your ability to revise. The photo in Figure 2.1 is one of the excellent pieces from the Image Warehouse (Media Design Interactive, The Old Hop Kiln, 1 Long Garden Walk, Farnham, Surrey, GU9 7HP, England. Tel: 0252 737630 Fax: 0252 710948 International +44 252 737630 AppleLink: Media Design). They provide a CD full of royalty-free images (in color) for you to use in your applications.

Figure 2.1 Man and Machine

Exercise

1. Give your Design mind the opportunity to scan the picture of "Man and Machine." Record your dominant impression in a circle. It can take the form of a polarity or a "contrary" if you wish.

2. Now cluster around it whatever you see, whatever you feel as your eyes explore the entire picture, and let your Design mind respond with associations.

3. Stay alert for the trial-web shift (aha!) that will spur your urge to write. When it comes, hold it fast in a focusing statement.

4. Now write your vignette, using whatever pertains from your cluster. Remember, clustering gives you choices; there is no need to try to squeeze in everything just because it's there. Choose from the rich array your Design mind has made available to your Sign mind to work in an integrated fashion.

5. Read your vignette aloud, listening for rhythms, images, metaphors, recurrences, tension, full-circle wholeness—all the techniques I have reviewed with you.

6. Now focus again on your dominant impression ("Man and Machine" should give you some ideas). This should be your point of reference for redesigning. Everything in your revised vignette should contribute to this central idea (whatever it is). Begin your word painting by cutting as much explanatory language as you can (edit out those useless adjectives and replace them with active verbs); strengthen your evocative language through recurrences, images metaphors, and language rhythms. Cultivate tension. Come full circle.

7. Now read your new vignette aloud. Your ear will tell you what still doesn't sound right. Listen and respond by making any changes that will pare it down and intensify the feeling you have created.

8. Now that you have produced your evocative whole, deliberately shift to a Sign-mind bias (the little blue nun) and read only to correct spelling, punctuation, grammatical, and typographical errors. If you have a tendency not to see these, try reading your vignette backward, which will enable you to catch errors you might not otherwise notice.

After completing your piece, count the words of your first vignette and compare it to the count of the second. Very likely the compression of the evocative vignette yielded fewer words, much tighter compression, and far greater intensity. The point is not how many words you use, but how effectively you use language. Every word should tell! ∎

Sample Answers to Chapter's Exercises

Cluster Words: Digital Scribe

Your clusters might contain words such as digits, fingers, writing down thoughts, monks of old, computers, linking, togetherness, communicating rapidly but with extreme precision, virtual books, electronic holy men, writing down words that vanish into pulses of energy, writing with sound, pictures and words.

A possible paragraph based on the above clusters might be as follows:

> The holy scribe sits at his terminal, waiting for the passion to grip his hands, encircle his brain, send electric impulses into his finger tips. He feels holy because he has such power in front of him. He can send his viewer into other worlds, where they can hear what he wants them to hear, touch what he wants them to touch, feel what he wants them to feel. The holiness he senses is his electronic religion: where his god communicates through him in quantum leaps, and where his mind is divided, forever panning over the endless possibilities, yet finally arriving at the perfect answer! Why? Because he is the chosen one: the digital scribe of the new century!

Write Four Lines of VRML Lyrics

The picture could be one like that shown in Figure 2.2.

> You started it, baby.
> My heart's a revolution
> Caught in the evolution
> the daring evolution
> of my first love.

Figure 2.2   The Evolution of Love

Rhythm Exercise

Here is a possible response using Poe's "Annabel Lee."

"Sara Lee"

For the day never dawns without bringing me coupons
    Of the bountiful Sara Lee;
And the stores never close but I see pungent rows
    Of the bountiful Sara Lee;
And so, in the night-time, I get down to kneel,
Near my scrumptious, my sumptuous, my snack and my meal,
    In her wrapper there by the Twinkies—
    In her cloak by the side of the Twinkies.

Metaphor Exercise

Here is a sample response.

It peeked its tiny head, eluding,
A scampering pewter hare.
The season's hues protruding,
From the frozen carpet bare.

The glowing firelight, peeping,
Silently lying there.
Spring hues gently keeping,
Hard it pressed, against, the frozen carpet bare.

Success, slow in coming, encouraging,
The bursting hues so fair.
That it may rise, flourishing,
Above, the frozen carpet bare.

To greet the new morn, rising,
Sprung forth the hues to dare.
Strong stem now sizing
Up, the frozen carpet bare.

The flower, now clear seeing,
'Twas not one, but a pair.
For close by there being,
Another, on this frozen carpet bare.

The sun greets the sky
As a lover caresses his lover's thigh
The warmth falls on the earth
Like his breath in her hair
And its light fills the sky
As her breath fills his being
And it is morning.

Taste/Savor Exercise

"I taste a good apple, but I savor apple pie. When tasting, one smacks the lips and chomps appreciatively. When savoring, however, one sucks in the flavors and ummms and ahhhs. I can develop a taste for rock-and-roll music, but classical symphonies must be savored to be truly relished." ■

MULTIMEDIA AWARENESS DEVELOPMENT

Now comes multimedia. This is a totally new dimension in the composition process because it provides you with the technology to communicate through and with a wider variety of media. However, to communicate with multimedia, you must first understand how to compose with your five senses.

In this part of the book, I will give you five exercises to practice using each of your senses (one exercise for each sense). What are your five senses? Touch this book. Read the words. Listen to the pages as you turn them. Place your nose on the page and inhale. Tear off a corner of the page and pop it in your mouth. You have now experienced this text with your five senses! This part of the book will also explore the theory and practice of hypertext.

But thinking with your senses requires practice. I recall one exercise that I give to my Freshman English Composition students to teach them how to do this. I tell them to get into pairs. Then, I tell one to blindfold the other one so he or she cannot see. Finally, I have the "sighted" one lead the other around campus and into "sensually stimulating" places. They might be led into the cafeteria, or the gym, or even into a biology lab where they are handed dissected frogs or other tantalizing tidbits. The "blind" student is told to write about experiencing life without the sense of sight. In other words, he or she can communicate with only the other four senses. The result is very interesting. In some cases, students learn that their other senses can be relied on; although in a large number of instances, they are fooled because they have not been used to employing these other senses.

In the world of multimedia composition, one can learn to use the senses by applying the technology available to each of the five senses. For example, *hypertext* (the ability to click on a word in the text that connects with another page of information or causes the viewer to "experience" some related event) gives the writer the ability to make the reader take control of his or her own "depth perception." In other words, by clicking the arrow or cursor on the word, the reader can discover more about that word or concept in your message or perhaps even be entertained in some outlandish way. As a result, the writer learns to link the hypertext to any of the five senses.

Hypertext is thoroughly discussed later, but an excellent example of linking to a sensory perception would be the one Scott Fisher gives in his text *Multimedia Authoring* (AP PROFESSIONAL) concerning the tuning of twin carburetors on an MGB. Instead of the description or the graph that is usually included in text-only tuning manuals, he included an audio clip recorded from the car itself, in three different states of adjustment: too rich, too lean, and "just right." Users who clicked on these links got to hear what the car sounded like if it were too lean, and could then make the adjustment accordingly as described on that screen. The location of the mixture-adjusting nut and the meaning of relevant terms were covered on the monitor. It is critical that readers of hypertextual writing be given prerequisite information that they may not have already read because the presentation is not necessarily linear (see *Multimedia Authoring*, Chapters 6 and 7).

Another example of using hypertext to link to a sensory perception would be the one I use in my multimedia application, Grammar Made Easy (see application on CD). In that text, I have a reference to the "present progressive tense," and the definition I give in the glossary is as follows:

> The present progressive expresses an activity that is in progress (is occurring, is happening) right now. The event is in progress at the time the speaker is saying the sentence. The event began in the past, is in progress now, and will probably continue into the future.
>
> *Form:* am, is, are + -ing

I wanted to be able to give my reader a sensory experience that showed this definition. So, I went to my software program 3D F/X, by Asymetrix Corporation, and I easily created the "spinning earth animation" that you can view on the CD accompanying this book. This animation did what only multimedia can do: it gave the user an additional learning link that sensually reinforced the typically "boring" grammar lesson. This is what you must learn to apply when you are writing for this new medium. Whenever you come across a new concept that is particularly complex, you must experiment with expressing that idea in a new sensory way.

With this in mind, I want to reproduce an article written by Scott Fisher that comes from the Writer's Connection newsletter, February 1996:

SINGING NEW SHAPES, BUILDING NEW COLORS: ADDRESSING ALL THE INTELLIGENCES

Last month, I introduced the theory of Dr. Howard Gardner and Dr. Tom Armstrong, that human beings possess seven intelligences—linguistic, logical, spatial, kinesthetic, musical, interpersonal, and intrapersonal.

This month I want to discuss how multimedia can let you reach people in ways individual media can't. Let's begin with a few exercises to get you in touch with each of the intelligences. Linguistic intelligence is the easiest to grasp in this format; if you can read this, or understand it when read to you, you are using your linguistic intelligence.

Logical intelligence deals in sequences. To understand logical intelligence, add the numbers of today's date. If the sum has two digits, keep adding the digits together till you reach a single-digit number. (For example, July 4, 1776 adds up to 32, so you'd add those digits together to get 5.) Now add up the numbers of the page on which this article is printed. Compare the two numbers. If the sum of today's date is greater than, equal to, or less than the sum of the page numbers, you used your logical intelligence. (The actual numbers don't matter—what matters is following the sequence.)

To understand spatial intelligence—often called "artistic"—draw a picture of how you think the intelligences are distributed in you. You can make a simple pie chart if you like; make a picture of your own head with regions of the brain drawn in different colors if you'd rather. As long as it's a picture showing the relationships, you have used your spatial intelligence.

Kinesthetic intelligence means learning via your body's motion and position. Close your eyes, reach down, and tie your shoes. That's your kinesthetic intelligence at work. Think how much more effective interactive screen design could be if it worked with the kinesthetic intelligence.

To understand your musical intelligence, say these syllables out loud: "Da da da dummmmmmm." Did you instinctively go lower on the fourth syllable (and then repeat the pattern a little lower down the scale, even if only in your head)? That's your musical intelligence (and Beethoven's genius) being irrepressible. How can this help you make your multimedia project more memorable?

For interpersonal intelligence, ask a friend or family member how they think interpersonal intelligence would show up in someone. Exchange ideas about it for a few minutes. Now consider how this exchange of ideas might benefit the collaborative team environment of the typical multimedia project.

Finally, there's intrapersonal intelligence. This is where writers spend most of our lives. Think back to a time when you were really in touch with yourself, when you were in the presence of your dreams and hopes, when you really knew who you were. Remember how it felt to be you that day? That's your intrapersonal intelligence at work

How do these intelligences relate to multimedia? To create the most powerful multimedia (or other kinds of writing), learn to cross-pollinate between all these different intelligences. As a writer, you're probably good at connecting linguistic and intrapersonal intelligence—looking into your own experience and converting it into language for others to share. In some of my other columns, I've taken you through several exercises to help build your spatial intelligence—storyboarding, for example, because the visual element of multimedia gets so much ink.

But what about music? In some cultures outside America, music is used to convey the history of the tribe, the people, the family. Here, we use it most effectively to sell cars ("See the USA in your..."), or on a good day to teach children the alphabet ("Now I know my ABCs").

How about kinesthetic intelligence? Imagine a connect-the-dots game where kids click on blinking icons in sequence, with the result being a large drawing of a number or letter on screen. As they move the mouse, their muscles are learning the patterns and shapes of the alphabet and the numbers. Adults might learn system administration, or sample a new product over the Web, in the same way.

Although I focus on learning, I haven't forgotten those of you in the entertainment or corporate multimedia fields. The entertainment benefits should be obvious: if you engage all the intelligences, it's a more rewarding experience than if you engage only one. As for corporate use, how many of you hear Mick Jagger's voice when you click the Start button on a Windows 95 system? (I know I do, but it's usually "You make a grown man cry . . ."). The more intelligences you can address, the better retention your users will experience—and that's important whether you're writing software for kids or on-line advertisements.

Now I will give you a chance to practice your sensory abilities. Please complete each exercise as creatively as you can. Remember, you are supposed to think of ideas that can most interestingly and most appropriately give your reader the experience of the sense under consideration.

Exercises

Remember the commercial of a few years back where hands tore into the skin of a ripe orange, and the vision of bursting flavor erupted into the air as slow motion droplets of gold sprayed against a black background? Or how about the fruit candy commercial that used colorful shots of fruit morphing into a river of sweet nectar waterfalls, and the candy would splash into this river in slow motion? As multimedia writers, we have to use one or two senses—sight (whether of words or of pictures) and sound. We must use our words and our images to transform sensory input of one kind (sound and sight) into as many others as are appropriate (scent, taste, touch). You may use any "connections" you find to do these exercises. Old literature textbooks are ample sources for ideas, as are any royalty-free CDs and other canned applications that assist the developer and digital scribe.

1. Sight

The first exercise tests your ability to think with your eyes. This will also test your multimedia awareness, mentioned earlier. In other words, you will have to "transform" the following sensory input into a visionary and auditory (remember parallel rhythms!) "experience" for the end user. In multimedia writing, one must always be thinking about how the user will experience your creation. Your task is to convert these impressions from other senses into a visual and stimulating image.

A. Show the flavor of fresh-roasted coffee.

B. Picture what an echo would look like.

C. Envision what wine tastes like.

2. Sound

Next, imagine that you must convert the following sensory experiences into a sound or a song that best represents that experience. Remember that you may not use songs from copyrighted works—but you may use original tunes you create on your own MIDI software!

A. What is the sound of lovers' first kiss?

B. What is the sound of greed (or some other deadly sin)?

C. The sound of a baby's first steps?

3. Taste

Try translating the following sensory experiences into something the user can taste:

A. The agony of a battlefield

B. Honeymoon night

C. Victory

4. Smell

Convert these sensory emotions into an experience the user can smell:

A. Passion

B. Hunger

C. Wealth or poverty

5. Touch

Create an experience that forces your user to use the touch sensation to understand the following:

A. Marriage ceremony

B. First day of school

C. A first date

Check your answers with the sample responses at the end of the chapter. ■

You should now be getting the idea of how multimedia writing works. You must make connections between the multimedia message you are creating and your viewer's senses. It brings all the senses into play, ultimately, and you end up mixing and matching the senses to create the best possible experience for your viewer.

Now that you are pumped up from all this creative activity, I would like to point out that hypertext is probably one of the most creative links you will use in multimedia writing. There are two major purposes for using hypertext. One, you can link your screen page with another page in a sequential order. This is done when you are moving your reader in a step-by-step process, and you want him or her to stay in a single direction. This is also called *unidirectional* hypertext. But the major purpose for using hypertext is to allow readers to bring their own context to the information. This is the crucial element in human creativity: putting together two existing ideas to give rise to a third new idea like striking flint on steel to cause sparks. When you structure a hypertext document, you make it possible for the readers to be present in a completely different context for each piece, or module, depending on which link they came from. Sometimes, however, you have to make sure they know A before they read B (as in Fisher's carburetor example earlier).

When I said that hypertext gives you depth perception, I meant that the writer can link a word with a definition or even with some other database, so that the reader can get an additional dimension about the concept under study.

The following chapter will discuss at length hypertext and the theory and practice of using hypertext.

Sample Answers

Exercise 1: Sight

A. One possibility would be to show the "Shakespearean Legend of the Coffee Bean." A beautiful tavern wench prepares the coffee by grinding it in a pewter urn and then placing it in an iron pot of boiling water. She also prepares heaping pans of sausages, potatoes, and eggs and bacon, and as she bends over to sniff the fragrant aroma of the coffee, we hear, accompanied by strains of the harpsichord, the sounds of men shouting and halloing as they trudge into the tavern and we hear the poet read in a VO (voiceover): *But O, it must be burnt! Alas, the fire of lust and envy have burnt it heretofore, and made it fouler; let their flames retire, and burn me, O Lord, with a fiery zeal of thee and thy house, which doth in eating heal.*

B. You could represent an echo by showing a succession of jump-cuts of beautiful women walking along in silky garments, as a voice sings his echoing song: *When as in silks my Julia goes, then, then, I think, how sweetly flows that liquefaction of her clothes. Next, when I cast my eyes and see that brave vibration each way free, oh, how that glittering takes me!*

C. You could try juxtaposing two images and using a morphing technique as well: a stumbling wino walks into a downtown liquor store and buys an expensive bottle of dinner wine. He then creeps into an alley, and suddenly it is transformed into a lovely, emerald-green glade, with birds, wildlife and flowers all around. A beautiful woman takes the old man by the hand and they sit inside a white gazebo. She takes two crystal glasses from her picnic basket and he pours the grape. The VO says, as they toast the miracle of the moment, *O, for a draught of vintage! That hath been Cooled a long age in the deep-delved earth, Tasting of Flora, and the country green, Dance, and Provencal song, and sunburnt mirth!*

Exercise 2: Sound

This exercise may have a variety of original answers, depending on your imagination and access to musical software or other instruments.

Exercise 3: Taste

A. You might show the first skirmish at dawn between American Civil War soldiers. As they fight, a young country boy watches, from high above on a hill, eating a large slice of watermelon. As the action becomes bloodier and men begin to fall and writhe in agony on the hard, dusty ground, the boy's eating becomes frantic: red pulp, black seeds and liquid are shown in extreme close-ups as they fly in every direction (his eating becomes a back-and-forth melody with the warfare below). In the VO, the words are chanted, dirge-like: *And now, like amorous birds of prey, rather at once our time devour than languish in his slow-chapped power. Let us roll all our strength and all our sweetness up into one ball, and tear our pleasures with rough strife. Through the iron gates of life: thus, though we cannot make our sun stand still, yet we will make him run.*

B. Once again, you could try juxtaposing images to create a taste quality: open on two lovers on their wedding night (dress clothes hung by the door). As he kisses her at the window, the full moon shines in and their lips begin to glow warmly as the camera closes in and the viewer can almost taste the kiss. But, as the camera pulls back from an extreme close-up of their lips, we discover it is now a mother kissing her child. As this is happening, the VO says, *Welcome! Though not to gold nor silk, to more than Caesar's birthright is; two sister-seas of Virgin-milk, with many a rarely-tempered kiss that breathes at once both maid and mother, warms in the one, cools in the other.*

C. Possibly show a series of jump-cut images of football players spiking the ball, basketball players slamming a dunk, tennis players acing a serve, baseball players hitting home runs, and then show the same men being slammed by the opposition, while over it all the VO: *Revenge, revenge! See the Furies arise! See the snakes that they rear, how they hiss in their hair, and the sparkles that flash from their eyes! Behold a ghastly band, each a torch in his hand! Those are Grecian ghosts, that in battle were slain, and unburied remain inglorious on the plain: give the vengeance due to the valiant crew.*

Exercise 4: Smell

A. Show a scene, (as in *Tom Jones*) of a couple who eat food ravenously as they, at the same moment, stare lustfully at each other, while the poet reads, *Then shall thy circling arms embrace and clip my naked body, and thy balmy lip bathe me in juice of kisses, whose perfume like a religious incense shall consume and send up holy vapors to those powers that bless our loves and crown our sportful hours, that with such halcyon calmness fix our souls in steadfast peace, as no affright controls.*

B. Over one-half a billion people live in hunger. Perhaps images of poverty could reflect that hunger as well. Juxtapose the dry, parched earth with close-up shots of the skeletal bodies of men, women, and children. Compare the razing of rainforests with the innocent gazes of the indigenous population. Over this all, in small screens, show the ravages of fire, flood, and famine.

The poet reads some of Alexander Pope's words over all these scenes to evoke the odor of poverty: *Lo! The poor Indian, whose untutored mind sees God in clouds, or hears him in the wind; his soul proud Science never taught to stray far as the solar walk, or milky way, yet simple Nature to his hope has given, behind the cloud-topped hill, an humbler heaven, some safer world in depth of woods embraced, some happier island in the watery waste, where slaves once more their native land behold, no fiends torment, no Christians' thirst for gold!*

C. One could turn around the answer in B and show wealth by juxtaposing the bounty of Nature with the bounty of material largess: mountains/castles, snow-covered trees/ermine-covered women, huge land turtles/huge tanks, etc. The VO might be something ironic, like: *See, through this air, this ocean, and this earth, all matter quick, and bursting into birth. Above, how high progressive life may go! Around, how wide! How deep extend below! Vast Chain of Being! Which from God began, Nature's ethereal, human, angel, man, beast, bird, fish, insect, what no eye can see, no glass can reach! From Infinite to thee, from thee to nothing.—On superior powers were we to press, inferior might on ours: or in the full creation leave a void, where, one step broken, the great scale's destroyed: from Nature's chain whatever link you strike, tenth or ten thousandth, breaks the chain alike.*

Exercise 5: Touch

A. This effect could be created by showing a hippie country wedding, with close-ups of the bride during the ceremony that match the lyrics in this famous poem by Marlowe: *Upon her head she wore a myrtle wreath, from whence her veil reached to the ground beneath. Her veil was artificial flowers and leaves, whose workmanship both man and beast deceives; many would praise the sweet smell as she passed, when twas the odor which her breath forth cast; and there for honey, bees have sought in vain, and beat from thence, have lighted there again. About her neck hung chains of pebble-stone, which, lightened by her neck, like diamonds shone. She wore no gloves, for neither sun nor wind would burn or parch her hands, but to her mind or warm or cool them, for they took delight to play upon those hands, they were so white. Some say, for her the fairest Cupid pined, and looking in her face, was struck blind.*

B. You could create this agony/ecstasy by using juxtaposed images again: a teacher scraping chalk on blackboard, a boy pulling a girl's hair, warm milk and cookies, blankets around children at nap time, a little boy sneaking a first kiss, a child running to mother at the end of the day and being enveloped in her arms.

C. This, too, could be an agony/ecstasy demonstration. Woody Allen creates excellent visuals of this first dating experience by showing a frenetic scene of knocking over aftershave lotion, spilling talcum, shorting out the electricity with the electric shaver, and cutting his face while trying to shave in a foggy mirror. This can continue into dinner with such scenes as smiling with chunks of broccoli between the teeth, trying to cut a huge piece of lettuce heart in the salad, sending a crab leg or lobster claw flying across at your date while you try to eat it, spilling wine when you pour, dribbling liquid down your front—you get the message. It could all end happily with a big kiss at the front door. ■

3

Hypertext: Theory and Practice

This chapter will cover the following:

- Hypertext defined
- Hypertext applications
- Links and nodes
- Anchors
- Process of hypertext
- Navigational dimensions and metaphors
- NoteCards
- Backtracks
- Bookmarks
- Cooperative authoring
- Guided tours
- Information retrieval

Conventional text is sequential in nature. In other words, there is a single linear sequence that defines the order in which text should be read. First you read page 1, then page 2, and so forth.

Hypertext is nonsequential and consists of interrelated units of information. These units are referred to as *nodes* and are the basic units of hypertext. There is no single order that determines the sequence in which to read the text, which means the user has the ability to navigate throughout the units in a random manner.

Nodes are connected by hypertext *links* and all links lead to the destination or source node, called the *anchor*. The number of links that can be supported is application dependent. In Figure 3.1, the nodes are A, B, C, D, E, and F. Notice that node A has three links and that numerous paths exist to any given node. It should also be noted that links are anchored to a specific location with a node, so that the user has the ability to click on the word associated with that link. This activates the destination node. Most hypertext systems also support a backtrack facility. For example, if we arrived at node D from A, the backtrack facility should provide the ability to return to node A.

Please note that nodes in frame-based systems and window-based systems are represented differently. In a *frame-based system,* frames have a fixed size. If the content information is too large, it is not

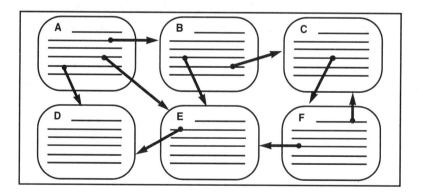

Figure 3.1   Nodes and links

possible to store it all in one frame, so it must be split into several frames. This type of a system also allows users to navigate by a system mechanism such as those found in Hypercard or Hyperties.

In *window-based systems*, windows contain as much information as needed. But it requires a hypertext mechanism and scrolling mechanism to navigate to the desired information. Some of the systems are Guide and Intermedia. In window-based systems, the hypertext systems designer has no control over nodes' display format, but windows may be of different size.

Links are the other fundamental unit of hypertext. Links may be explicit or implicit. An explicit link is defined by somebody as connecting an anchor node with the destination node. Implicit links are not defined by somebody but follow from various properties of information. Intermedia, for example, contains implicit links.

Links may be plain links, meaning they just connect two nodes. The links may be tagged with keyword or semantic attributes. Links can also be *typed* links to represent different types of relationships between nodes. The links can also be *superlinks* to connect a larger number of nodes. The superlinks may be a menu of the links or go to all the destinations at the same time. In some cases the system may choose the destination for the user.

Link anchors do not actually fit in the layered hypertext architecture. (Layered hypertext is hypertext that is connected by nodes.) In the layered architecture, links belong to the hypertext abstract machine level, but the location of the anchor node is dependent on the storage structure of the node media. Anchors become indirect pointers and the anchoring interface provides a translation between anchor identifiers in the hypertext abstract machine and the actual anchor values in the node data.

Many hypertext systems (for example, Intermedia, Hyperties) allow users to add new links to the primary material to customize the information space for their own needs.

Some Other Working Definitions

- **Icon:** This is a graphical representation of an object; these usually are what people will associate with the object. For example, in the Macintosh desktop system, the trash can is used as an icon.

- **Anchor:** This is usually the departure node in a link and it is joined to the destination node through this link.

- **Overview Diagram:** This is a diagram that presents the overall layout of the information space; this can be a great help to the user in the navigation of a document.

- **Backtrack:** Probably the most commonly used method of navigating large spaces is the backtrack, which returns the user to the previous node in the document.

HYPERTEXT VERSUS LINEAR TEXT

One of the main efforts in writing hypertext is in determining how to structure information in the hypertext network. This is quite different from writing linear reports.

The experience with the use of NoteCards [Trigg and Irish, 1987], which will be discussed further later in this chapter, indicates the need to give users a "strategy manual" about the design of hypertext networks and which useful conventions to follow.

The popularity of hypertext has led to many products which claim to be hypertext, but which fall short of the true definition discussed. Frank Halasz, from Xerox PARC, says a true hypertext system should include an explicit representation of the network structure. He further adds that the hypertext user should be aware of the placement of the current node within the entire system. NoteCards, for example, provides the capability of a dynamic overview in the form of a browser.

Some Advice for Authors of Hypertext

1. **Focus each node on a single topic.**
   Having a single topic for each node makes it easier to understand and recognize in overview diagrams, and also makes it easier for the author to know what links to construct.

2. **Make the nodes shorter than paper articles.**
   Reading speed is slower from screens than from paper, so the hypertext nodes should be short. Subsidiary topics, definitions, etc., need not be in the primary text. They can be in additional nodes.

3. **Use "clean" links.**
   Avoid adding unnecessary links between remotely related concepts. This will make it easier for users to navigate.

4. **Learn from examples.**
   A quick start in learning how to write hypertext is by picking up good authoring principles from existing hypertext examples.

Also, most hypertext systems possess one-directional links. In other words, the user can view all nodes reachable from the current node, but is unable to know links that lead to the current node. K. Eric Drexler has supported use of bi-directional links (links that can give the user a choice of directions). Drexler also states that future hypertext systems must support links across multiple forms of computer networks if hypertext is going to replace the publishing business.

In conclusion, hypertext systems must provide the user with an easily navigable structure. The interface should be intuitive, allowing the user to navigate with minimal cognitive effort.

NAVIGATIONAL DIMENSIONS AND METAPHORS

Navigational metaphors and dimensions often help users to better understand both their own movements in the document, and the overall structure of the information space.

For example, the interactive story *Inigo Gets Out* uses a metaphor related to Laurel's [1989] definition of personness in interactive systems. In this story, one dimension is represented by links to various pages within a single node, and the other is for the hypertext "jumps" between nodes. Movement within a node is seen as a linear, left–right dimension. Hypertext jumps are considered to be *orthogonal* to the page-turning dimension, and are visualized as an in–out direction.

Another example of an orthogonal dimension is the Aspen Movie Map. This hypertext map was developed by the city so users could explore the wonders of the famous ski resort. It can be operated independently of the geographical controls, and thus navigations throughout time and space are orthogonal in this application. Also, you may look at one of the catalog applications or my own Grammar Made Easy application on the enclosed CD. These are all fine examples of the hypertext orthogonal dimension in action.

NoteCards

Overview

NoteCards is a general hypermedia environment that is representative of workstation-based systems. It was developed by Randall Trigg and Thomas Moran at Xerox PARC to help people structure their ideas. NoteCards is a well-documented hypertext system and is famous in the research world.

This system originally could only run on the Xerox family of D-machines; only recently has NoteCards been made available on general workstations such as the Xerox Lisp machine. One reason for implementing NoteCards on the Lisp machine was that it provided the powerful InterLisp programming environment which makes it easy to program a complex system like NoteCards.

Basic Structure

NoteCards is designed around four basic structures:

1. Notecards
2. Links
3. Browser
4. FileBox

1. **Notecard:** This is nothing more than an electronically generated 3 × 5 index notecard. Each of these cards can contain some kind of editable substance—text, structured drawing, etc. NoteCards also includes a facility for adding new card types.

   The notecards can be operated as a window on the screen; these cards are standard revisable windows. Users can have as many notecards open on the screen as they want—though this can lead to a messy desktop quickly if the user opens too many cards.

   These cards can have different types depending on the data contained; the simplest card types are plain text or graphics. There are also at least 50 specialized types of cards available for individual applications that need special data structures.

2. **Links:** These are used to interconnect individual notecards into networks or structures of related cards. Each link is a typed, directional connection between a source and a destination notecard.

   The links are anchored by some icon at a specific location in the source notecard and on the other end. The whole destination notecard is called an anchor. The user can open the destination card into a new window on the screen by clicking on the link icon with the mouse.

3. **Browser:** This contains the structural overview diagram of the notecards and links. The browser card is an active overview diagram and allows users to edit the underlying hypertext nodes and links by carrying out operations on the boxes and lines in the browser. The user can also go to a card by clicking on the box representing it. The layout of the browser card reflects the changing structure of the hypertext document as the users add and/or delete nodes and links.

4. **FileBox:** This is used for the hierarchical nesting (map of the hierarchy) of notecards; each notecard is listed in exactly one FileBox. The FileBox is really a special-purpose note-card and so it is possible for a FileBox to contain other FileBoxes.

Navigation

The basic navigation technique used by the Notecards system is to move through the network by following links from card to card.

Another method is to create an overview browser card for some subnetwork (a collection of cards connected beneath the overview card, similar to subdirectories in Windows directory systems) and traverse the links from the overview browser card to the reference cards.

This system also provides a limited search facility; here the facility locates all the cards matching some user-supplied specification.

Overview Diagrams

Because hypertext relies almost exclusively on navigation, a tourist metaphor is a natural choice. One option is the guided tour. Typically, hypertext users are expected to explore the information space on their own, but maps should be provided regardless. An excellent example of using a hypertext map (MAPI) is the one at the Smithsonian Institution's home page (see Figure 3.2). This is a fine example of a guide for the Internet tourist. Netscape now has a plug-in that allows you to create these maps with a simple click. It is called Map This and is in version 1.10. Download it at **www.netscape.com**.

The space will normally be too large to display all of the nodes on one screen, so most hypertext systems provide overview diagrams to show different levels of detail. One system uses a global overview and a local view at the same time. An alternative is to provide a Zoom utility (represented by a magnifying glass icon) to allow the user to choose the level of detail displayed. There have also been attempts to design 3-D diagrams [Fairchild *et al.*, 1988].

A third choice is the fish-eye view [Furnas, 1986]. This type of overview diagram shows the entire space at once in varying levels of

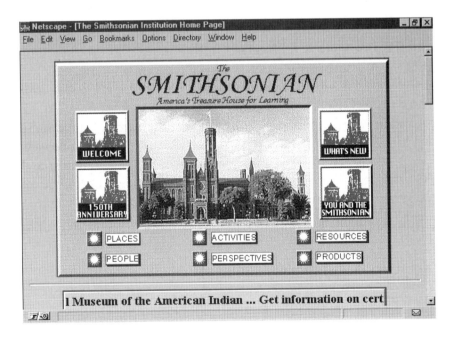

Figure 3.2   Hypertext map

detail. The nodes closest to the user are displayed in greater detail, with the level decreasing as the nodes get further away.

Not only can overview diagrams be used to show users the structure of the information space, but they can also help the explorer understand their movements through the space. To achieve this, the system should show the user's *footprints* (checkmarks used to mark nodes in the overview diagram to show where the user has been) on the map. To continue the tourist metaphor, landmarks can be a useful tool for the user. Tourists who visit Paris quickly learn to use a few key locations as a reference to their location. Similar utilities are common in hypertext systems.

The primary control structure in hypertext is the *goto* statement in the form of the jump. It should be possible to use methods that are similar to structured programming, as in the nested hierarchies of Guide.

Backtracks

The most important navigational technique is the backtrack, as discussed earlier. This technique allows the user to revisit the previous node. Almost all hypertext systems give the user some form of backtracking capability. Unfortunately, it is not always implemented consistently, which can lead to confusion on the part of the user.

The power of a backtrack facility is that it allows the user to browse at will with the certainty that familiar territory can be found by using the backtrack. This can be essential in building user confidence in the system. Any backtrack utility should fulfill two basic requirements:

1. It should always be available.
2. It should always be activated in the same way.

It should also be possible for the user to backtrack all the way to the first introductory node.

Bookmarks

Most hypertext systems allow the user to create bookmarks or place holders at nodes they think they will want to re-visit later. The major difference between bookmarks and *history lists* (another commonly used place holder or marker that allows the user to define a list of nodes that can be easily referenced later) is that a node is put in the bookmark list only if the user explicitly wants it there. This makes the bookmark list smaller and more manageable. In either type of system, the drawback is that the user might not realize that he/she will want to return to a given node until later. In the history list the difference is that the user cannot easily click to go there.

Some hypertext systems also provide history lists that allow the user to directly access any previously visited node. The nodes that users tend to want to visit via such a mechanism are usually nodes that have been visited recently, and a visual cache of a small number of the most recent nodes may be kept on the user's display. This can be in the form of miniatures of their graphic layout, or can be simple icons or even the title of the link.

Hypergate (a system that allows access to URLs on a top security basis—see Nielsen's work on hypertext) and some other systems allow the use of bookmarks. This history mechanism allows the user to define a list of nodes that can be easily referenced later.

GUIDED TOURS

The metaphor of a *guided tour* [Trigg, 1988] is the simplest solution to the problem of navigation, at least from the user's point of view. Such a tour may be thought of as a kind of superlink, connecting not just two nodes, but a string of nodes forming a path similar to the trails suggested by Vannevar Bush in 1945. Vannevar's trails were linked paths that the person journeying could follow by reading predefined trail markings along the way.

As long as users continue along the tour, all they are required to do is issue a Next Node command to see the next link.

In the Perseus system (Perseus 1.1 offers a single compact disc containing data that can be accessed as text, commentary, lexicon, encyclopedia, atlas, and illustrations), HyperCard software allows a user to construct links among them. Yet Perseus remains an imitation of the student's desk. All nodes have a path icon that the user can employ to move between links in a tour. The system also provides a path editor, which lists all the links in a tour and allows the user to add and remove links or rearrange the nodes in the path.

Guided tours are useful in orienting new users to the concepts of hypermedia because users are often in need of instruction about how to maneuver within the environment; they can also be designed for multiple special interests within a large document. The advantage of hypertext guided tours over *tourist* guided tours (tours that do not allow users to stray off the defined path) is that the user is not restricted to the tour and may leave to explore the rest of the Internet at any point, returning by giving a Return command. The drawback of tourist guided tours is that they defeat the spirit of hypertext by providing an essentially linear form of information.

HYPERTEXT AND REGULAR COMPUTER APPLICATIONS

Many computer scientists might say that hypertext is simply a collection of databases. However, there are distinctions that should be mentioned. A database is well structured, in terms of what type of data goes in, and often has predefined paths. A hypertext system has no central definition and no regular structure. Links are established for semantic reasons, not to satisfy a global definition.

For example, ThinkTank is a traditional program that some may consider to be a hypertext system because it allows users to establish outlines of reports and it has a hierarchical structure that allows users to follow a downward path. However, there is no path from a low-level object such as a paragraph to a chapter heading. This single fact eliminates ThinkTank from being classified as a hypertext system.

Hypertext systems should always allow the user to navigate intuitively (as in Windows editors, games, and interactive video). This is what some call "the hype" about hypertext because these applications are often not true hypertext. The control of the information moves from the author to the user. Systems such as multi-window editors are sometimes classified as hypertext because they allow users to move among units, but the user has to call up each additional window. Adventure games also make it difficult for users to find the appropriate link.

Interactive video (IV) is also often mistakenly referred to as hypermedia, but in fact, many interactive video systems are completely passive. The degree to which a user interacts with IV determines the viability of calling it hypermedia. However, IV should not be criticized without comment. It may provide the desired functionality without being hypermedia.

The Hype about Hypertext

Obviously, there is much excitement about the possibilities of hypertext, and, although much of this hype should be questioned, good reasons exist to suggest that hypertext is here to stay. The possibility of combining publishing, computing, and broadcasting opens the door to many new endeavors.

One example of this is NewsPeek, a hypertext system developed at MIT Media Lab, which offers the ability to record parts of the nightly news that only you desire. It also provides the potential to integrate other news media such as newspaper and wire services. Features like this are now possible due to the rapid explosion of the PC; however, the future will be determined ultimately by public demand.

Navigating Large Information Spaces

Cooperative Authoring

Nowadays, a project normally involves a group of people. This is also true for writing hypertext. Several problems arise under this collaborative environment.

1. **Disorientation** When more than one user works on a shared hypertext, an individual user will have trouble finding information he/she needs when changes are being made behind his/her back. Improved communication and coordination among the users can alleviate this problem.

2. **Authorization to change information** Each user owns some nodes, while certain nodes may be co-owned by people in the same group. The hypertext system might keep the identities of authors of nodes and links and use that information to determine authorizations and privileges to change or delete the information.

3. **Version control** The hypertext system needs to keep track of multi-author deleting, splitting, and redirecting nodes as well as changing links dynamically at any time [Delisle and Schwartz, 1987]. It can then inform the person making the change to update related links or nodes accordingly.

Information Retrieval

Another key component of hypertext is information retrieval, which is a search for specific data in a hypertext document that can be performed solely on the basis of navigation. However, this kind of movement search is impractical for a very large information space because it would take too long to navigate. Thus, it should be possible to let the computer do the work of finding the appropriate nodes.

Navigation alone is fine for a small space that is familiar to the user. If the information space is large and unfamiliar, then the use of queries is required to find data.

For example, search results can be integrated with the overview diagram by highlighting nodes that contain "hits." Superbook is one example of such a system.

If we have a hypertext in which the nodes have already been linked, we can utilize the information implied by the structure of the space to perform semantically meaningful searches. A hypertext document can be considered a "belief network": if two nodes are linked, then we "believe" that they are related in some fashion.

Query mechanisms may also be used to reduce the hypertext so that only the links relevant to the search topic are active, and only these links are shown on the overview diagram. This merger of traditional navigation and query methods could be the best of both worlds if properly implemented.

AN EXAMPLE: *INIGO GETS OUT*

The majority of the hypertext story *Inigo Gets Out* is presented in the first person, and the user must click on the places the cat wants to go. There are a few places where the story changes perspective to the second person, where the user directs the cat's movements by clicking on the cat rather than the destination.

A field study of kindergarten children using *Inigo Gets Out* [Nielsen and Lyngbaek, 1990] found that the students had no problem navigating through the story, but they often were confused at first by the change in navigational methods. This points to the need for a consistent metaphor in any hypertext system.

Exercise

Hypertext Challenge

Select a story from any children's book. *The Three Bears* could be a likely candidate. Now, using a word processor with hypertext abilities, create a variety of links, backtracks, and anchors. Invent imaginative places where the plot can go other than the routine ones. See how creatively you can link together the different choices the reader/user must make. Make believe your younger brother/sister or son/daughter will be reading this!

4

Creating Your Own Home Page on the Net

This chapter will cover the following:

- How to create your own home page
- How to publish and announce your presence
- How to get a free home page server listing

What do you do when have created your digital movie or written that best seller? Normally, you would try to get an agent to sell it for you (and I have supplied their addresses on the CD). However, you can set up your own presence on the Internet without an agent, without a publisher, and without all the money that these kind folks require! This, my friends, is what all the commotion is about around electronic artisan circles. If the little guy can get his stuff out for the masses to judge, then we can get rid of all those middle people who steal the profits. Gad, I can see my editor and publisher wince as I even mention such blasphemies!

In this section, I will show you how you can easily create a presence on the World Wide Web, and you do not have to pay anyone! Yes, there are costs (you did buy the computer and all the great stuff to go with it), but you still can get noticed without being taken in by the Web con artists who are soaking plenty of new people every day. Later in the book (Part IV), I will be telling you where to send to have someone else publish your stuff. I will even show you how to set up your own cyberstation without a computer! However, this section is devoted to showing the individual how to set up his or her own home page presence on the Net, so he or she can get noticed in a big way.

First of all, the best way to create a Web presence (and the easiest, from a non-techie point of view) is to use Netscape Navigator Gold 2.0 (download it free from http://www.netscape.com) and create a home page. I will be showing you pictures of the pages my wife, son, and I created to advertise our consulting business on the Internet. You can do this also, just as easily, and we hope you do. Whatever your personal or professional expertise or knowledge, you can create a home page that reflects your services or individuality in the best way. I now teach and consult about developing these service-oriented pages, and there are great opportunities for any digital scribe who can apply the concepts learned in this book.

Before I created my home page, I drew a storyboard of how it would be organized. Thus, I knew exactly what would go on my index page: a headline showing the name of our organization (Figure 4.1), hypertext links to our services (Figure 4.2), colorful and related graphics (Figures 4.1 and 4.3), a link to the Instructor page (Figure 4.3), and a link to our e-mail address (very important!) (Figure 4.7).

In Figure 4.1, you can see the general layout of Netscape Navigator Gold and how my Web page looks inside the browser. The great thing about Gold is the fact that you can load a file inside the browser to view it immediately after having created it. You can switch from Edit Document to View In Browser until you get it just right. I created the headlines on this home page using the handy color text

Figure 4.1

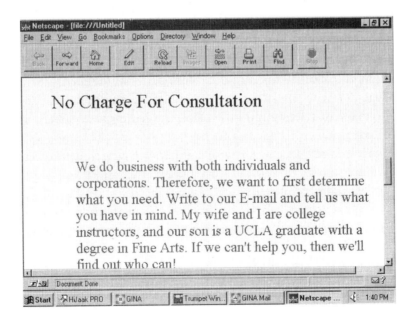

Figure 4.2

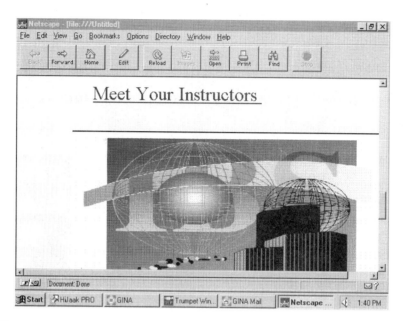

Figure 4.3

tool in the Options menu. On this first page, I wanted to let my user know just what my consulting business did. Thus, I placed the title of the organization, Contemporary Instructional Concepts, at the top, together with the slogan, "Where You Can Find Education Fast!" I made the slogan blink by using the handy text writing tool to create this effect. My wife and I differ as to its effect. She seems to believe it is too Las Vegas, and I think it jazzes things up. You can do what you prefer. Gold is really fast to use, and I finished this page in less than an hour.

In Figure 4.2, you can see where I added something about our talents as well as something about how we do business. It is good to maintain a friendly, personable voice on electronic Web sites because, unlike any other medium, the computer Web site represents a personal intrusion into mental and physical space. Your reader/user feels the need to connect to a human because the medium can be very alienating.

In Figure 4.3, I created a hyperlink to my first new page. This is done quite easily by clicking on the icon that looks like chain links. The "Meet Your Instructors" text is hyperlinked to a page of photos and hypertext (see Figure 4.4). In Figure 4.5, you can see the hypertext under the photo. This is linked to resumes of our experience (Figure 4.6).

It is fun to add a little humor whenever you can. Reading Web pages can sometimes be similar to those old Burma Shave signs that we read as we traveled across the highways of this country. We looked forward to seeing what the next sign would say. Another phenomenon of this nature would be the popularity of such sketches as "Fuzzy Memories" by Jack Handy. Any short and funny items you can place on your pages can perk them up quickly. Another great source for this type of humor is (believe it or not) *Mad Magazine*. They do a lot of little background items in the panels from which you can learn. However, you must be careful to make certain that your audience and your writing purpose can include a little humor. However, you

Figure 4.4

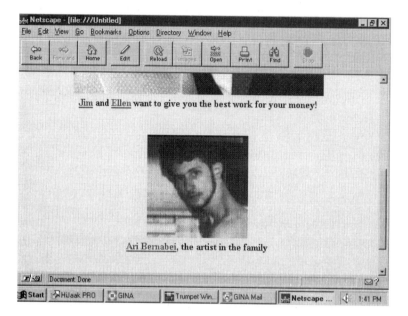

Figure 4.5

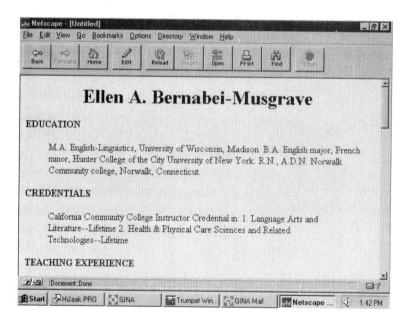

Figure 4.6

must not clutter your page too much with this stuff. Remember the 15-second span of attention rule!

In Figure 4.7, you can see that I added instructions for the reader to choose the item he or she needs from the hypertext list of our services (Figure 4.8). All of this information is important for the reader to know.

In Figures 4.9–4.11, you can see the artwork that we included to show off our son Ari's abilities. He also did the illustration used for the cover of this book (the hand and quill). Using links to show off your talents is the perfect way to demonstrate to your potential clients that you have what it takes. For example, I could have linked copies of my writing (fiction or nonfiction) to some hypertext in the index.html page. The user would then click and go directly to these samples.

Another great addition that has come about through the talents of Macromedia is the ability to play run-time files of multimedia directly from your Web page. That means you can also link these

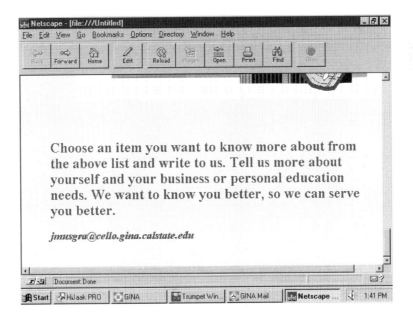

Figure 4.7

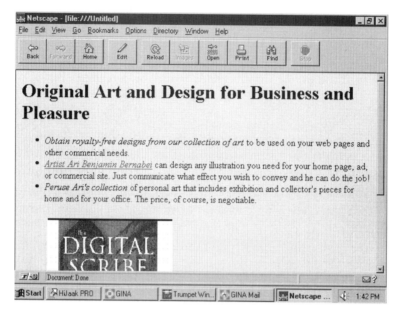

Figure 4.8

Figure 4.9

Figure 4.10

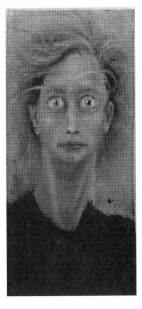

Figure 4.11

run-time applications to your Netscape home pages, and then the user may use Macromedia's Shockwave for playing Director files, or Multimedia World Wide Web (see CD-ROM) for playing Tool-Book files. I like ToolBook because you can play multimedia educational applications that keep track of the student's progress through the Administrator application. Macromedia provides no such vehicle (yet).

Now you may download your free copy of Netscape Navigator Gold (http://www.netscape.com) and see for yourself how easy it is to create a home page that can sell your service, product, or identity. Thousands are learning to do this every day, and the cost is minimal for an individual. You can use free Web sites provided by many organizations because they are sponsored by larger companies. They want your home page because it attracts business to the big fish. See the details of how to get a free Web page in Part IV of this book and on the CD inside the folder "Netguide."

Part II

Techniques of Prewriting for Electronic Media

5 | Storyboarding

Storyboarding is perhaps the most creative aspect of the digital scribe's job. Defined generally, storyboarding is the work the writer does before he or she creates on the screen. Unless one knows exactly what is going to go on the screen for the user to see, to manipulate, and to learn from, then the writer has not prepared sufficiently.

This chapter will cover:

- Three major categories of storyboard authoring
- Twelve Commandments of Storyboarding
- Specific techniques used within the three categories

THREE AREAS OF AUTHORING

The job of storyboarding can be categorized into areas of development or "technical authoring" that need to be done. Basically, there are three areas of storyboarding that are usually performed by writers of multimedia and authors on the Net:

1. Animation
2. Digital movies
3. Web page development

Each of these three areas has its own necessary procedures and talents, which we shall examine later, but first let us look at some of the similarities that all of these storyboarding tasks require. It must also be pointed out that these three areas are often combined to do certain tasks. For example, an advertising catalog could use all three storyboarding areas to fulfill the job. Animation could be used to demonstrate a product's use. A digital movie could show a message from the company president. And this could all be translated for the Internet into HTML and VRML languages. Digital scribes must be familiar with how to mix and match the areas and their skills, just as they must learn to do the same with the seven writing techniques that I covered earlier in this text.

TWELVE COMMANDMENTS OF STORYBOARDING

1. Visual design must be coherent for the message being communicated.

When you compose a storyboard, you must first make certain that the elements you are placing on the page are necessary for the enhancement or explanation of your message. In other words, if I were trying to attract an interest in automobiles, I would not include pictures of congested, smoke-spewing freeways at rush hour. I would instead include images of driving in natural surroundings, perhaps, or show how autos give one personal freedom on the roads. Visual coherence is the way the reader can easily link the media together in his or her mind. Without coherence, the page can become disorganized and cluttered. Remember the 15-second attention span rule!

2.   Media must not get in the way of the message.

Writing storyboards requires that you keep your media manageable on the page. That is, you must not let one graphic, animation, or text creation overpower your intent. For example, if I am trying to give information about how to apply for college on a home page in the Internet, I would not want a glitzy graphic of any kind taking up too much space. Instead, I would probably want to give the reader easily manipulated headers or icons that point to various departments within the organization where information can be found.

3.   Hyperlinks must be logical and appropriate to the purpose.

The information covered earlier in this text about hypertext and hypermedia applies here. The digital scribe should make certain that each location to which the user goes is planned out beforehand. That means that the storyboard should show what will happen when the user clicks on a word, an object, or a graphic. This must be done in language that the technical people on the project (if there are others) can understand. What type of sound file, what format of graphic, and what exact page location—all this information must go on notecards (see Chapter 3, "Hypertext: Theory and Practice"). Some writers use Mac HyperCards to do this, others use plain old 3" × 5" index card style. Whatever the methodology, it is important to make certain that each link is carefully outlined and detailed. Otherwise, there will *certainly* be problems in the developmental phase of the project, when the information is transferred to the final storyboard mock-up.

4. **One storyboard panel or screen must never show more than the reader can digest in 15 seconds.**

This is the cardinal rule in developing any application for the Internet or for multimedia. However, this does not mean that you cannot include a lot of information. On the contrary, your page may have links that take the reader to a multitude of places where words can be defined, concepts can be explained, and other informational events can occur. This rule simply means that on a single page there must not be more information (in text or graphic form) than can be read in 15 seconds.

5. **Storyboards must fit the project team's needs.**

The writer must design a form for the storyboard that fits the needs of all the members of his multimedia development group or any group that will be using these panels to create ideas. All members should agree that the storyboards can be easily read by all and that all will be able to understand what is communicated. This can prove difficult when the storyboard writer is located in a different department. That is why so many engineers have designed on-line storyboard methods, whereby the whole team can access the storyboard frames to give individual input that can then be immediately accessed and thus understood by all who are involved. It should be remembered that some of the first storyboards were designed for the Disney animators. These were simply giant wall murals that all involved could see and write on to get an immediate reaction. This team spirit has continued down to the present-day multimedia work group. Thus, before drafting your storyboard outline, the writer should make certain that it fits the needs of every person on the development team.

6. **Most storyboards (even the ones for technical projects) should have some element of entertainment for the project members.**

This is a commandment that gives the digital scribe a chance to have some fun. Whether it is pasting yellow smiling faces, telling jokes, or adding Java moving applets, the scribe can do a lot to enliven an otherwise tedious task. This can often lead to a breakthrough in the team's creativity (they access their creative child, as discussed in Chapter 1).

7. **Which comes first, the chicken or the storyboard? In this instance, the chicken must come first, if by "chicken" we are referring to the overall "intent" of your creation.**

Just as written communication must have a purpose or intent, storyboards must also have a purpose for which they are created. In other words, storyboarding is not, on its own, an end. Some people are confused, I suppose, by animation storyboards in their final "shooting" or photographed form, which sometimes sell for thousands of dollars as art. Even though they are artistic masterpieces, they are still only one link in a story that was previously thought out all the way through to the end in some other form (usually paragraphs). This is the "story" in storyboard.

8. **Storyboards should be flexible.**

You must keep extra copies of storyboard templates, cards, or other media on hand so that members of the development team can easily change formats, switch designs, or even start over. Without flexibility, storyboarding can become a tedious and even dictatorial task. I know that the famous film director Alfred Hitchcock personally created his detailed storyboards and reportedly refused to let anyone change them, but we are not all geniuses. Most of us must remain flexible enough to accept criticism, change our techniques, or even change the content of our creations.

9. **Storyboards must be alive.**

The cardinal rule of shooting digital movies is "don't shoot unless it's moving." This same rule can apply to most storyboards. Something should be happening within your frame, even if it is a small movement. A great example occurred when cameras were focused on the surviving Kennedy family at the funeral for John F. Kennedy. They all stood at erect attention, and there was no movement to speak of, until John-John raised his little hand and gave that now-famous salute to his daddy. That single motion made the scene come alive.

10. Storyboards must use color whenever possible.

This rule points to the fact that we are visual beings. Unless the colors are planned beforehand, the entire effect could be lost on the user. That is why it is a wise storyboarder who gathers the required information about which palettes will be used in the story frames. This information can go in the "Graphics and Video" column on the sample interactive module page (see Figure 5.1 and the CD).

11. Storyboards must show sound use whenever possible.

Most multimedia projects require that the writer insert the audio to be played, whether it is speech, music, or sound effects. Note that the sample interactive module page has a column for "Audio." The writer must insert what will play on this screen.

12. The final commandment says that storyboards must be organized.

This means that the writer must make certain that the frames are numbered and that the administrative details are inserted wherever they are required. Note that the example interactive module page has places for the following: Client/Project Title, Module Number, Module Title, and Rev. # (revision number). All of this information should be inserted so that the storyboard can be kept consistent and logical. In addition, page numbers can be inserted (usually handwritten because they can change order often).

PROCEDURES AND TALENTS

Now we shall examine specific procedures and talents that go into each of the three authoring areas: animation, digital movies, and Web page development.

Animation Storyboards

Animation requires a specific type of storyboarding that must be used with care and with artistic flair. You can see the simple application of an animation storyboard in the sample panels from a fifteen-year-old artist's Mac HyperCard program (see Figures 5.2 through 5.4). This required some artistic talent but not much, and the colors were easily inserted with a simple paint program.

It must be noted, however, that the digital scribe may only need to refer to the artist's work in his interactive storyboard script (see sample and Figure 5.1). The information, such as "art scene 1," would go in the column labeled "Graphics and Video."

What talent is required from the writer is his or her ability to see the story take place and to write what animations should occur. This, in fact, is the very talent described in the article by Ken Melville later in this book (see Chapter 9). The writer must have this "visionary" talent, even if her or she is not an artist. Most multimedia projects have art departments to work on the writer's vision, so there is not much to worry about. Also, there are excellent software programs that can duplicate characters for your animation, and then you tell them what to do (see the description of 3-D Choreographer in Chapter 8).

Digital Movie Storyboards

Digital movies require another type of storyboarding talent, in addition to the artistic one. The movie planner must also be able to

Module Title

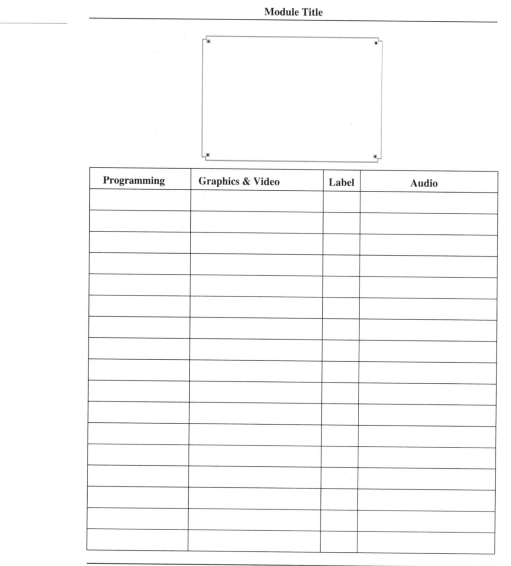

Programming	Graphics & Video	Label	Audio

CLIENT\PROJECT TITLE - MODULE NUMBER - MODULE TITLE - Rev. #

Figure 5.1

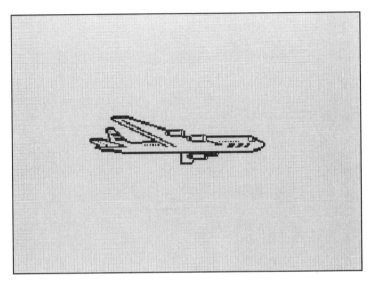

SCENE 1: We see a plane flying through the sky.

Figure 5.2

SCENE 2: Inside plane facing the movie screen with people in the foreground.

Figure 5.3

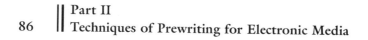

SCENE 3: Zoom in on old lady and fat man, both are watching the movie.

Figure 5.4

see what motions make good drama. In other words, the storyboard writer for movies must see as the camera does, and know exactly what will add to the overall movement of plot, character, and dramatic conflict. For example, suppose you were planning the opening scene to a story that pits brothers against each other during the American Civil War. What action would you describe to show the viewer how these characters will soon be having to go against each other? Perhaps you could have a scene where they are both trying to impress a local country girl they both like. They both are trying to climb a large oak tree to see who gets to the top first. By showing this rivalry early in the action, you are demonstrating or telescoping the future conflict, when they go their separate ways—one brother to the North, one to the South.

The storyboard is the most important step in making a movie. When you have finished the storyboard, you have essentially made the movie. Some marketing people prefer to use storyboards as a tool for getting funding. In this case, the storyboard must be extremely fancy and detailed.

However, in most cases, the storyboard is simply a blueprint of the movie that the director and the cinematographer follow. The storyboard can even be thumbnail sketches on the back of a napkin . . . just so long as it is clear what happens in every shot of the movie.

Many storyboard artists will prefer a natural drawing program like Fractal Design's Fractal Painter 3.0, which is available for both the Macintosh and the Windows PC. When used with a 6 × 9 or larger Wacom tablet, the program gives the feel of working with paper. Also, Fractal Painter has been specially designed to do production work in Hollywood. Fractal Design also has a great program for beginners called Dabbler II.

Animated storyboards (called *animatics*) for digital movies are an excellent idea. This is an example of the mix-and-match rule mentioned earlier. In this instance, we are mixing animation technique with movie technique. Still-frame storyboards are limited since they do not show the timing of each shot. This knowledge can save as much as half the cost of shooting the motion picture.

By simply putting each storyboard frame into a nonlinear editing program like Premiere or VideoShop, the storyboard can become animated to clearly show the timing of each of the shots of the movie. Then the director only needs to shoot the necessary shots without shooting extra coverage.

Storyboard programs such as Storyboard Artist can create Quick-Time movies, while Storyboard Quick does not. As mentioned earlier in the case of animation, simple storyboards can be created in HyperCard if you know how to write simple programs in that application. The advantage is that all the still frames can be linked together in a book.

In HyperCard, create a master document with one frame on each page. Type the dialog under each blank frame. Remember that each shot will average five seconds long and range from three seconds to seven seconds. If the dialog is longer than five seconds, break it up into two or more shots.

Print the blank storyboard sheets and draw the storyboard by hand, not by using the computer. Using the computer is inefficient in HyperCard.

For finished storyboards, print the same storyboard sheets full-sized for drawing in more detail. Use simple stick figures to show the location of the actors and where they are facing. Nothing fancier is required unless you are trying to impress investors.

Another alternative is a 3D virtual reality program such as Virtus WalkThrough Pro or Virtus VR (see samples on the CD), since these programs let you look at the scene in 3D through various lenses and at various angles. QuickTime or AVI movies can be created of each shot, or still images can be printed out. Walkthrough programs are much faster to use than normal 3D animation programs.

When you create the digital movie storyboard, consider the mood of the scene. This will determine what lens you should use. Both wide-angle and telephoto lenses distort the image. A normal lens does not.

A wide-angle lens makes the scene seem cold, distant, strong, and unfriendly. A telephoto lens makes the scene look warm, close, soft, and friendly. A normal lens makes the scene look plain, dull, and boring.

Indicate how much of the background should be seen. If everything in the scene must be in sharp focus, then you need to have greater depth of field. A greater depth of field can be obtained by using a wider angle lens or by decreasing the size of the iris of the lens (which makes the lens act like a pinhole camera.) The iris can be made smaller only if you switch to faster film or add more light. A zoom lens usually has a poor depth of field and a limited close-focus distance. Always use prime, not zoom lenses, if you can.

Also make notes on the storyboard if the camera is looking up or looking down on the subject. If the camera looks up, the figure will look more powerful and threatening. If the camera looks down, the figure will look weak and insignificant. One of the finest movies to view for its use of camera angles for dramatic effect is Orson Welles's classic *Citizen Kane*.

If the camera moves in the scene, indicate that by drawing two frames. The first indicates where the camera starts and the other indicates what the camera sees when the movement is finished. Then draw an arrow between the two frames to indicate they are part of the same shot.

The camera is moved for three reasons:

1. **To give the scene a sense of depth.** If the camera moves to the side even slightly, it gives the scene a sense of depth. The rate of movement of all the objects in the scene shows the relative distance between all the objects in the scene. Even the slightest movement turns a flat 2D image into a 3D image.

2. **To follow the action.** Caution: Too much motion can cause seasickness.

3. **To transition between one action and another.** This is called an *in-camera edit* and can be very graceful.

Never zoom the camera lens in or out if you can help it. Always move the camera in or out. Zooming only magnifies an already flat image while moving in the camera (dolly in) magnifies the scene while adding 3D depth to the scene.

Remember the Golden Rule of motion pictures, which is "If it doesn't move, don't film it!" If the actors do not move in a scene, move the camera instead, even if it is only three inches (the distance between our left and right eyes).

Web Page Storyboards

Writing storyboards before you create Web pages can be crucial to your design. This is especially true when you are designing pages that have multimedia applications such as Java applets, sound, Shockwave for Director, Multimedia World Wide Web or World Wide Web Kiosk (to play Asymetrix ToolBook applications), or any of the many VRML and other such interesting possibilities. Never before in the history of on-line page development have there been so many creative possibilities for the digital scribe to make a living in the Web page or home page development task.

Storyboards for Web pages must include all of the information necessary to keep track of the placement of multimedia applications and hypermedia (see Chapters 3 and 4). If you have it all written down, then the task of placing these items on the screen becomes organized and easy.

Development of Web pages is especially important because the hyperlinks for Web page development are often changes in address (URL) rather than simply movement from one file to the next. Therefore, you are apt to get bad connections very easily unless you make your links solid. There is no better way to ensure this than to have accurate and detailed storyboards. As you will see in the next chapter, unless these storyboards are detailed, the mix-and-match rule will be very difficult to apply. The final development of the project (whether by a team or by an individual developer) must be organized and easy to follow.

6

Web Page Authoring

This chapter will cover the following:

- Defining communication
- Structures of Web page communication
- How to compensate for browser drawbacks
- How to best use graphics
- Using image maps
- Web etiquette
- How to create a style guide
- Basic navigation techniques
- Basic forms of the Web page
- How to design for browser differences

WHAT IS COMMUNICATION?

The communication process is what happens when people interact. The basic process is as follows: A source (person) projects an intention through an interface for an audience to interpret meaning.

The steps that occur are

1. The source has an intention that he or she wants to project
2. The source projects the intention to an interface
3. The interface is interpreted by an audience
4. The audience forms some meaning based on the interface

Before starting a site, the author of Web pages must first identify the source, the interface, and the audience in order to identify the message and what projection media to use. One must also have a concrete idea and use it as the anchor (see Chapter 3, "Hypertext: Theory and Practice") during a site's development. The best way to test the effectiveness of a well-designed site is to evaluate the interpretations of sample audiences and incorporate some of the suggestions in the site. In fact, this book is an example of this idea in action!

STRUCTURES OF WEB PAGE COMMUNICATIONS

The basic organizational structures of Web pages are of the following types: linear, hierarchical, circular hierarchical, and clusters. These structures provide ways to categorize many types of data into linked nodes. The author must completely know the subject matter in order to choose the right structure. Often, it is best to use a combination of the different organizational structures in different parts of the site.

For example, introductory nodes present a traditional table of contents in a hierarchical structure. Then within each chapter, the linear structure connects the chapter sections. Each chapter becomes an independent cluster. Each sentence may contain circular references to other nodes within its chapter or outside its chapter.

Choosing the Correct Medium for the Message

As we all know, the Web supports a wide range of media types. Every message has an optimal medium for its conveyance to the audience. A Web writer must choose which media form best fits a message or source contents.

BROWSER DRAWBACKS

The Web's strength, its movement across a spectrum of platforms, is also its weakness. Some users access the Web from locations with a fast Internet connection, like a T1 line that enables them to retrieve large images, sounds, and other files relatively quickly. On the other hand, some users access the Web from a slow modem connection that can cause large files to take minutes or hours to download. Web designers need to consider ways to present data quickly and also aesthetically by different link speeds. This often means avoiding unnecessary graphics and supplying workable navigation alternatives to graphical image maps (MAPI).

Various browsers display Web documents in radically different ways. Some browsers, like Lynx, use only a single-font text display for all HTML documents. Other browsers, like Netscape, use not only graphics, but proprietary formatting codes that are incompatible with other browsers.

As if these differences were not enough, the browsers are also displayed on a wide range of computers and monitors. The monitors may be black and white or 8-bit or 24-bit color; the screen may be a nine-inch screen or a two-page display. Graphic designers used to the paper medium have the foresight to know how the page will be laid out and can usually place graphics at exact locations. However, a Web page designed for a large monitor may create a navigational nightmare for small-screen audiences, who find themselves endlessly scrolling around the entire Web page. Therefore, Web designers find that they must design graphics and layouts that can translate to a wide range of displays.

- **Using Graphics** A picture is worth a 1000 words (or more). Literally. Choose carefully.

- **Using Text** Text is incredibly versatile and efficiently transmitted.

- **Using Links** Links define the way users travel through a site.

- **Using Sound** The Web is quickly becoming the new radio.

- **Using Movies** The nature of movies makes them a conceptually perfect match to the Web, but the bandwidth and file size constraints still limit how often they can be used.

HOW TO USE GRAPHICS

Images can give one a taste of a physical location, can invoke emotional qualities, and can express numerical data. Try to use the following when designing Web pages:

- **Motifs** Recurring design patterns within a set of graphics unifies the elements (see also the section entitled "Recurrence" in Chapter 2).

- **In-line Graphics** These provide visual separation and pacing. But be courteous to low-bandwidth users.

- **Image Maps (MAPI)** Images with links require implied usage of hot regions that show on the map itself and are easily recognized by the user.

- **Toolbars** Simplicity and functionality are the toolbar's best features.
- **Mastheads** Mastheads, the topmost graphic on a page, are quite often used to unify.

Uses of Images in Web Page Designs

Real-world Images

Images such as scans of photographs give the viewer a literal impression of the real world. They interpret the texture qualities as an element that actually exists in some other place.

Optical Illusions

Graphics can represent many things that do not exist in the real world. For example, some graphics (like holograms) depict optical illusions that do not have a physical correspondence.

Emotional Qualities

Graphics do not have to have a literal reference. They can represent emotional qualities like the process of actually creating art. The development of modern art was a response to the development of photographs. Artists felt liberated from merely depicting the real world and could thus begin to fill canvases with emotional value.

Quantitative Data

Graphic charts are often the best way to present large sets of data. Unlike a linear sequence of numbers, the visual dynamics of a chart can create a visual map that highlights many hidden dimensions of the data set like trends and averages. Graphics can also be a visual map to a set of data.

Motifs (recurring patterns)

Most Web sites contain a series of graphics. Sometimes, graphics do not seem as if they belong together. This disparity is often caused by the lack of developed motifs (recurring design patterns within a set of graphics).

Consider the design dynamics of fonts; for example, the Times-Roman family. Each character in the family looks as if it belongs with the rest of the characters because there are underlying patterns in which the characters are built. Even though the h and the m characters are different formations, they seem to belong to a similar family. Notice how the width of the curve starts off small and grows as it arches over to the base. The height and the width are consistent for each instance of this arch formation. The bases extend out to the same width, and the width of the stem is identical. The motifs, the constraint patterns, are tools that are used to design every element in the graphic set. The motifs tie the individual characters together and make them into a type of family.

Standard Icons

The design of new graphics always incorporates colors and forms that are based on other sources. Every time a color is used, it infers a certain emotional quality. Each shape can be reduced to primal archetypal symbols like water and fire. Every aspect of the graphic conveys some information at a conscious or subconscious level.

In the design of icons, it is usually helpful if one uses accepted standards for visual representations. Under usual conditions, the most effective stop sign is one that is familiar to the audience. For example, many applications use a magnifying glass icon to symbolize the Find or the Search command. Even though the connection between the magnifying glass metaphor and the Find command is not readily apparent, many users have become accustomed to this usage. It is as if they learned that a strange symbol like glass stands for the shhh sound. The magnifying glass has become part of a new basic alphabet for visual icons. Utilize this alphabet in order to reduce the time it takes for the audience to understand the meaning of symbols. This works especially well when you are working with educational Web pages. Children are naturally metaphorical, as I explained in the section on writing.

In-line Graphics

Many visual artists use the Web as a way of advertising their artwork. This usage demonstrates the true utility of offering graphics in a Web site because the content is the graphic and not text. Naturally, a piece of visual art cannot be fully expressed in words. It must be represented by the actual work or at least a photographic approximation.

However, one must be courteous to the audience trapped behind a slow link to the Web. It is often best to provide a preview by offering a low-resolution version of the graphic with a description and information about the full graphic file, like its size and type. The descriptive text should include keywords that will help locate your image through the use of searching tools. Sneak peeks of the art give your users a chance to judge their interest level before actually waiting to download the complete file.

Space

Graphics are often inserted between text as a way of separating the flow of separate items of text. In cases where the text flow contains a variety of late-breaking items, like Sports pages, the spacers are helpful in identifying when one point begins and another ends.

If graphics are used as spacing, try not to make them so big that the user loses his sense of location. If a large separator graphic is displayed on a small monitor, the user may not take the time to scroll to the next section of text.

Image Maps (MAPI)

Image maps are graphics containing hypermedia regions, that is, links to other page nodes. A common usage of image maps is to provide an overall visualization of a particular site. For example, a museum can offer an architectural layout as a way of showing the location of different attractions (see the sample Web page from the Smithsonian Institute in Chapter 3). A mouse-click within the boundaries of a room will load that room's Web page representation. Image maps give the user an establishing shot perspective of a location so that they can immediately survey the entire site's content.

Some image maps are cluttered with too many icons and hypermedia regions. This may distract the audience from the central pieces of information and may confuse them. Optimize the path to key data by having important graphical elements that are easily perceived as the interactive hypermedia content.

In addition, make sure that the hypermedia regions are obvious. Sometimes, this is accomplished by giving these regions a similar border. For example, some image maps, like in Macromedia (see CD), simulate the look of a button. This makes it very obvious to the user exactly where the hypermedia links are. It may seem creative to have image maps with obscure links, but that will often lose the audience's attention, so it is usually an unwise practice.

Always Supply Text Navigation

Sites designed around image maps should provide optional navigational mechanisms for users without graphical browsers. If an image map is followed by a text link, the text-only image browsers will display that text as the main part of the screen.

The Smithsonian Institute page (see Figure 3.2) can also be shown through a text-only browser. If you visit this site, you can note how the text that was not a main part of the MAPI page becomes the main focus of the text-only page. Providing the alternative text path increases the audience range that can navigate through a site.

Keep Graphics Ordered by Their Function

Separate the graphical regions by functionality.

Keep Graphics in the Same Family

A readable image map contains elements that often fit together as a family and are within the same context. Sometimes, external elements are introduced that can confuse the interpretation of the image map. For example, let's assume we wanted to add a search feature to the museum map above. One way to do this would be to place a magnifying glass directly over the graphic of the museum layout.

The problem with this solution is that it is hard to immediately differentiate between the borders of the rooms and the overlaid magnifying glass. A quick glimpse at this image might suggest that the magnifying glass is a round room in the corner of the museum. It might also suggest that the entire picture is an abstract collection of lines and circles. Effectively rendering depth on a two-dimensional plane requires a lot of experience. The audience is also given a significant amount of interpretation overhead. Avoid overlapping graphics because it adds unnecessary noise. There is a distinction in the result between clicking on a room and clicking on the magnifying glass. The rooms are hyperlinks to different page areas, but the magnifying glass is linked to a query form. The search utility is thematically apart from the site because it performs a transaction on its contents.

In the above picture, the search command would best be represented by a button beneath the museum layout. It provides a visual distinction between the resulting action if the user clicks on a room or on a button. It improves the user's metaphorical connection that a button is expected to trigger some sort of function. Therefore, the best result is achieved.

WEB ETIQUETTE

The following are the usual expected "helpers" you should supply on your Web pages:

- A style guide
- A standard look for your site to give it cohesiveness

The best way to ensure consistency is to start off with a style guide describing the various ways to present data.

- Basic navigation (simple interactivity)
- Basic forms (easy to input)

Other Forms of Web Etiquette

Keep the Noise to a Minimum

Most people have to pay some sort of a price for the time it takes to download data. Every piece of content in a site should be worth its weight in bytes. Step back from your page offering and objectively judge the relevance of every graphic and every file that is there. Is the data within context? Should it be placed elsewhere? Is there something distracting the user from the important data?

Be Considerate of Bandwidth

Bandwidth is the biggest design problem Web designers must face. The Web enables you to design with rich media types, but gives a tiny straw with which to deliver such rich data.

Therefore, until wide bandwidth becomes generally available, one must judge the size of offered files. Text files should be small enough so that they can be downloaded in a reasonable amount of time, usually less than five to ten seconds.

Graphic files can take more time to download, usually 30 seconds. The graphic files do not need to be huge. Question how much resolution each graphic really needs to offer. Most browsers will not usually display a graphic that is larger than 72 dots per inch and 640 by 480 pixels. If the graphic is larger than that, then the user ends up scrolling to see the entire picture, which often reduces its impact.

Name and Date the Page

Identify yourself and your organization on every page. The audience will often want to know who to reference or contact when they are interested in your content.

Avoid Dead Links

As a site is created, often files are moved or misplaced, which may affect inter-document and cross-site links. Always go back and reference each link and make sure that they are still functional.

Provide Complete File Information

When a large file is being offered, always provide the file type and size next to each link. This is courteous to the audience, who may have to patiently wait for minutes or hours to receive a large file.

Be Considerate of Various Browsers

It is reasonable to pack a site with design elements for high-end graphical browsers, but make sure to test the pages on the low-end text-only browsers. Usually, one can accommodate both types of browsers with a display solution.

HOW TO CREATE A STYLE GUIDE

Design a site to provide great content in an insightful structure. Try not to explore with new user interface elements unless that is the central focus of your site. If an unconventional element is used, it may call too much attention to itself and detract from the actual content. The audience wants to be able to navigate the Web with the utmost of ease. Avoid detracting from their visual flow.

One of the best ways to ensure a smooth visual flow is to be consistent with the boundaries of your site. Many word processors and page layout tools encourage the use of style sheets, that is, a certain set of definitions used to describe the way different elements will look.

Develop sheets for your Web site and stick with them. Create style sheets for each type of page, which usually includes the following:

- **Index Page**   Type of navigational device that will be used to present all of a site's data.

- **Content Page**   Page containing text or graphics that is the primary content of a site.

- **Embedded File**   Description of how in-line graphics will look on the page.

- **Typical Form Layout**   What are the standard elements that will be found on all "typical" data entry forms?

Each style sheet usually displays

1. The placement of logos
2. The navigation paradigm
3. Embedded file information
4. Standardized development tools

In reference to item 4, depending on the type of tools you use for a site, files can end up looking completely different. If you use a text editor to directly write HTML, you have more control over how the page will ultimately appear. (Netscape Gold 2.0 is especially effective for this.) However, if the source files are being written in a custom editor or a shrink-wrapped editor like Microsoft Word or Frame-Maker, the files will have to be converted to HTML using a filter package. The filters may apply certain types of formatting conventions or introduce you to their types of visual design.

Before you develop multiple pages, identify all components of the editing process, including what editors, filters, and directory structures will be used. By standardizing the way the files and content are actually built, the pages will more likely look the same.

Increase User Learning

Style sheets and a consistent development environment will make all of a site's pages look similar. This enables users to expect certain types of behavior and data formations within a site. That expectation reduces the amount of time it takes them to navigate and feel comfortable with a site.

BASIC NAVIGATIONAL CONCEPTS

There are several ways to present the nodes and links that make up a Web site. Choosing the right navigational devices can have an impact on how the user perceives the ease of getting around a site. Each device is best suited for a particular type of site structure. Carefully identify the data that you are providing in a site. How does it lay out? What are the central nodes? Is there an abundance of clusters? Are the nodes laid out in a linear or circular hierarchy? After identifying the structure of your site's data, choose the devices that seem to work best with the information.

Overall Navigational Concepts

Always let the users know where they currently are, where they can go, and where they have been.

One of the biggest problems with hypermedia is that users are constantly traveling between a range of contexts. Every time they move from one page to another, they have made a contextual jump.

When you read a book, one chapter ends and another one begins. The physical nature of the book, the very fact that it is in your hands, is reassuring. You know that the previous chapter did not disappear and you have developed a certain amount of confidence that the chapter will stay around after you're done with it.

A Web browser is a new media form that is still unfamiliar to users. They cannot look forward to much from the way it presents information. There are no reassurances or built-in paradigms that ensure that a page or chapter will stay there. The server may die, the page may disappear, or the browser may crash. The new hypermedia is not as familiar, which causes users to be wary of the new space they explore.

It takes some time to be comfortable with the page order that most browsers provide. It takes even more time to trust in something you cannot see. The fact that users are always jumping contexts makes one navigational concept very clear:

- Make users incredibly comfortable by providing visual equivalents for their immediate context (for example, metaphorical symbols like the magnifying glass).

Composition of Web Pages Viewed as Film Editing

Consider the way different cuts are assembled in a film. When most films show a scene, the scene is composed of many different camera angles, including close-ups on actors and medium shots of the entire room. The shots establish the relative locations of the different elements by always carrying over visual elements like the edge of a desk or the corner of a room. This reassures the audience that they are observing events in a constant contextual space.

Always Have a Way for the User to Review

As the user flips from page to page and node to node within a site, every node can be a more comfortable place if it does not lose the mental connection between the previous node. Creating links to the previous nodes reassures users that they have not entered a brand new world because there is continuity between pages. (This is equivalent to the transition in written communication.)

Provide Associations

Provide visual cues like text or graphical links that provide paths to new and related locations. The links suggest possible relations to the current contextual node.

Avoid overwhelming the user by providing too many links on one node. Only show links that are immediately relevant to the current node's position in the site.

The Basic Forms of the Web Page That the User Sees

- **Home** The home page (index) is the first page users see as they enter into a site. It usually provides some sort of introductory text and a listing of the site's contents.

- **Book** A linear list of pages is the most basic form for a Web site.

- **Flip Cards** A card structure that acts like a deck of index cards.

- **Deep Cards** A hierarchy of nodes that can be represented with links to the ancestor node.

- **Outline Viewpoint** Multiple node levels that are displayed in one page.

- **Topographical View** A topographical view that gradually presents more information to the audience.

Types of Complementary Navigational Aids

- **Index** An index provides a way to find keywords quickly.

- **Linked Overview** Linked introductory text is used in addition to another navigational structure as a way of explaining the central concepts of a site.

- **Change Log** A listing of modifications made to a site helps frequent users find new content.

- **Searching Engine** A searching capability is an interactive way of helping users find their targets.

- **Navigational Paths**   Providing a path identifier of the current location within a site orients the user.

HOW TO DESIGN PAGES FOR BROWSER DIFFERENCES

It is difficult to compensate for the wide range of browsers that will access a site's data. There are few guarantees that the design of a page will be consistent between two machines. Several tactics can be used to provide both a graphically satisfying view of data and a perspective that scales down to text-only browsers.

Use Multiple Browsers

The most useful approach to creating designs is to have various browsers readily available to you. Try out designs made for high-end browsers and see how they scale on text-only browsers. Do not save this exercise for the end of the project. Try out some initial designs and view them concurrently. Find out ways of pushing the graphical presentation while providing navigational paths for text-only browsers.

Optimize the HTML Tags

HTML provides many different ways to present data, including numbered lists, indented lists, and descriptive entries. These formats are optimally interpreted by most browsers. Use the HTML formats instead of fighting them.

Provide Multiple Paths

Often, sites create more than one navigational path. One contains the in-line graphics and the other contains only text. If the resources are available, this approach is useful. However, it does create more maintenance overhead because any change to the site needs to be updated in more than one place.

Avoid New HTML Extensions until They Mature

Although it may be crafty to use every new feature that comes around, try to limit the use of HTML to the most widely supported standard.

Use In-line Graphics as an Index

A simple way to provide a graphically rich perspective of the data while catering to text-only browsers is to use descriptive entry lists with a complementary in-line image.

Tables: Using Preformatted Text

The Table feature may not be available on many browsers for some time. Using preformatted text gives you a close approximation.

Put Large Graphics in a Small Screen

Consider this trick for fitting large graphics on small screens: Sometimes masthead graphics are created that are designed for large-screen monitors. The disadvantage of large mastheads is that browsers running on smaller screens tend to clip them. One way to avoid this problem is to segment the graphic into smaller components if such boundaries exist in the graphic.

If the graphic is offered as two files, each containing one of the words, the image will appear as initially designed on large screens and scale down to small screens because the browser will place the graphics on top of each other.

When designing larger mastheads, keep in mind that they may need to be tiled for smaller screens. The graphics should work equally well next to each other as they do on top of each other. If elements on the graphic bleed outside of the boundaries, make sure that the features match up in both orientations. If a grid is used as the background, the offsets should be designed so that they line up across or down.

7

Surveys

This chapter will cover the following:

- Why the Japanese succeed in marketing
- Ben's List to Obtain Employment as a Freelance Anything
- How to create needs assessment surveys

The Japanese have proven to be successful in sales and marketing because they have taken elaborate pains to make certain their consumers want the product or service they are offering. In fact, if they discovered that the consumers did not show much interest in a product or service, then they would drop it completely. Not so, I am afraid, with American business. You see, it has to do with cultural differences. Whereas in Japan, the individual is raised to think of society's needs first and one's own needs a distant second, in America, most children are raised to think about themselves as being number 1 on the hit parade. What other country could gamble away billions of dollars a year with lotteries, Las Vegas and Atlantic City meccas to "the one big win"? All of this money is being gambled away because our culture has an almost mythological belief that one person will be the exception and will beat the odds. It is true, America does create some very prominent individuals ("superstars"), but many times the little person is left alone, dreaming get rich quick glory ideas that never come true.

In Japan, however, where the population saves rather than gambles, the individual is seen only in terms of how one can contribute to the society at large. Thus, police in Japanese society still live and work in their community's neighborhoods, practically unarmed and un-afraid; in contrast to America, where tanklike police cruisers with attack dogs and special armaments roam neighborhoods that, as civilians, they have never even visited or acknowledged.

Get the idea? What all this leads to is that if you want to be a successful entrepreneur in America, you had better learn who your consumers are and what they really want. And the only way to do this effectively is to copy the Japanese marketers and construct a good survey questionnaire.

I know. You are now saying, "Oh boy, not another one of those boring marketing forms they ask you to fill out when you are ready to go somewhere, and they take hours to answer."

No. I am not referring to those types of surveys. What I propose is a "need survey." For example, why do you think these lengthy "lifestyle questionnaires" get developed in the first place? Well, most American marketers go on the assumption that if you find out how much people make and what they do, then you can convince them that they need a certain product by fancy advertising. That is why those things are so intruding!

The Japanese, on the other hand, construct "need surveys" to send to their consumers because they truly want to find out what these people need! That is right. They want to give people what they want.

Thus, advertising, in the small role that it plays (compared to the megabucks spent in the American marketplace), becomes a simple vehicle of humor and "family bonding" between the business and the consumer. Japanese companies, on the whole, are more worried about the long-run investment than they are about high profits right away. Thus, it makes sense, does it not, to be extremely interested in constructing surveys that show a special interest in their customers' needs.

And this is where you as the digital writer can learn a good lesson. You should not work on the usual American premise of "I have this great idea for a product or service. Now, all I have to do is pay a high-priced ad firm to convince the buyer he or she needs it!" Wrong! This is not a long-term investment at work. For example, Ben, a struggling artist, just graduated from UCLA with a degree in Fine Arts (of all things!). He happens to be a very talented young man, but he is also in the doldrums because he does not believe he has the technical know-how to succeed in the big bad world of America. To a certain extent, I agree with his assessment of this society. We do rely too much on a person's technical knowledge going into a job. And, indeed, one does have to be able to use computer graphics software to do business for most people these days. But the School of Fine Arts is to blame, in my opinion, because they did not require students to learn computers as part of their curriculum.

However, I believe that Ben has something to give that business people need. He has a creative ability to draw and capture images that provoke interest. That is all that is needed, really. Computers do *not* do this. Computers are merely the tools used by great artists to make their work faster and (in some cases) easier and more accessible.

Ben can succeed as a freelance artist without computers if he will just follow the following check-off sheet. I am going to include it here in the hope that you are filled with the enterprising fortitude that Ben seems to be lacking at this point in his life.

Thus, if you want to succeed as a freelance anything, just follow these steps (or keep them taped to your computer and think about how much you distrust authority).

Ben's List to Obtain Employment as a Freelance Anything

1. Gather addresses and phone numbers of printers (over 20 employees) from the phone book or from a library source book (ask a research librarian).

2. Memorize your "sales pitch." It should contain information about what *you can do for the clients* (stated in a positive, can-do attitude). Give them an idea of your rates (hourly, by the job, etc.). Tell them you can provide samples of some of your work or references if the clients want to see them.

3. Call at least *five* phone numbers each day. If you get some interest, tell them you want to meet them personally to set up details of your sales brochures, business cards, and so forth to be located at their place of business. At the very *least*, you should get them to commit to having your phone number handy in case a client wants a job done fast—you can do it! Emphasize that your work is professional and that you want to increase the overall business of the establishment.

4. Go out to the business (printer, publisher, what have you) and get to know the owner. Don't settle on talking with the "manager" or some flunky who lacks the authority to hire you. Only the *boss* can make such decisions. Your future work depends on having the head honcho like you and your work.

5. If you get commitments, make a card file listing the various places where you may be getting work. Call them every week (even if they don't call you) to touch base and to see how things are going. They will forget you exist if you do not bug them. The same goes for any clients you get. The best

advertising is "word of mouth." Satisfied clients can act as references, telling a new client what a pro you are (so you don't have to).

6. Look at yourself in the mirror each day and tell yourself what a hardworking, creative, and dynamic person you are. Fake it until you make it!

Now, my right hemisphere must connect what I just gave you to the main purpose of this chapter. The connection occurs when you realize that when one becomes a service to his or her clients, one is providing for those people's needs.

A needs assessment is done to determine what you can do to help people. It is used a lot in professional education. The employment development department does an employee assessment survey to see who is not satisfied with the way business is being conducted and why the person feels that way. Caltech's Industrial Relations Center provided such a service, and the companies who used our information later said that their employee attitudes and productivity increased dramatically.

The need survey I suggest for the digital writer is similar. That is, you can use the Internet relay chat sessions and the multitude of BBS locations (see list on the CD) to ask people what they need! That's right. You have at your disposal one of the most fantastic communications devices known to humanity, and all you have to do is use it. With over 30 million people on the Net worldwide (and numbers are growing daily), you can reach quite a few samples by posting messages in some key spots.

I will be including some services at the end of this chapter, in case you do not want to go it alone in this venture, but I want you to understand that word of mouth advertising is still the best type around. Thus, I would much rather you were pleased with this book and told a friend about it, than if my publisher were able to "hard sell" it through the "right ads."

The message, however, is still more important than who you get to deliver it. That is why I want to emphasize communication and delivery, to you, the digital scribe of the new era. Consumers out there will, most likely, want to save money or enjoy life more by using your service or product. Therefore, your message must relay that you are interested in their welfare. Sounds easy, doesn't it? Well, you may be surprised to know most advertising in this country (USA) ignores this basic fact.

How can you create assessment questionnaires that get an honest response? Box 1 shows a sample form that you can alter and change to fit your specific needs. It includes most of the questions that you would need answered to begin a business or service of some kind.

Please note that the questions pose no kind of threat to the individual. There is no hint that you will call later, or that they have to fill in their names or addresses. This anonymity is very important. You need to get honest answers.

Questions 1–4 are aimed at seeing what is out there in the way of needs. Questions 5–10 may seem obvious, but you learn about people and how they think by getting these responses. You can tailor these questions by adding specific requests. For example, if you are starting a publishing consulting business, you could substitute *publishing* wherever I have mentioned *product* or *service*.

A recent editorial in *U.S. News and World Report* by John Leo, "Decadence, the Corporate Way," sums up my interpretation of what big companies are paying for with their big money in advertising:

> Freedom from responsibility. It works like this: Advertisers are focusing more and more on the emerging market of "people who do only what they want to do," that is, people who yearn to be completely free of all restraint, expectations and responsibilities. This is a familiar '60s product now tinged with '90s pessimism. So a socially subversive, pro-impulse, anti-rules and anti-restraint message is casually being built into more and

---

Box 1

Assessment Questionnaire

I am trying to start a new business or service, and I need your input. Could you please answer the following so I can learn how I can serve you better?

1. What bothers you most about local businesses? Be specific.

2. What services could be provided to you that would save you the most time and energy? Give at *least* three examples.

3. If you could order three things from a company or an individual, what would those things be?

4. If someone could do some service for you to free up your time, what would that service be?

5. What are your recreational interests? How much money do you spend on hobbies per week?

6. Do you think big corporations are cold and uncaring toward customers?

7. Do you tell your friends about products or services that you like?

8. Do answering machines and computerized advertising questionnaires bother you?

9. Besides having a greater income, what in life do you do that improves your lifestyle?

10. Do you appreciate businesses and services that put the customer's needs first?

---

more campaigns, often with the help of hired psychologists and focus groups (page 31).

Leo goes on to cite examples of Calvin Klein ads in which young people pose in a variety of "opening scenes from a porn movie," as he describes them. I tend to agree with him on a major point of contention: Advertisers have forgotten about the consumer's true needs. When sex, "do your own thing," and anarchy become marketing trends, you know that advertisers have strayed far from the Japanese ideal of society first.

I do not want you to think that I idealize Japanese society. They put so much stress on their young people to achieve that these kids lose their "child within" at a very early age. Thus, Japanese children are today being taught to smile, believe it or not, and they are often experiencing loss of hair and other physical manifestations of "adult pressure" disease.

Possibly this is because they were shut off from the West for those many hundreds of years. However, after their resounding defeat in World War Two, they picked themselves up and became an industrial power to be reckoned with, mainly because they take the time and make an investment in researching their consumer audience before they make any plans to market. And this is my main point: Take the time to know your market's needs before you advertise.

Once you have determined the service, product, or information you want to market by researching your customers, then you must select the means by which you transport the message to them. I have included some sample software on the CD with which you can create a variety of applications for your customers' needs. Box 2 shows what you can do with each type. I am not going to go into depth as to how you can market your product, service, or information on-line; there are a plethora of consultants, books, and articles out there from which you can choose. However, my first dictum still stands: If you spend the right amount of time researching your need base with the potential buyer, then you will have more than enough word of mouth advertising to make your endeavor worthwhile.

Macromedia has announced a plan to work with Netscape to produce multimedia documents that can be accessed over the Web. Shockwave for Director is now available from Macromedia (download your copy at www.macromedia.com). Multimedia ToolBook, however, was the first application to have tools that allowed users to play their multimedia applications from a web browser (not available from Asymetrix, so don't ask!). They are called Multimedia World Wide Web, World Wide Web Kiosk, and a virtual reality author and player, VRXplorer. I have provided copies of these tools for you on the CD. You must have Asymetrix ToolBook to use them. Paolo Tosolini, of Southern Illinois University, developed these programs, and they are being perfected. Go to his web site to get updated versions as they become available.

These Internet multimedia communication programs will allow direct contact between application developers and will also allow users to retrieve multimedia applications (sound, video, animation) and play them via the Web! This is truly a gigantic breakthrough for network communications. Once the bugs are out, the uses will multiply every day (see Part IV). However, I have included some mailing labels on the CD that you can use to send out your stuff. I have divided them into three groups:

1. Publishing addresses
2. Software products and games addresses and BBSes
3. Literary agents

Simply put the right-sized labels into your single-feed printer and run off these macros! Just remember that an excellent-quality "rifle approach" is much better than a shoddy "shotgun approach." In other words, first determine who wants your stuff before you spend a lot of money sending it out.

If they do need whatever it is you have in mind, then, by all means, use the best possible packaging you can afford. The next few chapters will discuss the variety of packaging software out there for you to use.

Box 2 — Software to Develop Your Message

1. **Multimedia ToolBook, Macromedia Author/Director.** With this software, you can develop interactive documents that include animation, sound, text, and graphics and that can be packaged as "run-time" applications to be loaded on the user's computer system. You may also create interactive kiosks with these tools. Soon, they will be able to be placed on the Internet and accessed by web browsers such as Mosaic and Netscape. My personal preference is ToolBook because of its easy use and friendly, nontechnical interaction. However, you can give them both a try and see which one you prefer. (ToolBook not on CD.)

2. **Catalog on Disk for Windows** creates customized, interactive catalogs featuring a Page View displaying product details and a Column View showing product tables like short-form catalogs. It has a nice mix of text and graphics. It is possible to have "on-screen ordering" for customers. The software includes setup and run-time software.

3. Inexpensive, e-publishing software includes **Writer's Dream, Dart, Orpheus,** and **NeoBook.** These are also available as shareware from BBSes and on Net sites. Some multimedia is possible, but they are definitely "low-end" tools.

4. Creative writing tutorials include **Dramatica for Windows** and **Writepro.** The former is for developing screenplays and "Hollywood formula" stuff, and the latter is for teaching creative writing technique. They are both excellent for the beginner. In addition, there is a sample of **Scriptor,** a fine professional screenplay formatting software for the game and interactive movie developer. (Dramatica not included on CD.)

8

Match the Software to Your Needs

This chapter will cover the following:

- Software categories
- Word processing software
- Creative assistance software
- Multimedia software
- Virtual reality and 3-D graphics software
- Other software applications
- Animation software
- Movies, graphics, and sound software

It is extremely important for you to pay attention during this chapter. Many would-be digital scribes spend thousands of dollars on software that they never use and will probably never have a need to use. Why? Simply stated, they listen to the Bill Gateses of the world, rather than to their own abilities and their own professional expertise.

It is my theory that most of the "new market" that has still to embark on the computer media revolution has yet to discover their own need to use the tools out there. Certainly, these cynics are aware of computer technology in a vague, mostly confusing way: the supermarket scanners that are rumored to be fixed by the owners to read high prices; the businesses that have computerized, impersonal telephone answering devices that comedians like Steve Martin love to satirize: "Hello. You have reached 555-2806. At the sound of the beep, you will speak to a live person"; finally, perhaps the only personal uses they have for computers are to keep addresses of clients or do simple bookkeeping chores. Yes, they figure, there is no real need to have a computer that does everything but butter your toast in the morning. They are correct. However, unless I am mistaken, these same people do need to know on which side their toast is buttered because they are missing out on a marketing bonanza that will begin to dovetail into the most dynamic and profound communications integration since radio got a cathode ray tube for Christmas.

Of course, I am speaking about when the Internet combines with television technology and we begin to see interactive home shopping malls where users can stroll between lifelike stores and actually charge for whatever they see that strikes their fancy! Game parlors will also be there for the adventurous, sampling the most realistic computer CD-ROM and cable games that money can buy.

In addition, buyers will be able to "plug in" and listen to music and other sounds, watch movies, or see a multitude of animation and other special 3-D effects, while at the same time deciding which product to purchase. The proving ground for this fantastic technology is now on the Internet, and once these technical advancements are perfected by the thousands of engineers, scientists, and teachers, the world will be ready for a real adventure.

The digital scribe of the 21st century will be able to use the media to its best advantage. I am going to give you the latest information about the programs I have found to be valuable to the person who needs to establish his or her own path, learn with the fewest number of technical difficulties, and put a message out on the airwaves for all to see and hear.

I have broken down the software into three categories of purpose:

1. Word processing (including the latest HTML, SGML, and VRML editors)
2. Multimedia (the best programs for the money and the best results)
3. Graphics and animation (including the best utilities to go with categories 1 and 2)

Please be advised that I do not know what purpose you have for getting into the production of electronic media publications. However, I will be giving you all a special bonus chapter aimed at giving those among you who need an extra inspiration some specific ideas about what to create for a public that is savvy about this medium and wants to experience it all! I often do this for my students. These are ideas that give them the impetus to go on to become entrepreneurs and inventors! It is my belief that the books on the market today about writing for the Internet and other electronic media do a good job of showing examples of what is out there in the way of technical information, but they really do not illustrate by giving readers specific suggestions that are just waiting for a creative mind to do them justice. That is why books like the *For Dummies* series are so successful. People want straight talk and straight advice, and it must be communicated to them in simple terms.

As you can see by my earlier chapters, I have spent some time giving you exercises to strengthen your creative thinking skills (and you are not finished yet). However, as a professional writer and communicator, I know that the only authentic test of a digital scribe is when the scribe can actually try out an idea and see if he or she can make it work! My next chapter will be giving you that chance, so stay tuned.

WORD PROCESSING

For now, let us take a look at the latest word processing software for the truly creative writer, the scribe who wants to be on top of things and prepared for all the new technology. I have spent many months cruising the Web, sifting through computer books and magazines, and doing my best to spend countless hours (ask my wife!) to evaluate the leading software in each of these three categories. I evaluated each program with an eye to a user who has some typing skill, a little bit of technical and computer knowledge (certainly not at the programmer level), and (most important) a desire to see electronic media used in its most creative and interesting way.

WordPerfect Corporation has some new developments that make using its programs a delight. Envoy is a program that lets you communicate with others on-line as you edit and draft your documents in the word processing software. For example, suppose I wanted someone to share in the development of a chapter in this book. All I would have to do would be to use Envoy to hook me up to the Net with a few easy clicks, and *voilà*, both of us can share our insights live and in real time! You can imagine the implications this will have for the speed of technology development. Books will be completed in less time and with more accuracy, and editors and writers will be able to exchange important content information right over their computers. Another great use for Envoy is instructional. I teach college composition, and I find there is a time lag before I can get back to students with important feedback. In addition, I let many students learn how to critique by doing, and this software would allow my Net surfers to plug into each other's word processing software and give it the old "two heads are better than one" try.

WordPerfect is also coming out with some new software for HTML and SGML editing. However, for those who like to put together their own packages, you can hunt on the computer software search engine with Netscape. One of the thrills of the Net is the fact that "backyard mechanics" can still put together inexpensive, high-quality Macintosh and IBM software "hotrods" via the shareware available. Of course, for those who are getting into this business to make money, you want the best possible package, with all the headaches taken out beforehand. WordPerfect's new HTML editor does the job with style.

WordPerfect also makes IBM-compatible products such as Presentations 2.0 for DOS. This software allows the user to create business presentation slide shows very easily. In fact, any digital scribe who needs to express a message fast and with color, graphics, and sound will find Presentations 2.0 the best application available. The sound application can play MIDI and digital files, but make certain that your user has the room on the hard disk to play them (and a proper sound card)! Many developers do not plan where they will be distributing their applications, and the result is a presentation that never gets played! That can mean thousands of dollars in contracts if you want to get the job, so make sure you plan ahead. Because most new computers have built-in speakers and a sound card for mono, this is usually not a problem, but the space requirement can be a big problem.

The reason I like WordPerfect software is because all of their documents are compatible with the HTML conversion, so the digital writer can easily convert a document into a file to be placed on the Internet. Other word processing software also has HTML add-ons, but only Novell offers a copy of Net Publisher free to those who already own WordPerfect 6.1 for Windows. You may download a copy at http://novell.com. Click on What's New. You can research software yourself by using the Netscape browser (CUSI software search engine).

Of course, there are a multitude of HTML, SGML, and VRML editors out there (see samples on the CD), but most of them are not allied with a major word processing package like WordPerfect (yet).

HoTMeTaL and WebWizard are the most interesting because of their easy interface, and I would even recommend HoTMeTaL over the WordPerfect SGML edition if you need a tutorial. You can download any or all of these experimental programs (at your own risk—but Net cruisers come in all shapes, sizes, and levels of courage), but I would recommend a reputable company like WordPerfect because of its technical service and its compatibility with most other programs. Even though capitalism creates a multitude of competitors, thus keeping the big boys honest, some companies want to keep your business, so they create compatible products.

WordPerfect, for example, came out with WordPerfect 6.1 Word Processing for DOS, and I (and many others) became turned off, but for reasons other than compatibility. The ease of the 5.1 version was just not there, because (in my opinion) they tried to add too many bells and whistle gimmicks. This result is caused by the phenomenon I was discussing earlier in my chapter about marketing strategies. I assume the heady successes of WordPerfect 5.1 created a "halo image" around the engineers/creators, who were able to sell management their stuff without really questioning the users out there (me included) about what they needed. Thank goodness, with the news of the HTML and Envoy programs, WordPerfect is back in the groove again! In fact, the Windows version of WordPerfect 6.1 is the software I am using right now. And I just received my prerelease version of WordPerfect 6.1 (SGML edition). This is the cutting edge because I can create home pages for the Internet without a special editor! That's right, all the WordPerfect documents are easily converted to HTML and SGML format for easy reading on the Net. This is a real breakthrough, and I am using it in my workshops on home page creation. I am sure other companies will be coming out with similar versions for their own software, but I am pleased by the quality of Novell Corporation.

Informed digital scribes, however, can remedy this would-be problem of "technology hype" by first reading reviews in computer magazines, talking to nerds, and even buying books like this one, before they plop down their hard-earned money for the latest upgrade.

CREATIVE ASSISTANCE

The next class of word processing software for the digital scribe is what I call *creative assistance applications*. These are the multitude of software packages that assist the electronic writer with formatting manuscripts and creating original stories. As far as I know, no program does both tasks for you (perhaps you will one day create one!). Some programs format your text into an acceptable structure for submission to editors and publishers; other programs help you come up with the right story lines and characters for creative projects.

The best formatting and Hollywood-type idea software comes from the same company: Screenplay Systems, Incorporated, 150 East Olive Avenue, Suite 203, Burbank, CA 91502. It is the producer of Scriptor, professional screenplay formatting software, used by many of the pros in Hollywood. It also sells Dramatica for Windows, a creative story-line software that does a number of left-brain tasks for creative minds who want creative ideas that will satisfy and a story line that can sell.

Scriptor is good because it provides the three formats most needed by the digital scribe: television screenplay format, movie screenplay format, and stage play format. There are variations on these (interactive games, for example), but this is the software I would recommend for the serious writer. It works with most of the major word processing software, so it is easy to convert the text created in the word processing format into the Scriptor engine.

Dramatica is a unique way to get your story into shape for Hollywood consumption. Through a series of questions concerning genre, plot, theme, and character, the writer arrives at the one story form that consistently supports the chosen elements of the narrative.

What is unique about Dramatica is that it gives sample ideas from other screenplays and novels, and it also supports interesting ways to manipulate characters and their motivations. This program lets you begin with 32,768 potential storyforms. As you make the choices by answering storyforming questions, that number will diminish until it reaches 1.

Also included on my list of interesting software for the digital scribe who needs to learn the craft of writing for short stories and novels is a creative writing tutorial called WritePro. I include a review copy of this software (Lesson 1) on the CD. Sol Stein has created an excellent educational and interactive program that lets the writer learn by doing. As he says in his introductory letter:

> Within minutes of opening the package, WritePro will start guiding you step by step to create believable characters— heroes, heroines, villains; develop suspenseful, page-turning plots; use dialogue that jumps off the page; start a novel or story that hooks your readers immediately; decide which point of view to use for maximum impact; write description, narrative, and scenes your readers can see and feel.

Most of these claims are indeed true. If you need a basic instruction about how to create publishable stories, then this is the program for you. I personally heard Stein's presentation at a writing seminar and was impressed by his down-to-earth, practical instruction. He certainly does not try to con people into believing they can be creative storytellers overnight. He does, however, believe that a writer with a creative idea can learn the techniques to put that story into its best shape. If you have ever wondered whether you could put words into characters' mouths and watch them work out their problems in a dramatic situation, then you can most likely learn from these excellent lessons. As a teacher of writing myself, I wholeheartedly recommend this program for the beginner who wants to learn creative writing basics.

MULTIMEDIA FOR THE MASSES

One who is new to writing for electronic media would probably want to use programs that provide (1) the easiest interface between user and software, (2) the best quality graphics and movies, and (3) the best professional assistance to the new user. These are the three most important stipulations when evaluating most software programs. In addition, technical assistance and the contacts each company makes within the scientific and academic communities are important. It is important that the company selected be creative, but one also would want them to be looking for the latest technology that puts the user first—not technology for technologists. We already have too much politics for politicians, and technology for technologists is just as bad.

With this in mind, I favor a company in Washington state, Asymetrix. Even though Macromedia had a track record with animators and graphic artists, I found their multimedia software to be much too inclined toward technical apparatuses that took too long to learn and were easy to confuse during the heat of the creative moment. Of course, in the not too distant past, when a whole team of people worked on a project, there were always computer programmers who could explain the intricacies of this technology to the others. However, now that companies like Asymetrix have put together multimedia creation packages that can be run by one person, the pressure is on for high quality and ease of interface.

Once more, I use my example from the marketing chapter. Asymetrix has probably learned a lot from its clientele, who have tended to be less technical types like teachers and college students. Macromedia, on the other hand, has always been rooted in the heart of the Silicon Valley near San Francisco, and its immediate interest was to develop engrossing "toys" for the miraculous computer wizards who could follow all kinds of complex instructions and still get the job done. Frankly, most people lack the resources or time to learn the complex technical interfaces that Macromedia Director and even Author demand. Director is a fine animation creator, and Author has an interface that can put together some pretty impressive applications.

With Asymetrix ToolBook, animations can be created in the same program, and the interfaces are smooth, logical, and fast. Both companies have excellent graphics tools and sound interfaces, but only ToolBook has a CBT edition for the important job of creating interactive applications for education. This is a highly lucrative aspect of the digital scribe's job because more and more companies are utilizing multimedia to train employees and present instruction to clients. Macromedia has one small mention in their collateral advertising of a company that has "produced Authorware Professional macros" that will help you to train employees, but you have to buy the expensive macros from *another* company and then figure out how to run them in your Authorware application.

Asymetrix ToolBook CBT edition, on the other hand, provides all the tools necessary to create highly creative and interactive educational software, using animation, movies, sound, and full-color, three-dimensional effects. Most important, ToolBook CBT also has an Administrator program that lets the user track student progress, assign instructional books or modules, and print out detailed reports of the individual weaknesses and strengths of the students who use the applications. Figure 8.1 is a sample of what the Administrator application page looks like.

I have included one demo on the enclosed CD that I created using Asymetrix ToolBook CBT. It is called Grammar Made Easy, Module One. My wife, Ellen (an English as a Second Language instructor with 20 years experience in the classroom), and I worked on it over several weeks. I used another handy program, AddImpact!, (Gold Disk, Inc., P.O. Box 789, Streetsville, Mississauga, Ontario, Canada L5M2C2) to create interesting add-on animations that are ready to embed as OLE (Object Linking and Embedding) applications in my ToolBook lessons. I found this was an even faster and handier way to add animation effects in what would otherwise become a boring chore for students to learn.

With Macromedia's Author, on the other hand, I could not get any kind of educational application to run effectively. The animations had a number of bugs, and no facility could track scores or assign values to the questions. Macromedia may be an attractive application for creating commercial animations and games, but as

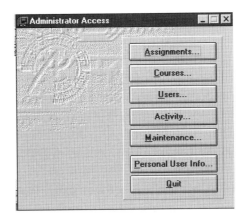

Figure 8.1   CBT Administrator page

an educational tool it has much to learn from its competitors. Of course, if you are interested mainly in creating CD games or entertainment applications, then Macromedia may be just what you need.

There are also multimedia software programs on the low end of the professional scale, and they can be purchased for a lot less money. In fact, I suggest that, if you are totally new to multimedia development, you should try one of these programs before investing in Macromedia or even Asymetrix. Writer's Dream, Multimedia Workshop, Q-Media (a nice Canadian product for business applications but not too good for education or entertainment), NeoBook (NeoSoft Corporation's variety of programs, including NeoPaint and NeoShow—I had a difficult time getting these programs to run on DOS), Dart, and Orpheus are all programs that you can buy for just a little money, yet you can learn how multimedia applications are developed. The only drawback is that these applications have only average graphics and it is difficult to impossible to distribute these as run-time files (files that can be loaded onto your customer's hard drive and played—without the client purchasing the entire software). Writer's Dream has this ability, but then it is only a book-format application with no fancy animation or movie abilities (see my e-book novel example, *Russian Wolves,* on the CD). Neo-Soft is a good application (the best, along with Q-Media, of the low-end multimedia software) that can be loaded as a stand-alone application (royalty free) on either Windows or DOS. This is unique because both Macromedia Authorware Professional and Asymetrix ToolBook 3.0 require Windows for IBM applications. Neo-Soft is also a lot less expensive, but the results are good enough to learn on and to develop some interesting titles that can be distributed to customers who have older hardware. As I mentioned, however, I had a problem with memory management in DOS, but I am certain you can work that out with the technical advisors at Neo-Soft.

Another multimedia application that got my attention was Catalog on Disk for Windows by Curtis Software. This software will let you create full-color catalog documents that can be loaded as stand-alones and as disk versions. Product records include mixed text and graphics. Page and Column Views are linked; clicking switches views. Customers can browse or search. On-Screen Ordering simplifies and automates placing orders. Catalog can create customized Title Screens with the company's logo, list box of product lines, and option buttons. Information can be imported from a database or graphics and text can be pasted in using the Windows Clipboard. Version 2.30 supports catalog creation from layout design through media production. The professional edition is very expensive, but it is well worth the investment for a company on the rise. I have included a sample demo on the CD.

VIRTUAL REALITY AND 3-D GRAPHICS TOOLS

Vistapro 3.1 for Windows from Virtual Reality Laboratories, Inc. (2341 Ganador Court, San Luis Obispo, CA 93401; phone 805-781-2254), lets the user create realistic, color three-dimensional settings for your fiction or multimedia applications using real-world data from the United States Geological Survey and extraterrestrial data from NASA. The software is easy to install, and you can use the Makepath Flight Director and AVI Builder to create your own animated movies. Ground or aircraft flight simulations are possible with this unique product, and you can add trees, snow, rivers, and other geographical details to make your setting as lifelike as you wish. This program is a good addition for the multimedia digital scribe who wants to give his or her user the most realistic experience possible.

I must also mention Asymetrix 3D F/X because it is, in my estimation, the best and easiest to use three-dimensional animation program available on the market. The reason I say this is because 3D F/X takes all the complex maneuvers out of getting your animation to run. It has a catalog of predrawn models, surfaces, predetermined paths for your models, and a way to "drag and drop" them into a preview window, so it is easy for even the most nontechnical user to learn. The graphics and motion are clear, colorful, and realistic; you can even adjust the lighting of your models and text for the best possible 3-D effects. You can increase productivity by working with solid models rather than wireframes, and you can extend the application with OLE 2.0 support and Microsoft Office compatibility. It can export a variety of file formats including AVI, BMP, and TGA with alpha channel transparency. You may also import 2-D graphics, metafiles, Autodesk 3D Studio and AutoCAD (.DXF) models, video, and other graphic elements. You may view a sample effect in my Grammar Made Easy application on the CD. After clicking on the picture in Figure 8.2, the three-dimensional planet Earth spins into the picture accompanied by some classical music. Here, I am not only showing a fine animation, but I am also teaching the present progressive verb tense to English as a Second Language (ESL) students. The entire animation was created in less than five minutes! That is why I recommend Asymetrix 3D F/X to my readers who want easy, visually arresting 3-D software that they can import into a variety of multimedia documents for a variety of purposes.

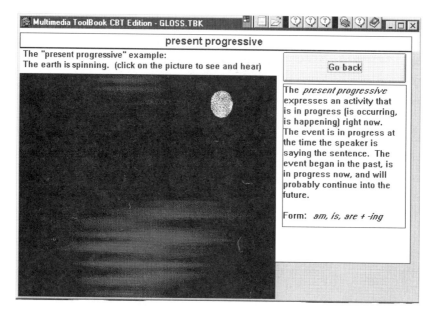

Figure 8.2   3D F/X application in Grammar Made Easy

PhotoMorph2 is a unique program from North Coast Software, Inc. (P.O. Box 459, 265 Scruton Pond Road, Barrington, NH 03825; phone, 603-664-6000; fax, 603-664-7872; Internet, 4386449 @mcinmail.com). With this program, you can create your own special effects, like those you see in Hollywood movies and in TV commercials. PhotoMorph is Windows software and powerful enough to meet the needs of the professional but easy enough to have you making your own morph movies in minutes. The features include morphing, warping, distortion, and transition effects; blue screening, chroma key, alpha channel; 256,000 transition combinations; colorizing and titling of video clips; storyboarding and chaining of multiple clips; an autoplay feature for constructing multianimation presentations; a complete image editing facility for cropping, rotating, scaling, and titling; importing of 15 popular formats, including AVI, PCX, GIF, Targa, TIFF, BMP, JPEG, OS/2 BMP, Macintosh PICT, and Amiga IFF; and output to Microsoft's

Video for Windows AVI format, Autodesk's FLC Flick format, or individual 24-bit frames. Video for Windows Runtime is included in the package, allowing you to distribute your movies as AVI animations (royalty free). If you do not have the money to invest in Adobe's Photoshop, which is probably the best image enhancement and editing program available, PhotoMorph2 is probably the best bet at a reasonable price. The morphing effects are especially interesting, and they provide you sample applications that you can use immediately. So, the next time you want to morph Hillary Clinton into Bill, or vice versa, use this program! Figure 8.3 is a sample page from PhotoMorph2.

OTHER APPLICATIONS

Many programs are available on the Internet that you can try for nothing. I got hold of a demo called Home Space Builder that lets you create 3-D interactive, virtual reality houses, museums, and

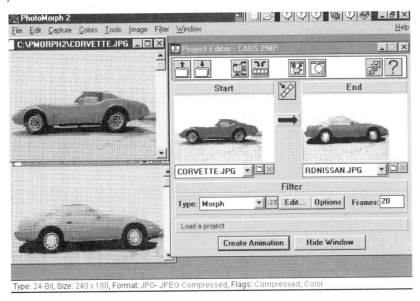

Figure 8.3   Working page from PhotoMorph2

stores that you can decorate with your product's message in the form of pictures, sound, and animations, which can be seen as one "walks around" your creation. In addition, you can add URL addresses (other locations on the Net where readers are taken when they click on your object) to your tour, and thus your users are transported to wherever you want them to go. I will refer to this application when I describe some possible creative applications in the next chapter. Figure 8.4 is a sample page from Home Space Builder.

Notice that you can use the maneuvering instrument to walk around and see what your viewer will see. You then add the different objects, URL links, and other interesting applications as they fit your message. I have included a demo copy of this application on the CD so you may try it out. Figure 8.5 shows what the digital scribe sees when walking around the church.

I have included another excellent virtual reality creator, Walk Through Pro 2.0 by Virtus Corporation. You can create shopping malls and other structures that may be accessed by your "walker/user."

A variety of 3-D viewers are also available from the Internet files. You are able to access and view a variety of 3-D and virtual reality (VR) graphics using WorldView on the Internet. This company also makes an editor so you can create your own applications to place on the Net.

ANIMATION TOOLS

A variety of animation software programs are available to choose from, and they can be accessed using the same search engine (CUSI) that I mentioned earlier (Netscape 1.1). Or, you may call the companies directly to get demo copies. During my evaluation, I found some applications that can increase the entertainment value of most multimedia software programs like Asymetrix ToolBook and Macromedia Authorware. Of course, Macromedia has Director 4.0, one of the best (yet, sadly, also very complicated) animation software

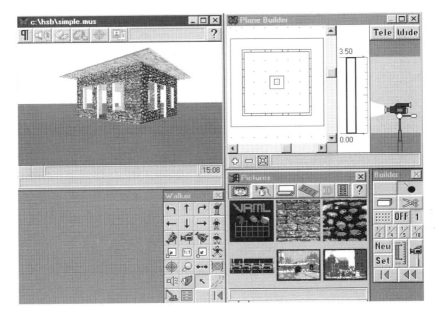

Figure 8.4 Sample from Home Space Builder

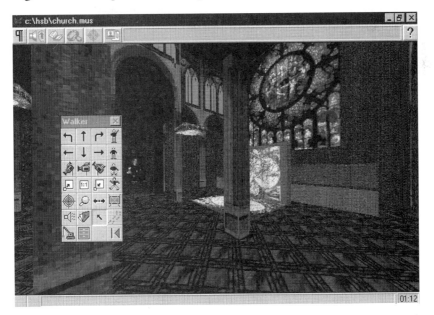

Figure 8.5 View from inside the church

programs on the market. For the professional animator, one of the high-end products, like AXA Animation Series (AXA Corp., 17752 Mitchell, Suite C, Irvine, CA 92714; phone, 714-757-1500; fax, 714-757-1766) will produce professional animations as seen in TV commercials and cartoon series. However, unless you have some animation experience and are indeed serious about producing total animation products, I would opt for a simpler version to use with the multimedia software.

If you are an artist who can create animated characters, then you may want to buy a program that lets you create. The best program (and very inexpensive) that I have seen and that my artist friends tell me is excellent is The Animation Studio (Disney Software, 500 South Buena Vista Street, Burbank, CA 91521; phone, 818-841-3326, 800-688-1520; fax, 716-873-0906). This is a full-featured animation and paint program that utilizes current animation techniques characteristic of Disney-style animation. The exclusive "onion-skin" feature allows users to view four cels at once. The Animation Studio contains Disney animations, audio effects, and tools to assist in creating and learning about animation.

However, for those of us who are not professional animators, some programs let you create animations with less stress on the right brain. I reviewed many programs that claimed to fit the need, but only two were satisfactory for the digital scribe.

I would choose a program like AddImpact (mentioned earlier) or 3D Choreographer 1.5 (Anicom, Incorporated, P.O. Box 428, Columbia, MD 21045; phone, 800-949-4559; fax, 919-933-9503). These are easy-to-use, graphically attractive animation software programs that let the digital scribe create with flexibility.

Specifically, AddImpact 1.0 instantly brings the dynamic impact of multimedia to any Windows OLE-compatible program. AddImpact's innovative floating tool bar (see the sample graphic in Figure 8.6) pops up inside the current application, letting users quickly and easily add voice animation (already prepared!), animated graphics and text, sound effects, and even music. Everything you add is

Figure 8.6   AddImpact 1.0 in Windows Write

automatically embedded in the current document for easy distribution to others (Gold Disk, Inc., 3350 Scott Boulevard, Building 14, Santa Clara, CA 95054; phone, 408-982-0200, 800-4653375; or fax, 408-982-0298). Figure 8.6 is a sample working page, showing how AddImpact works in a Windows Write word processing program.

Notice that the application animation is simple, but the best feature of AddImpact is that you can import any packaged animation you may get from a CD collection of royalty-free artwork. That makes this program especially valuable because it has the OLE ability.

3D Choreographer 1.5 enables you to think in terms of movement, not frames, providing a much more intuitive and natural method of creating animations. You simply specify commands for your animated actors to follow, and the program will automatically generate the animation. It's that easy. To change your animation, you merely issue different commands. There is no artwork to draw and no complex three-dimensional concepts to learn (although you can import 3-D graphics to animate). The animation concepts are easy to learn, and I was able to create a high-quality, finished product in 15 minutes. Figure 8.7 shows a sample menu page from 3D Choreographer.

MOVIES, GRAPHICS, AND SOUND APPLICATIONS

The digital scribe of the new era must have access to many multimedia software applications and also to the newest media to hit the computer industry: movies. A number of software programs let you work with movies, and I will mention two that I found to be superb: Adobe Premiere 4.0 and Asymetrix Digital Video Producer. Adobe's product is excellent (and costly), but if you are professionally developing

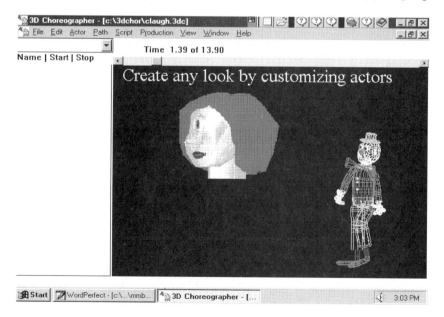

Figure 8.7   3D Choreographer menu page

video, this is what you need. Users can simply gather the clips and arrange them in the order in which they want them to play, capture QuickTime or Microsoft video for Windows movies from videotape, import titles from Adobe Photo-shop or other programs, export a filmstrip to Adobe Photoshop for painting, set critical editing options with a mouse click, and choose from a broad range of special effects and transitions. The program supports the use of all common media types and video content in AVI and QuickTime formats.

However, for a less expensive alternative, you might want to try Asymetrix's Digital Video Producer. This program does most of what Adobe does and has the oh-so-friendly "drag-and-drop" feature that makes frame editing and other complex tasks much easier to accomplish.

Remember, however, that all VCRs made in the last ten-plus years (for sale in the U.S.) support one of two kinds of cable: RCS jacks, which are the standard "stereo-cable" jack cables, and 50-ohm coaxial cables, which are the standard "cable-TV" cables. What you need is a computer that is compatible with VCRs (such as a fast 486 or an AV Macintosh as a minimum), and one that has a video card into which you can plug your VCR's output. And you almost literally cannot have too much memory—the more RAM you have, the smoother your movies will be. Digitizing video is easy, though there are some technical (as well as aesthetic) things to remember about light, slow panning, and zooming and contrast. A good source for finding out more is a book by Scott Fisher, *Creating Interactive CD-ROM for Windows and Macintosh* (AP PROFESSIONAL). Otherwise, you can obtain "canned videos" from royalty-free companies that produce them in CD format.

Speaking of canned resources, every digital scribe should have a library of available royalty-free (you can't get sued for using it!) artwork, movies, sounds, and graphics to use when needed. Four companies that I found to be superb are Adobe's Image Club Graphics Inc. (U.S. Catalog Fulfillment Center, c/o Publisher's Mail Service, 10545 West Donges Court, Milwaukee, WI 53224-9967; phone, 800-661-9410), where you can find just about any artwork, photograph, and graphic you need; Media Design Interactive (The Old Hop Kiln, 1 Long Garden Walk, Farnham, Surrey, GU9 7HP, England; phone, 0252-737630; fax, 0252-710948), makers of some superb art collections (see the sample in Figure 8.8); Educational Renaissance (2474 Woodchuck Way, Sandy, UT 84093-2742; phone, 801-943-0841), makers of high-quality sound effects (I used their Sound Effects for Multi Media, Vol. I in my Grammar Made Easy demo); and Gazelle Technologies, Inc. (in San Diego; phone, 619-693-4030), makers of some fine photographs and videos on CD. The quality from these companies is excellent, and you can rely on them. In addition, you should check out the Internet to download free graphics, videos, and sounds. However, sometimes you cannot trust whether the person who placed them on the Net was careful about copyright restrictions (see my chapter on legalities and the digital scribe). Check with that individual personally to be certain. You really cannot afford a traffic ticket when you are just starting to enter the information superhighway on-ramp!

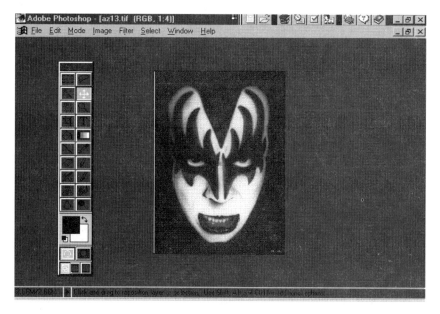

Figure 8.8   A boy named Gene as seen in Photoshop

By the way, in case you were wondering how I was able to capture the graphics from other software and place them in my word processing text, I used the wonderfully versatile program HiJaak Graphics Suite, which allows you to paint, draw, enhance, capture, convert, trace, search, and find all your graphics in a few easy clicks of the mouse. Used in tandem with a well-stocked, royalty-free graphics, art, and photo collection, you can do just about any image task required. You can find out more about this excellent tool for Windows and Macintosh at Inset, 71 Commerce Drive, Brookfield, CT 06804-3405; phone, 800-DR INSET; fax, 203-775-5634.

The next chapter will take you on a little brainstorming session. I have collected a variety of business, educational, and other application ideas that I think may interest you. This is my "bonus chapter." If you are the creative digital scribe that I think you are, you may possibly "steal" one of these ideas and create your own product! Feel free to do so. As Henry David Thoreau once said (did I quote him before?): "You may build your castles in the air, but then you must lay the foundations for them here on earth."

9

Productive Ideas

This chapter will cover the following areas:

- Where do I send my work?
- Interactive game treatments and the business of CD-ROM games
- Creative ideas for women scribes (or anyone who can use them!)
- Creative ideas for work and entertainment
- The home page store front
- Students on the Net
- Various exercises

This section will be covering some suggestions about how you can make money from your digital writing abilities. I will also give you some assignments (in case you are learning this inside a college classroom) that are practical and informative. You should have some multimedia software to do these assignments, and you should be able to complete the instructions that I give you. My book does not focus on technical, step-by-step movements within a particular software program. Instead, I have purposely chosen to review software applications that are easy to learn and present the least trouble technically. Therefore, I will be concentrating my exercises upon your creative writing skills and how well you can think with your senses, and you can use other books to give you the detailed technical instructions (or learn on your own, the way I did) to finish the assignments.

Frankly speaking, this chapter was one of the main reasons I researched and wrote this book. I saw that there were innumerable technical and what I call "toots and whistle" books on the market, but very few of them gave the reader any profitable suggestions to apply their knowledge. One of the exceptions, in my opinion, is Colin Haynes's classic book *Paperless Publishing* (New York: Windcrest/McGraw-Hill, 1994). You may download a free electronic version off the Internet at the publisher's home page address. This book gave me the inspiration to write *The Digital Scribe* because I saw the writing on the electronic wall, so to speak. Many consumers were getting bombarded with books that explained how to market, how to sell, and how to work the variety of software and hardware on the market. But none, as far as I could see, taught the consumer how to use that knowledge practically and profitably. Haynes does this, and I hope I do it, too.

However, as I am a classroom teacher as well as a digital scribe, I want my readers to learn something about writing and creating. It is well and good to know the technical side of the computer revolution, but now it is time for the nontechies to get a chance.

Enough lecture. Now we get down to ideas, the very heart of creative thinking. Without ideas, my students would still be staring in space, hoping some lightning bolt would strike them with inspiration or perhaps a fellow student would serve as their Muse (or even write the paper for them). We adults all know, however, that it takes hard work to be creative, and it also takes hard work to put that creative idea to work.

I will be giving you suggestions that I believe will make excellent applications on the Internet and as CDs or even as businesses, and I want you to take the ball and run. Run until you reach the end zone and spike it like Natrone Means (or fill in your favorite NFL runner).

WHERE DO I SEND MY WORK?

The Net has some excellent resources for finding on-line and print publishers. One of the best addresses to reach these bookstores and publishers is

http://www.vmedia.com/shannon/publ.html

When you get there, your page should look like Figure 9.1.

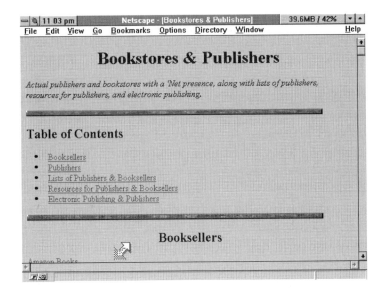

Figure 9.1   Bookstores and publishers (via Netscape)

I have also enclosed some address label macros on the CD for you to use. You should send a cover letter with each submission (especially to print publishers) and include some clips of previously published work (if you have any). In the interactive game market especially, it is important that you have some title credits to your name. I am going to include some possible treatment examples, but be aware that unless you have a definite connection in the industry, it is very hard to break in. Box 1 shows a sample treatment of a game I proposed to Broderbund Software.

Box 1 | **Treatment for CD-ROM Game: "Gene Wars" or "Family Values"**

This interactive adventure game is based on my science fiction short story, "Family Values" (copy enclosed). The year is 2518 in Sandicalfor, a megalopolis controlled by the Reverend Fathers and their "families" (militant warriors and genetically engineered youths programmed to fight).

The drawback is that there are also pockets of "natureborns," those remaining people who were born and raised in the old-fashioned way with a nuclear family and parents. The Family Police arrests these natureborns and imprisons them on a remote island off of Mexicalfor run by the Sturgeon Family. They produce a gladiator competition show wherein natureborns are forced to fight an assortment of genetically created monsters in a battle arena.

The purpose of the game is for the user to rescue the natureborn woman, Reewa Hin, from the Sturgeon Family Prison Colony. The user takes on the persona character of Vince Palmer, a genetic engineer in the Palmer Family of Sandicalfor.

Together with his partner, Billy, they set out for the Sturgeon island, but, first, the user must attempt to earn points to be able to create genetically engineered combatants to help him or her in the attack. The user must fight a series of six mutants on a televised "Gladiator Battle Royale" inside the Sturgeon Family Sports Complex.

The two partners may fight (individually or as a team) or the user may choose Reewa Hin to fight; they may choose an assortment of weapons (flesh lasers, electronic swords, neutron grenades). For each battle won, the user can score 50 points. The user may restart if he or she fails.

The user who compiles 100 points or more (a maximum of 300), may then go to the "genetic creation lab," where he or she gets to assemble five warriors for assistance in the onslaught to rescue Reewa Hin from her gladiator prison. The user gets to choose from a variety of genetic DNA prototypes, including elephants, dinosaurs (a variety), lions, gorillas, alligators, wolves, cheetahs, NBA basketball players from the 20th Century, NFL football players, eagles, hawks, and any other beasts that can be suggested by my development team. The user will be able to click and drag parts of these animals/beings and stick them together to form the "ultimate fighting warrior."

There will be a total of 30 different screens in this game, and the user will be able to explore such sights as the Palmer Family Breeding Hospital (where the test tube male members of the Palmer Family are created), Reewa Hin's Primo-gladitorium (where the user can work out and eat with Reewa and the other natureborn prisoners/gladiators), Reewa Hin's flight (where the user gets to experience Reewa Hin's transformation into a flying woman), The Sturgeon Family Mutant Compound (where the user gets to see, hear, and "test drive" the assortment of mutants created by the Sturgeon Family genetic scientists, including Harpies (winged eagles/women), Devils, and other mythical monsters, Max Horseman's Apartment (where user gets to hear about the history of the Sturgeon Family Sports Complex and view the assortment of memorabilia), the Primogladitorium Caverns (where there are a variety of rooms where mutant monsters are kept that must fight in the daily battles over The Family Television Channels Netplay).

The user must battle the assortment of Sturgeon Family mutants and human guards, as he or she takes Reewa Hin to the top of the Sports Complex to the waiting Jet Copter. The user who succeeds in getting into the copter and taking off gets to experience the "Flight to the Natureborn Mountains," where they grow wings and fly out of Vince Palmer's apartment and over the megalopolis of Sandicalfor—Vince and Reewa as eagle beings—where they can live in peace away from the warring city, and at long last experience the age-old tradition of a natural family. Indeed, the essence of Family Values.

Notice that I have not really done any technical script writing here. Most of the game market is still controlled by computer programming people, and unless you can convince them that your story is a worthwhile interactive game, you will have little chance of writing the final script for them.

Although writing games seems the most lucrative and glamorous part of multimedia creation, I would advise the newcomer to seek other avenues first to gain recognition—then, if you are still set on creating games, you can send the producers a well thought-out treatment or even a speculative script.

At a multimedia game developers' conference in San Jose, I was particularly amused and educated by a presentation given by Kenneth Melville of Digital Pictures, Inc. He has permitted me to include the text of his speech in my book. I think you will get the idea of the problems the gaming writer has to face after you have read this satirical, yet honest presentation. There is some good, practical advice in here, so pay close attention:

I would like to start out with a few words about the Holy Grail of interactive writing, the interactive movie. Nobody really knows what the hell they are, but a lot of money is being spent to make them. For the screenwriter entering the interactive arena, it is something comforting to relate to: hey, after all, it's just a movie with buttons, big deal. Well, in practice this Holy Grail has turned out to be more of a Trojan Horse for the writer: It gets you in the door of a potentially lucrative new market but once you're there, you look around and realize: My God, I'm trapped in GEEKWORLD, what are they gonna do with me? The answer is, they're going to try to turn you into one of them. It's not as bad as it sounds, but . . . almost. I'll get back to this hostage thing later, but first . . .

If you attended any media conferences (except this one) in years past, technologist spokesmodels informed us that Hollywood was kaput! Yes, you and I were going to be writing, directing and starring in our very own interactive feature films by now. Well, If you've checked out some of these cine-interactive blockbusters lately you're guessing that Ed Wood must be back and *he's* makin' 'em. If you think about it, the guy was a major interactive pioneer . . . *Glen or Glenda* . . . the very first FMV role-playing game.

What I'm trying to say here is that if there are any frustrated screenwriters out there who are hoping to whip out an interactive movie script this weekend for some quick cash . . . get a life. The genre may not even exist.

What happened? Okay, here's the Top Six Reasons that interactive movies have floundered:

Number 6. Filmaking is a highly refined art form requiring specialized technology. The average American secretly longs to be Kato Kaelin. 'Nuf said.

Number 5. 900 page scripts.

Number 4. HELL CAB! HELL CAB!

Number 3. You're the protagonist . . . and you can't talk!

Number 2. An hour of video for 200 thousand bucks. Can you say "student film?"

And the number 1 reason interactive movies don't work: If the script sucks, you wrote it.

In summary, these things have been blurry, blotchy, jerky, mucho expensive, semi-interactive boondoggles answering questions that nobody's asked: Movies ain't broke—don't fix 'em. Game consumers, especially the 16 and older crowd, have become extremely gun shy of the whole Hollywood/ FMV thing: to them it means a lousy game with limited control and repetitious video clips.

Okay. All right. You knew this tragic scenario couldn't end like this, you're writers. Where's the third act? Well, it's not finished yet. That's your job. Here's how it starts out:

EXT. AMERICA—SUNRISE

- PC's and game consoles are finally starting to deliver reasonable quality computer graphics, animation, video and audio. This means that the player can actually read subtle character expressions and understand what they're saying. The lack of this up to now has been a huge impediment to effective storytelling, forcing the writer to create simplistic, over-the-top, cartoonish situations, characters and dialog.

- Even better, the inevitable convergence of broadband cable and the net will create a huge market. Forget point-and-click interactive TV: This is totally post-linear stuff: a real-time immersive multiplayer environment with staggering possibilities. Get with the program . . . or should I say, the *anti*-program.

- No, interactive movies still don't work. But who cares? This nonlinear stuff does work, in its own goofy kind of way. More on that later.

Let's get back to the hostage situation. We'll call this part "A Survival Guide to Interactive Writing." You get the gig and cash your advance check. That's your first mistake. Then they throw you in a room with somebody called the game designer. I want to make one thing perfectly clear. This person is your natural enemy. I don't have a visual aid to show you, but . . . they'll look something like . . . uh . . . Noah here. He's a good example. He'll seem friendly at first, but don't be deceived. He'll be drinking your blood before the lunch break.

Here's the problem: He's created a game called . . . let's call it Sword Shark—a fencing game based on *The Three Musketeers*.

It's played from the first person point-of-view of D'Artagnan. You say, "Excellent. I will give D'Artagnan an opening soliloquy worthy of Dumas. Noah says, "Forget it. He can't talk. He's us. We could be a woman, we could be a child. That would break the suspension of disbelief. Besides, how would we select what to say? Put Text Buttons on the screen?" He laughs gaily and breaks into the derisive sneer common to the Interface Police. He informs you that any one of the Three Musketeers standing before your character may be selected. "What if you click on Porthos?" he asks. You are inspired and gush forth: "Porthos will reveal his character in a clever skit mocking Cardinal Richelieu . . . "

"Stop!" cries Noah. He then whips out a flow chart the size of a bedsheet and his index finger stabs at a little box in the upper left hand corner. "Says here Porthos fights us."

You appear dazed. Noah shows us two little boxes connected to the first one.

One says Win and the other Lose.

"I need dialog for these," he states, flatly. You are reinspired. You take the Win box. Let's see . . . uh . . . The vanquished Porthos is lying in a cart of mule dung as his companions make merry at his expense. Porthos says something like "Your swordsmanship, sir, is a match for Cardinal Richelieu himself! My companions and I . . . "

Noah leaps to his feet. "No, no, no. That's too long for the player to go without making another decision. Besides, Richelieu is the boss of level 26. He's not in this part."

Noah presses on, relentlessly . . . "I was thinking of three possible lines from Porthos appropriate to our degree of skill: (a) 'You're pretty good, D'Artagnan,' (b) 'You're awfully good, D'Artagnan,' and (c) 'D'Artagnan, you're no slouch with that weeny roaster.'"

Your mind wanders to the ominous stack of unpaid Writer's Connection bills behind your toaster... You manage to choke out:

"Noah, that really ... really ... works for me. This is so exciting ..."

By now you have correctly deduced that the interactive writer is below krill in the game company food chain. Things could be worse. They could be out of Plankton burgers at the company cafeteria.

You can see here ... the heart of the problem is the dreaded *E* word: *Exposition*. There, I've said it. Noah is right, of course. His game design requires that every word out of your characters' mouths advance not the plot, for all practical purposes there *is* no plot in the traditional sense, but advance *the game*. The player is mainly interested in succeeding in the game and therefore wants to hear *useful stuff* all the time that relates directly to his or her progress. For the most part, dialog that expresses character depth and motivation requires a pace and verbosity that players find, frankly, frustrating. They want clues, they want path choices, they want *information*. They'll stomach a little punchy payoff jargon if it's kept to humorous or arch one-liners, but even that can get tedious after the fiftieth play of the game.

Exposition. In the gaming world, it's mostly all you'll be asked for. It crowds out nuance, humor, repartee, emotion, development. And since the player wants to get right at whatever the game's about (shooting, exploring, fighting, etc.), it effectively crowds out *character*. It's very difficult to introduce a non-stock character if there's no screen time to allow them to reveal or explain themselves. You'll be left with a very confusing, half-baked persona. That's why there's so many stereotypes in games and the interactive genre.

It is generally assumed that the player cares more about the unique qualities and surprising variations within the game play than they do about the necessary evil of the characters that populate the world. Also, the simpler and more obvious the backstory the less noninteractive screen time needs be devoted to it. Game designers get very nervous if more than a few seconds go by without a required action from the player. And as for plot, the player essentially creates the plot themselves as they proceed down the success path of the game.

Even worse for the hapless writer, the occasional great line of dialog or clever bit of business they get to slip into the product repeatedly hammers at the player like water torture with each subsequent replay of the game. That better be some killer nonexpositional dialog to survive the fiftieth play. That's why players routinely blow by all the dramatic scenes after the first play of the game: Once is enough.

So in this guerrilla war between traditional writing virtues and gaming requirements, the designer is the Doom guy with a chain saw and your script is an ESRB-approved red stain on the floor . . . *if* . . . and only *if* . . . you try to hang on to your musty old Syd Field Writer's Bible. Well, snap out of it! Welcome to the Sewers, punk! Relax . . . pretend it's a game . . . maybe it'll even be fun . . .

Drill number one: Forget drama. You're writing hyperdrama. Minimalism is supreme. Every first time interactive writer *overwrites*, big time. It's almost impossible to *underwrite* for the medium. There's no time to set up gags; there's no time for your character to enter, exit, cross the room, nothing. Things happen, *now*. Short, declarative lines. And they better be good. One of the few saving graces of the medium is what I like to call *The Rocky Horror Picture Show* syndrome. If your lines are catchy and classic enough, instead of the player blowing through all your work on the hundredth play of the game, they'll actually sit through it and chant the dialog along with your character in a mindless nirvana of gaming bliss. It's a lot more work for you, but it pays off.

Drill number two: Always put yourself in the player's chair—what do you want from this world? If you really think about it, you actually *do* want a story, you *do* want surprises and plot twists and fascinating characters. Storytelling is still important, it's just needs to proceed from the players' actions and explorations. Not your rigid, predigested, linear, writer-as-God mind set.

Drill number three: Make the player earn these plot surprises and character payoffs through their own cleverness and hard work. If you can make that happen, you're thinking like a game designer, and the dynamics of your script and those of the design will begin to merge and reinforce one another. And Noah will give you a big kiss.

Okay, now . . . let's look at this as a business for a minute. Is there work out there for you? The answer is probably, and those are a lot better odds than you'll find in the TV and movie industry. Two main forces are at play right now: New hardware is coming to market with radically improved program quality—Playstation, Saturn, M2, DVD, MPC3 for PCs and eventually set-top boxes bringing in massive amounts of interactive data and entertainment.

The slightly downbeat side of this for writers is that these systems can generate extremely realistic, high-speed, polygon-based computer graphics. This gives the consumer a highly immersive and engaging arcade-style world in which video and its attendant story and characters is largely irrelevant. Some of the biggest game companies are growing skeptical of the need for any full-motion video at all. This is not quite as disastrous as it sounds, as the highly articulated animated characters, humanoid or not, that can be generated by these platforms will still need a good writer behind the curtain to bring them to life.

Right now is the best time to try to break into the industry. That's because the individuals at interactive companies who hire writers are still relatively open to unsolicited scripts. They'll still read unrepresented relative unknowns. Why? For the most part, Hollywood agents haven't shmoozed, wined, dined and generally mesmerized them yet. These creative directors, producers and product development people are usually not products of the TV and film industry and haven't got a Rolodex full of agents to whom they owe favors. In short, they're low-flying stealth targets for the ICM and CAA crowd. But...

This is changing. Agencies have had their consciousness raised concerning the interactive world. Some of this came about when they noticed that a number of their film and video director clients were being well paid for interactive productions that were quick shoots and a great fit between series or features. This created a relationship with the interactive company and before you knew it, scripts began arriving by the boxload at Big Game Company, Inc. The only upside of this is a big one for you, the starving writer: These established writers demanded and got bigger bucks than those who came before them. They also negotiated ironclad contracts that are becoming the norm to everyone's benefit.

On a side note to this, interactive is still a relatively wild and wooly industry compared to the elaborate set of standards and practices in Hollywood. The WGA has yet to wrestle with the murky overlapping that can occur between the designing of and the writing of an interactive product. By example—A number of years ago, I was hired by Really Big Game Co. to write a mystery game. The job was a writing assignment only, no design. They were paying only for a script. The design was to be forthcoming. I researched the period and locale and worked up many drafts of character bibles, sample dialog, scenarios, etc. waiting for the design spec, the actual game structure, to hang the story on but none was ever developed. Eventually, the company became unhappy when they didn't get a finished script. When I reminded them that I never got a game design, they replied, "Well, you know, in a mystery game, the script *is* the design."

This kind of manipulation can be minimalized by following a few simple rules:

1. Don't trust anyone! If you're not represented by a licensed agent, get an experienced entertainment lawyer to negotiate an equitable contract. Or use the pending deal to attract and/or establish a relationship with a good agent who'll handle it for you. You won't regret it.

2. Spend a lot of time with the interactive company clarifying terms and responsibilities relative to the specified creative tasks. Then make damn sure the contract accurately reflects these understandings.

3. Once you've begun, expect a certain amount of creative give and take between yourself, the designer, the director and others on the creative team. Don't expect to get any design credit unless you've contributed in a major way to the final design. A good designer really kills his or herself to deliver that final design spec, so give them a break. Conversely, be extremely protective of your writing credit! It should be understood that design elements which affect plot and character are just that: design elements.

Okay, what about the future of interactive? It's going to be here real soon and it's not going to be either static or stable or boring.

You got a VR helmet, an SGI-quality graphics chip, and a high-speed hookup into a multiplayer net service. So, what's in it for the writer? Not much except an entire world to create. Sure, if the designer wants to give the player a gun and make him run around shooting at everybody, you can take a hike. But what if there are no guns? What if there are nonplayer characters, NPCs, rendered in 3-D who can talk. What if they're complete with personalities, weaknesses, needs, jokes, whatever. Artificial Intelligence sufficient to generate fully realized, realistically spontaneous people is a long way off. But not if you define your characters to take very simplistic actions and have very simple responses.

What does the world look like? What can I gain and lose out there? What are the central conflicts that drive this place? This is creative territory as well suited to a writer as a game designer. What are the dramatic possibilities when an on-screen player surrogate, or Avatar, meets and engages another? Is there dialog? Action? Barter? Out of the primordial ooze of lifeless graphics explodes an endless, self-generating society, and you get to design the Genesis Bomb that blasts it into being.

Now, moving over into the nuts and bolts department, make sure you're using a late-model word processor or scripting software program that can output and import a variety of standard formats like Word RTF. Get a fast modem, hook into an online service so you can e-mail your clients easily and a fax machine will save your butt, too. You wouldn't believe how many writers are using junk like Wordstar on 12-year-old machines incapable of connectivity. This provides a lot of headaches for the producer, as none of the files are compatible in either direction and you can't e-mail anything. We even had a guy who "hand wrote." That stuff is all very charming, but interactive scripts are complicated and rewrites are endless because of frequent design changes. I use "Final Draft" on a Mac. They've finally worked out most of the bugs. It automates practically everything and has an absolutely killer multiple revision mode with auto "A" and "B" pages and selectable colors. Pure gold when you're cranking towards a deadline.

A couple of notes on script formatting: I use standard screenplay format with scene numbers keyed to the design flowchart. Then I'll include a lot of game design description including interface and miscellaneous graphics utilization in the appropriate places within the script. This proves invaluable to help the production folks understand the gaming context and motivation of the dramatic action, as well as get a better sense of the final screen presentation and dynamics of the product. The difference is, I'll center and italicize that material so the production manager and the director don't associate it with anything they have to budget or shoot.

Finally, I'd encourage you to play and experience the interactive games and edutainment products that speak to the genre you'll be writing in. When I meet with a writer for the first time who has opinions about a specific product's gameplay, interface, graphics, stories or characters, I start to feel a lot better about working with them. It's just human nature. If a writer shows no interest in interactivity, there's concern that they're not going to get it, or get into it. An ace writer who's ambivalent about interactivity is usually useless to a project. I've seen many crash and burn before the first draft. I'd much rather have a less experienced writer who's really excited by the boundless and sometimes bizarre possibilities of the medium. That person's likely to have the sustained interest and energy to take them through the wringer of the development process. And if they knock out a great script that not only "conforms" to, but "enhances" and "expands" the designer's vision . . . that would be cool, too. That's the real Holy Grail of interactive writing. Thank you very much.

K. Melville
Writer's Connection Seminar on Multimedia Development
June 1995

Create a Game Treatment

Using the sample game treatment in this chapter as your model, create an interactive game treatment. You may choose any genre you wish (science fiction, adventure, western, mystery, etc.), but be certain that you know which companies you want to send this to.

This means you must first research via the Net or the library to find out what types of CD interactive games are being published. Try aiming your treatment at a publisher who is smaller than normal because these are more likely to give a new writer a shot.

Follow these steps as you develop your plan:

1. What does the user have to accomplish in your game?

2. How does he or she accomplish it? Are there different skill levels involved?

3. Who will be your protagonist? Who are the villains? What are their various skills or magical powers?

4. What reward can the user win at the end of your game?

5. What puzzles, mysteries, or clues must be solved or gathered?

6. What makes your game different from the rest?

When you have responded to all of these questions (or most of them), put your proposal in paragraph form. Is your game challenging? Does it seem possible to accomplish? Will it keep the user moving in a positive and exciting direction? If you think you really have something, try sending it out! Stranger things have happened. You just may hit the right pair of eyes.

I hope you enjoy doing the exercise (see box, p. 159). If you are working on a team in a computer lab, I hope you get the chance to develop your game. Remember that teams must cooperate. Let the programmers do their stuff, and do not be afraid to aim at a new market: perhaps a game women may be interested in or maybe something children could play along with adults. I would personally like to see someone come up with an interactive soap opera CD. Many of my female students said they would love to play the "Goddess of the Soaps" if they could manipulate the variety of possible calamities in these characters' lives. Please, if you come up with a successful idea for a game, drop me a line at my e-mail (musgrave@mail.sdsu.edu). I want to include you in my next book!

Box 2 shows another example of a game treatment, this time aimed at the edutainment market. Please note that this game must contain both interesting experiences and educational content for the user. Tests have shown that many inner-city kids respond to edutainment tutorials more than to teachers in a conventional classroom setting. The reason is twofold: (1) these students are already accustomed to televised play, and (2) they are enthusiastic and interested in participating and earning their way through a series of problems, which reinforces the lessons. They feel that they have an intellectual and physical (motor skills/hand–eye coordination) investment in the outcome.

It is very rewarding to see students who have never really responded inside a classroom take so naturally to interactive edutainment games. There is a lot of pressure from teacher groups against this type of learning, but I think that the learning statistics will speak for themselves (see, for example, "New Ways to Learn," *Byte,* March 1995).

Box 2　Treatment for Grammar Learning Game: "Quiz Show!"

This game would consist of two stages: one, the student (up to four may play at a time) chooses his or her persona (from a collection of characters, ethnically representational). The one stipulation is that the original character must be dressed in homeless garb—that is, circa 1995 Goodwill. Also, the character must demonstrate (with a click and sample dialogue) a lack of proficiency with the English language (makes many grammar errors in speech).

Therefore, the student must get his or her character into some kind of intense grammar training to build up the character's skills so he or she can compete on one of the quiz shows. The user may *not* enter the second stage of this game until he or she scores enough points (1,000) to be able to pay off the studio director to get on the chosen show. (This is sort of a twist on the movie *Quiz Show*.) The "Grammar Training" consists of going through the hypertext handbook and studying the rules of grammar, logically organized in five sections to correspond with each of the five quiz shows located in stage two of the game, and then taking the tests at the end of the chapter screens to rack up enough points to get on the show. Whenever the student misses a quiz question, a variety of "grammar goons" play imaginative pranks on the student's persona (such as pulling down his pants, throwing pies in his or her face, goosing, tickling, and any other funny stuff I and the development team can devise). The handbook chapter screens will cover the following grammatical areas: punctuation, joining ideas together, sentences and structure, parts of speech, and consistency and parallelism.

In stage two, once the student has "earned" the thousand points and has bought a ticket to the quiz show, the fun really begins. The five quiz shows are as follows (each has a robust and loudly attired M.C.). "Wheel of Torture" is a game of punctuation skills, wherein each time the contestant answers a correct answer, he or she gets to choose a favorite "torture" from the many available (by spinning the "wheel of torture"), including getting tossed in the air on a blanket by five NFL linebackers; sitting in a chair inside a dunk tank, while the opponent gets to throw baseballs to hit the target that will send the opposition splashing in the drink; and getting kissed by an assortment of monsters who slobber, grunt, and groan all over the hapless victim.

"Hollywood Tears" is a game of joining together ideas, whereby the contestants must "join phrases together properly" by clicking and dragging a variety of animated celebrities and placing them together so their "bubble words" (phrases inside text bubbles over their heads) join together in the proper way. The "phrases" will consist of funny rhymes and sentences that will cause the audience to cry with laughter. Whenever the celebrities are properly joined, the contestant scores points, and the celebrities perform in a variety of silly ways. If the contestant misses a question, the persona will begin to cry for 30 seconds.

In "The Engagement Game," contestants are asked grammar questions about sentences and proper structure. The purpose is to get an engagement after the show. The questions are humorous sentences having to do with relationships. For example, "Is this sentence parallel? I like a date who brings me squirting flowers, but not squirting guns." This would be accompanied by live animation that "shows" the sentence, and the participant gets squirted in the face, if he or she misses the question.

"Peril!" is a game where the contestants answer a variety of questions about parts of speech. Once again, animations illustrate the variety of silly questions, and the participants become the butt of most of the jokes.

"Don Juans and Vamps" is a quiz show about punctuation that uses the TV game show "Studs" as its model. Contestants must learn the sounds of each punctuation mark (this takes an explanation, but in brief it concerns a spin on a routine that comedian Victor Borge has performed for many years, whereby he reads text and makes the special "sound" of the punctuation mark each time he gets to the proper places). Thus, the contestant must click on the punctuation mark and drag it to the spot in the given sentence where he thinks it belongs. Once it is there properly, the "sound" is made and it is embedded inside the sentence. Whenever the contestant clicks on the "hear sentence" icon, the wave file will play the sentence being read with the funny punctuation sounds added for effect. The sound effects of punctuation will be hilarious when combined with sentences about men and women who think they are romantic and sexual dynamos.

The student who wins all five quiz shows gets to the Presidential Ball to meet and converse with a variety of celebrities and dignitaries (similar to the scenes in *Forrest Gump*—animations or .avi), and try out his or her newly mastered grammar skills. Each animation celebrity will have a particularly difficult grammar question, and when the student clicks on the animation he or she will see and hear it asked. The student then must type in the correct response. If the answer is incorrect, President Clinton will play his saxophone in a rather loud and obnoxious manner. If it is correct, Hillary Clinton will give the student a big, wet kiss. Once the student answers all the questions correctly inside the Presidential Ball, he or she is designated "Grammar Quiz Show Champion" by the First Family.

Now that you have seen what it takes to create a game treatment, you can understand why it is important to have a clear idea of what you want to create before you create it. Unless the digital scribe is prepared to give each and every detail of instruction to the designers and programmers, and to work closely with them to make certain that the words are succinct and usable, then he or she will not be successful in the game market.

However, as we shall see, other areas of digital design can be even more lucrative and creative for those who want to write and connect with the masses. For example, there is a huge, untapped market for women on the Internet.

CREATIVE IDEAS FOR WOMEN SCRIBES

It is important at the outset to let you know that I am aware of the "gender-specific problem." I do not want to make it a gender issue, but the facts are there. Many more males use computers and computer technology than do females. As I mentioned earlier, I have a

Create an Edutainment Game

For this task, I want you to create a treatment for an edutainment game that can both teach something and also provide entertainment to the user. These types of interactive games are very popular with children, but you do not have to aim at the children's market. Just be certain you answer the following questions as best you can before writing the treatment paragraphs:

1. What skill, lesson, project, or destination will your user(s) learn?

2. Will there be a quest or a rivalry of some kind?

3. Will the user(s) score points or answer questions? How?

4. Why is it important for your user(s) to be in your game world? Will they create the gaming world?

5. What kinds of interactive tasks will your user(s) have to accomplish?

When you have answered the five questions, try putting your plan into paragraph form, using the sample treatment I gave you as a model. Go over it a second time and make corrections. Make certain you have given all the technical information necessary to put your game into action.

theory about why this is true, but suffice it to say, I am here to give all the wonderfully creative women out there a boost of support. As a college writing instructor, I see women writers who are generally much more creative than my men. Men, as a rule, are linear beings. That is, they are logical, exacting, and task-oriented creatures who do well in math and science, but who have historically done less well in the more "creative" areas of endeavor like English and the humanities.

I do recognize that if you are reading this book you most likely are a technically savvy woman. Thus, when I mention the fact that many women have not become computer literate, I do not mean you. It is my belief that if I can get women to get out there on the Net to enthusiastically develop new concepts and new ways of looking at the same reality, then the quality of the Internet will improve. The best way I know how is to give the women out there a challenge. A female student who took a summer school class from me was an extremely bright person: She was a junior in high school taking a college-level composition course, who has since gone on to Stanford. After I had challenged her all that summer to create more and more and to develop her innate talents, she paid me the highest compliment a teacher can receive. She said, "Mr. Musgrave, my teachers in high school never really challenged me the way you have. I want to thank you for that. I need to be challenged to do my very best. My concert piano teacher does this, and I respond. I like to be challenged!"

My challenge is to give you some ideas. These ideas can be used to create your own new reality. I want you to focus your energies on creating something of which you can be proud. Do not let the technicalities of computers deter you. I have suggested software that is easy to learn, so you should spend the time to learn it. Every new era of creative challenge must be met by those who are unafraid to learn the tools of that era. You must not fear these technical challenges just because males have done most of the technical creation. A Freudian psychoanalyst could write a doctoral thesis on the language of naming in our masculine computer world: hard drive, RAM, crash, slip access, information superhighway, boot up, on-line, zipped, and downloading—all terms that have definitely masculine connotations. A woman who enters this world had better be prepared to get "flamed" if she cannot compete.

Women *are* competing in the gaming world, for instance. Some of the best and most creative game designers are women. Most interestingly, they are better in the area of edutainment, rather than with the violent destruction games like Doom and Descent. The ideas I give in the exercise box (p. 166) will challenge you to try your hand at a variety of areas of program design and information manipulation. Note that these exercises are not exclusively for women.

I will then continue with some other ideas that you may use to make some money on the Internet. Perhaps one of my ideas will lead you to yet another, better, idea. I want you to let your creative mind go wild, and I want you to follow through on your creativity. Remember those "castles in the air." This is your chance to build your own dreams. I also want you to teach one of your sisters who may not be as technically literate as you are. She may have new ideas that can be expressed best in multimedia or electronic form, and you can give her a start!

Creative Ideas for Work and Entertainment

1. Design a concept for an interactive "family story game" wherein the user must make choices for family members based on their individual character make-up, profession, and motivation. Create three families that are rivals in some way and must compete for some reward outside the family. Romantic love (e.g., Romeo and Juliet) is always a good way to make interesting interactions between characters as the lovers try to overcome family differences (cultural, racial, or otherwise) to be together. Also, it is always entertaining to plot a variety of possible "scenarios" to show what will happen when the user makes a specific choice. For example, suppose one family is "underhanded and evil," and the other is "honest and good." What happens when they each try to nominate their father or mother to run for town mayor? It becomes a real feud. Each choice becomes important to the user because it may influence the coming election. This can be filmed using live actors, so screenplay format is preferred.

2. Design a service or retail store or other mall-type shopping place wherein the customer's individual needs are taken care of. For example, it is possible to create "virtual bodies" based on the physical measurements of the "shopper" that are input into the database via the keyboard, at an on-line shop location on the Internet. The user could then "see" his or her own form and "try on" a variety of clothing, hats, and shoes. See what I mean? Use the Home Builder software combined with some 3-D animation program to create the clothing and figures. The virtual reality technology is here. You just have to write how it will work!

3. Create a publication or home page where people can go to learn new "cost saving ideas"; this could be modeled after the popular newsletter *The Penny Pinch Press,* which gives readers a variety of ways to cut corners in a recession economy. Your newsletter, however, can be interactive (graphics, sound, movies, etc.). You can show rather than just tell the user how to save. You should cluster and brainstorm to discover the best ideas. Write a possible outline or treatment.

If you feel uncomfortable with the technical side of creativity, take heart; many programmers out there are dying to meet some digital scribe full of creative ideas like you have. They can help you get your ideas and treatments into a form called a "demo," which will be your calling card to the Internet and to publishers on-line, about whom I will be telling you more later.

I hope you see what innovative opportunities there are in cyberspace for the digital scribe who wants to go beyond action games. Other ideas could include developing an interactive home page that serves as a counseling center for abused people; making a storytelling home page, where you provide multimedia "re-creations" of old nursery rhymes and Mother Goose stories (these are free from copyright restriction laws, so they are safe to use); developing a virtual reality beauty parlor or unisex salon, where the user can "try on" a variety of haircut and hairdos (the basis of this would be that the user would send you a scanned [digitized] picture of himself or herself on which you would show what the hairstyle would finally look like); or creating a multimedia psychic page, where the user could participate in seances, play a Ouija board (with the computer acting as the "other"), or have a fortune teller gaze into a crystal ball (like those arcade gypsies of long ago). Of course, any or all of these projects could cost the user a bit of money, depending on how you set it up. Credit card purchases are now coming on-line, and there are always the shareware and the SoftLock Corporation methods (see the section on "Ways to Sell Your Ideas," Chapter 13). What is lacking right now are creative people like yourself to implement these ideas by working with your friends and computer nerds to see the visions come into reality. Once again, if you use one of these ideas (or you come up with a better one), please drop me a line and tell me how you accomplished it; I will be overjoyed to know!

The Home Page Store Front

All of these ideas could serve as "come-ons" for your business or service. You could actually own and operate a business or service that this home page represents, and the user who has fun with your interactive creativity can call you by e-mail (or by fax or phone) and find out where you do business. This is especially true of your business if it is providing a product and you give potential customers an on-line catalog to choose from (see sample catalog-maker software on the CD). However, service businesses could also benefit from these specialty home pages (as I have illustrated with the beauty and unisex salons). Pet grooming, child care, and other service businesses would be excellent examples of home page store fronts.

THE SMALL-BUSINESS CREATIVE TYPE

In the classes I teach at a couple of junior colleges in San Diego, California, I get a lot of students who enroll who are interested in starting their own business—trade, service, or other types. This is my direct solicitation to these people: There is a great opportunity for you to create your own store front on the Net! Imagine. The average income of a person on-line is $73,000 per year, according to most marketing analysts like Netscape. Now, imagine all the business these users need for their automobiles, their plumbing, their landscaping, their—just about every service you can think of!

I want to give the small-business entrepreneurs out there a chance to create a calling card that will get business fast. By using an HTML editor (samples on the CD) you can create a home page on the Internet and start taking orders for business (see the exercises in the

Figure 9.2 Sample portion of a home page from the Internet

Store Front Home Page Exercises for Small Businesses

Even if you are *not* a tradesperson, you can benefit from doing this exercise. After all, tradespeople would love to hire you if you could create a fancy home page for them to reap the new business engendered by your creativity.

1. Pretend that you are a plumber. What interactive home page could you create using the sample software I have discussed in earlier parts of this book (catalog builder, Home Space Builder, HTML editor, etc.)? Draw a sample page and include a headline, "hot words" (words you click to get somewhere else or to put some animation, sound, or movie into action), and graphics that relate to this profession. What else could you include that would be humorous, practical, or that would set you apart from the competition?

2. Pretend that you own an automotive repair service. Do the same as in exercise 1, except relate your items to the specific profession of automotive mechanic. In what ways can you show that you care? What sounds, movies or animations would help you sell your service? Again, draw a sample home page. Give the details about what will happen when the user clicks on the variety of buttons, hot words, or pictures.

3. Finally, imagine you are a used car dealer. How can you best represent the automobiles you are selling to the people who might be interested? Perhaps yours could be a rendition of what we in San Diego call the *Automobile Shopper* magazine. What new multimedia "gimmicks" would you include in your design of the home page that would stand out for your Net surfer? Once more, draw a sample home page. Give the details about what happens when the user clicks on your interactive icons.

box). However, you should consider making your home page more interesting than the next person's by adding all the "extras" you can think of. That means if you must create sound files, add a little music, or even develop a 3-D virtual house (using the sample software on the CD), then you will do it! I know you are up for it because only you know how your business can help others. Figure 9.2 shows part of a home page on the Internet.

It is worth the investment to get your business listed on Bulletin Boards (BBSes) and to create your own home page because e-mail is inexpensive and taking orders electronically saves time, space, and money. You can get others to do it for you (see SoftLock Software on the CD). There are also many free Web sites where you can place your ad. I will talk more about this in "How to Submit Your Work in Cyberspace" (Chapter 13). Finally, you should approach your local Better Business Bureau, Chamber of Commerce, or other small-business group so that you can network and exchange ideas. Digital scribes who like PR or marketing writing might find a lucrative niche by working with local businesses to set up low-cost, useful Web sites for community entrepreneurs.

STUDENTS ON THE NET

I hope you were waiting to hear this—all you students out there. Yes, there is an opportunity for you to contribute to this growing world of electronic connections and communications. In fact, if this book is being used as a text, you have already started on your way to becoming a professional digital scribe. The only thing that separates a professional from an excellent student is money. And the Internet is the place where you can be as influential as any professional—if you just give others what they want.

Perhaps you want to reach your peer group. One idea, if you are an art major, could be to start a "T Shirt by Order" business. Your home page could consist of an input database where customers could sign in and order the design of their choice (selected from the many full-color designs you have placed on the page for them to browse). Perhaps you could have some music for them to listen to as they browse through your awesome collection of original prints, or you could build a T Shirt Villa, a virtual reality house that has T shirts on the walls instead of pictures. The "walker" could click on the T shirt and order it. Finally, they can indicate the shirt size by clicking on a T shirt logo. Presto! You have your first sale!

Home Page Exercises

1. Create a home page for people who want the latest information on your favorite musical group. Choose the group, research some possible interactive attractions you could place on your page, and then do a rough outline that shows what will happen when the user clicks on the various hot words, pictures, buttons, or other interactive devices. The more creative you can be, the more your user will want to return! Make certain you include the headlines and text on the home page.

2. Create a possible home page for your high school or college. Collect possible graphics, photos, sounds, and other interesting items that a user would want to see and experience to learn about your school. Once more, draw a rough outline that shows, in detail, what will happen when the user interacts with the page.

3. Design a possible home page that advertises your service. Perhaps you babysit, clean houses, or tutor. Or maybe you do freelance artwork or writing/computer consulting. What headline, text, and interactive devices would you have to call attention to your service? Could you add some sound files? Draw the outline and show, in detail, what your service page would encompass.

This same idea can take on a variety of forms. One group created a line of greeting cards aimed at the black population. They used churches and other neighborhood groups to market their designs, and people ordered through the community groups. The first year they made $15,000. The second year, $150,000! This can also be done on the Internet. If your home page reflects the designs of your greeting cards, the customers can order right from the page by clicking and filling in the order form.

Now that you get the hang of what I mean, I want you to try the exercise in the box.

Now that you understand how everybody can participate as digital scribes, it is time we let you in on the legal aspects of authorship. There are great differences when it comes to copyright restrictions and other legalities in electronic publlshing as compared with print media. The next chapter will give you information about those differences and how you can publish and not perish!

Part III

The Digital Scribe and the Law

10

The Legalities of Electronic Media

This chapter will cover the following:

- Definition of copyright
- Who can claim copyright
- General principles of copyright
- National origin of work
- What works are protected
- What works are not protected
- How to secure a copyright
- Works created before 1978
- Registration procedures
- How to investigate a copyright
- Serial or magazine copyright law

Digital scribes must be aware of copyright laws and restrictions that apply to creative work in electronic media. The information presented has been researched using the latest laws available, although the laws are always changing, and I suggest you seek counsel if you have any serious business or legal questions.

Congress is presently reviewing electronic media copyright law. There will most likely be many changes made, so it is wise that you consult the Congressional Web pages regularly to keep abreast of the news. Many countries, for example, have done away with copyright law on the Internet because it is almost impossible to enforce. If, for example, I download a document from Finland and publish it as my own, who is going to keep track of the authorship? The law becomes very flimsy when it comes to this type of publishing, and Congress is going to do some heavy thinking on the issue before we know the result.

But first, you should be aware of the general laws regulating artistic creations, in general. The following is a basic outline of general copyright law and how it works. It is taken verbatim from the United States Office of Copyright, and you can obtain an electronic version free of charge.

WHAT COPYRIGHT IS

Copyright is a form of protection provided by the laws of the United States (title 17, U.S. Code) to the authors of "original works of authorship" including literary, dramatic, musical, artistic, and certain other intellectual works. This protection is available to both published and unpublished works. Section 106 of the Copyright Act generally gives the owner of copyright the exclusive right to do and to authorize others to do the following:

- To *reproduce* the copyrighted work in copies or phono records

- To prepare *derivative works* based on the copyrighted work

- To *distribute copies or phono records* of the copyrighted work to the public by sale or other transfer of ownership, or by rental, lease, or lending

- To *perform* the copyrighted work publicly, in the case of literary, musical, dramatic, and choreographic works, pantomimes, and motion pictures and other audiovisual works, and

- To *display* the copyrighted work publicly, in the case of literary, musical, dramatic, and choreographic works, pantomimes, and pictorial, graphic, or sculptural works, including the individual images of a motion picture or other audiovisual work.

It is illegal for anyone to violate any of the rights provided by the Act to the owner of copyright. These rights, however, are not unlimited in scope. Sections 107 through 119 of the Copyright Act establish limitations on these rights. In some cases, these limitations are specified exemptions from copyright liability. One major limitation is the doctrine of "fair use," which is given a statutory basis in section 107 of the Act. In other instances, the limitation takes the form of a "compulsory license" under which certain limited uses of copyrighted works are permitted upon payment of specified royalties and compliance with statutory conditions. For further information about the limitations of any of these rights, consult the Copyright Act or write to the Copyright Office.

WHO CAN CLAIM COPYRIGHT

Copyright protection subsists from the time the work is created in fixed form; that is, it is an incident of the process of authorship. The copyright in the work of authorship *immediately* becomes the property of the author who created it. Only the author or those deriving their rights through the author can rightfully claim copyright.

In the case of works made for hire, the employer and not the employee is presumptively considered the author. Section 101 of the copyright statute defines a "work made for hire" as

1. A work prepared by an employee within the scope of his or her employment or

2. A work specially ordered or commissioned for use as a contribution to a collective work, as a part of a motion picture or other audiovisual work, as a translation, as a supplementary work, as a compilation, as an instructional text, as a test, as answer material for a test, or as an atlas, if the parties expressly agree in a written instrument signed by them that the work shall be considered a work made for hire...

The authors of a joint work are co-owners of the copyright in the work, unless there is an agreement to the contrary.

Copyright in each separate contribution to a periodical or other collective work is distinct from copyright in the collective work as a whole and vests initially with the author of the contribution.

GENERAL PRINCIPLES

- Mere ownership of a book, manuscript, painting, or any other copy or phono record does not give the possessor the copyright.

- The law provides that transfer of ownership of any material object that embodies a protected work does not of itself convey any rights in the copyright.

- Minors may claim copyright, but state laws may regulate the business dealings involving copyrights owned by minors. For information on relevant state laws, consult an attorney.

COPYRIGHT AND NATIONAL ORIGIN OF THE WORK

Copyright protection is available for all unpublished works, regardless of the nationality or domicile of the author.

Published works are eligible for copyright protection in the United States if *any* one of the following conditions is met:

- On the date of first publication, one or more of the authors is a national or domiciliary of the United States or is a national, domiciliary, or sovereign authority of a foreign nation that is a party to a copyright treaty to which the United States is also a party, or is a stateless person wherever that person may be domiciled or

- The work is first published in the United States or in a foreign nation that, on the date of first publication, is a party to the Universal Copyright Convention or the work comes within the scope of a Presidential proclamation or

- The work is first published on or after March 1, 1989, in a foreign nation that on the date of first publication, is a party to the Berne Convention or, if the work is *not* first published in a country party to the Berne Convention, it is published (on or after March 1, 1989) within 30 days of first publication in a country that is party to the Berne Convention or the work, first published on or after March 1, 1989, is a pictorial, graphic, or sculptural work that is incorporated in a permanent structure located in the United States or, if the work, first published on or after March 1, 1989, is a published audiovisual work, all the authors are legal entities with headquarters in the United States.

WHAT WORKS ARE PROTECTED

Copyright protects "original works of authorship" that are fixed in a tangible form of expression. The fixation need not be directly perceptible, so long as it may be communicated with the aid of a machine or device. Copyrightable works include the following categories:

1. Literary works
2. Musical works, including any accompanying words
3. Dramatic works, including any accompanying music
4. Pantomimes and choreographic works
5. Pictorial, graphic, and sculptural works
6. Motion pictures and other audiovisual works
7. Sound recordings
8. Architectural works

These categories should be viewed quite broadly; for example, computer programs and most "compilations" are registrable as "literary works," maps and architectural plans are registrable as "pictorial, graphic, and sculptural works."

WHAT IS NOT PROTECTED BY COPYRIGHT

Several categories of material are generally not eligible for statutory copyright protection. These include the following, among others:

- Works that have *not* been fixed in a tangible form of expression. For example, choreographic works that have not been notated or recorded or improvisational speeches or performances that have not been written or recorded.

- Titles, names, short phrases, and slogans; familiar symbols or designs; mere variations of typographic ornamentation, lettering, or coloring mere listings of ingredients or contents.

- Ideas, procedures, methods, systems, processes, concepts, principles, discoveries, or devices, as distinguished from a description, explanation, or illustration.

- Works consisting *entirely* of information that is common property and containing no original authorship. For example: standard calendars, height and weight charts, tape measures and rulers, and lists or tables taken from public documents or other common sources.

HOW TO SECURE A COPYRIGHT

Copyright Secured Automatically upon Creation

The way in which copyright protection is secured under the present law is frequently misunderstood. No publication or registration or other action in the Copyright Office is required to secure copyright (see Note). There are, however, certain definite advantages to registration (see page 194).

Copyright is secured *automatically* when the work is created, and a work is "created" when it is fixed in a copy or phono record for the first time. "Copies" are material objects from which a work can be read or visually perceived either directly or with the aid of a machine or device, such as books, manuscripts, sheet music, film, videotape, or microfilm. "Phono records" are material objects embodying fixations of sounds (excluding, by statutory definition, motion picture soundtracks), such as audio tapes or phonograph disks. Thus, for example, a song (the "work") can be fixed on sheet music ("copies") or on phonograph disks ("phono records"), or both.

If a work is prepared over a period of time, the part of the work that is fixed on a particular date constitutes the created work as of that date.

PUBLICATION

Publication is no longer the key to obtaining statutory copyright as it was under the Copyright Act of 1909. However, publication remains important to copyright owners.

The Copyright Act defines publication as follows:

> "Publication" is the distribution of copies or phono records of a work to the public by sale or other transfer of ownership, or by rental, lease, or lending. The offering to distribute copies or phono records to a group of persons for purposes of further distribution, public performance, or public display, constitutes publication. A public performance or display of a work does not of itself constitute publication.

Note

Before 1978, statutory copyright was generally secured by the act of publication with notice of copyright, assuming compliance with all other relevant statutory conditions. Works in the public domain on January 1, 1978 (for example, works published without satisfying all conditions for securing statutory copyright under the Copyright Act of 1909) remain in the public domain under the current Act.

Statutory copyright could also be secured before 1978 by the act of registration in the case of certain unpublished works and works eligible for ad interim copyright. The current Act automatically extends to full term (section 304 sets the term) copyright for all works including those subject to ad interim copyright if ad interim registration has been made on or before June 30, 1978.

A further discussion of the definition of "publication" can be found in the legislative history of the Act. The legislative reports define "to the public" as distribution to persons under no explicit or implicit restrictions with respect to disclosure of the contents. The reports state that the definition makes it clear that the sale of phono records constitutes publication of the underlying work; for example, the musical, dramatic, or literary work embodied in a phono record. The reports also state that it is clear that any form of dissemination in which the material object does not change hands, for example, performances or displays on television, is *not* a publication no matter how many people are exposed to the work. However, when copies or phono records are offered for sale or lease to a group of wholesalers, broadcasters, or motion picture theaters, publication does take place if the purpose is further distribution, public performance, or public display.

Publication is an important concept in the copyright law for several reasons:

- When a work is published, it may bear a notice of copyright to identify the year of publication and the name of the copyright owner and to inform the public that the work is protected by copyright. Works published before March 1, 1989, *must* bear the notice or risk loss of copyright protection. (See discussion on "Notice of Copyright," which follows.)

- Works that are published in the United States are subject to mandatory deposit with the Library of Congress. (See discussion on "Mandatory Deposit.")

- Publication of a work can affect the limitations on the exclusive rights of the copyright owner set forth in sections 107 through 120 of the law.

- The year of publication may determine the duration of copyright protection for anonymous and pseudonymous works (when the author's identity is not revealed in the records of the Copyright Office) and for works made for hire.

- Deposit requirements for registration of published works differ from those for registration of unpublished works. (See discussion on "registration" procedures.)

NOTICE OF COPYRIGHT

For works first published on and after March 1, 1989, use of the copyright notice is optional, although highly recommended. Before March 1, 1989, the use of the notice was mandatory on all published works, and any work first published before that date must bear a notice or risk loss of copyright protection.

(The Copyright Office does not take a position on whether works first published with notice before March 1, 1989, and reprinted and distributed on and after March 1, 1989, must bear the copyright notice.)

Use of the notice is recommended because it informs the public that the work is protected by copyright, identifies the copyright owner, and shows the year of first publication. Furthermore, in the event that a work is infringed, if the work carries a proper notice, the court will not allow a defendant to claim "innocent infringement," that is, that he or she did not realize that the work is protected. (A successful innocent infringement claim may result in a reduction in damages that the copyright owner would otherwise receive.)

The use of the copyright notice is the responsibility of the copyright owner and does not require advance permission from, or registration with, the Copyright Office.

Form of Notice for Visually Perceptible Copies

The notice for visually perceptible copies should contain all of the following three elements:

1. *The symbol* © (the letter C in a circle), or the word "Copyright," or the abbreviation "Copr." and

2. *The year of first publication of the work* (In the case of compilations or derivative works incorporating previously published material, the year date of first publication of the compilation or derivative work is sufficient; the year date

may be omitted where a pictorial, graphic, or sculptural work, with accompanying textual matter, if any, is reproduced in or on greeting cards, postcards, stationery, jewelry, dolls, toys, or any useful article), and

3. *The name of the owner of copyright* in the work, or an abbreviation by which the name can be recognized, or a generally known alternative designation of the owner. For example,

© 1992 John Doe

The © notice is used only on "visually perceptible copies." Certain kinds of works—for example, musical, dramatic, and literary works—may be fixed not in "copies" but by means of sound in an audio recording. Because audio recordings such as audiotapes and phonograph disks are "phono records" and not "copies," the © notice is not used to indicate protection of the underlying musical, dramatic, or literary work that is recorded.

Form of Notice for Phono Records of Sound Recordings

The copyright notice for phono records of sound recordings[1] has somewhat different requirements. The notice appearing on phono records should contain the following three elements:

1. *The symbol* ℗ (the letter P in a circle), and

2. *The year of first publication* of the sound recording, and

3. *The name of the owner of copyright* in the sound recording, or an abbreviation by which the name can be recognized,

---

[1] Sound recordings are defined as "works that result from the fixation of a series of musical, spoken, or other sounds, but not including the sounds accompanying a motion picture or other audiovisual work, regardless of the nature of the material objects, such as disks, tapes, or other phono records, in which they are embodied."

or a generally known alternative designation of the owner. If the producer of the sound recording is named on the phono record labels or containers, and if no other name appears in conjunction with the notice, the producer's name shall be considered a part of the notice. For example,

℗ 1992 A.B.C., Inc.

Note

Because questions may arise from the use of variant forms of the notice, any form of the notice other than those given here should not be used without first seeking legal advice.

POSITION OF NOTICE

The notice should be affixed to copies or phono records of the work in such a manner and location as to "give reasonable notice of the claim of copyright." The notice on phono records may appear on the surface of the phono record or on the phono record label or container, provided the manner of placement and location give reasonable notice of the claim. The three elements of the notice should ordinarily appear together on the copies or phono records. The Copyright Office has issued regulations concerning the form and position of the copyright notice in the *Code of Federal Regulations* (37 CFR Part 201). For more information, request Circular 3.

PUBLICATIONS INCORPORATING UNITED STATES GOVERNMENT WORKS

Works by the U.S. government are not eligible for copyright protection. For works published on and after March 1, 1989, the previous notice requirement for works consisting primarily of one or more U.S. government works has been eliminated. However, use of the copyright notice for these works is still strongly recommended. Use of a notice on such a work will defeat a claim of innocent infringement as previously described, *provided* the notice also includes a statement that identifies one of the following: those portions of the work in which copyright is claimed or those portions that constitute U.S. government material. For example,

> © 1992 Jane Brown. Copyright claimed in Chapters 7–10, exclusive of U.S. government maps.

Works published before March 1, 1989, that consist primarily of one or more works of the U.S. government *must* bear a notice and the identifying statement.

UNPUBLISHED WORKS

To avoid an inadvertent publication without notice, the author or other owner of copyright may wish to place a copyright notice on any copies or phono records that leave his or her control. An appropriate notice for an unpublished work is as follows: Unpublished work © 1992 Jane Doe.

Effect of Omission of the Notice or Error in the Name or Date

The Copyright Act, in sections 405 and 406, provides procedures for correcting errors and omissions of the copyright notice on works published on or after January 1, 1978, and before March 1, 1989.

In general, if a notice was omitted or an error was made on copies distributed between January 1, 1978, and March 1, 1989, the copyright was not automatically lost. Copyright protection may be maintained if registration for the work has been made before or is made within five years after the publication without notice, and a reasonable effort is made to add the notice to all copies or phono records distributed to the public in the United States after the omission has been discovered. For more information request Circular 3.

HOW LONG COPYRIGHT PROTECTION ENDURES

Works Originally Created on or After January 1, 1978

A work that is created (fixed in tangible form for the first time) on or after January 1, 1978, is automatically protected from the moment of its creation and is ordinarily given a term enduring for the author's life plus an additional 50 years after the author's death. In the case of "a joint work prepared by two or more authors who did not work for hire," the term lasts for 50 years after the last surviving author's death. For works made for hire, and for anonymous and pseudonymous works (unless the author's identity is revealed in Copyright Office records), the duration of copyright will be 75 years from publication or 100 years from creation, whichever is shorter.

Works Originally Created Before January 1, 1978, but Not Published or Registered by That Date

Works that were created but not published or registered for copyright before January 1, 1978, have been automatically brought under the statute and are now given Federal copyright protection. The duration of copyright in these works will generally be computed in the same way as for works created on or after January 1, 1978: the life plus 50 years or 75/100-year terms will apply to them as well. The law provides that in no case will the term of copyright for works in this category expire before December 31, 2002, and for works published on or before December 31, 2002, the term of copyright will not expire before December 31, 2027.

Works Originally Created and Published or Registered Before January 1, 1978

Under the law in effect before 1978, copyright was secured either on the date a work was published or on the date of registration if the work was registered in unpublished form. In either case, the copyright endured for a first term of 28 years from the date it was secured. During the last (28th) year of the first term, the copyright was eligible for renewal. The current copyright law has extended the renewal term from 28 to 47 years for copyrights that were subsisting on January 1, 1978, making these works eligible for a total term of protection of 75 years. However, the copyright *must* be renewed to receive the 47-year period of added protection. This is accomplished by filing a properly completed Form RE accompanied by a $12 filing fee in the Copyright Office before the end of the 28th calendar year of the original term.

   For more detailed information on the copyright term, write to the Copyright Office and request Circulars 15a and 15t. For information on how to search the Copyright Office records concerning the copyright status of a work, request Circular 22.

TRANSFER OF COPYRIGHT

Any or all of the exclusive rights, or any subdivision of those rights, of the copyright owner may be transferred, but the transfer of *exclusive* rights is not valid unless that transfer is in writing and signed by the owner of the rights conveyed (or such owner's duly authorized agent). Transfer of a right on a nonexclusive basis does not require a written agreement.

A copyright may also be conveyed by operation of law and may be bequeathed by will or pass as personal property by the applicable laws of intestate succession.

Copyright is a personal property right, and it is subject to the various state laws and regulations that govern the ownership, inheritance, or transfer of personal property as well as terms of contracts or conduct of business. For information about relevant state laws, consult an attorney.

Transfers of copyright are normally made by contract. The Copyright Office does not have or supply any forms for such transfers. However, the law does provide for the recordation in the Copyright Office of transfers of copyright ownership. Although recordation is not required to make a valid transfer between the parties, it does provide certain legal advantages and may be required to validate the transfer as against third parties. For information on recordation of transfers and other documents related to copyright, request Circular 12.

TERMINATION OF TRANSFERS

Under the previous law, the copyright in a work reverted to the author, if living, or if the author was not living, to other specified beneficiaries, provided a renewal claim was registered in the 28th year of the original term. The present law drops the renewal feature except for works already in the first term of statutory protection when the present law took effect. Instead, the present law permits termination of a grant of rights after 35 years under certain conditions by serving written notice on the transferee within specified time limits.

For works already under statutory copyright protection before 1978, the present law provides a similar right of termination covering the newly added years that extended the former maximum term of the copyright from 56 to 75 years. For further information, request Circulars 15a and 15t.

INTERNATIONAL COPYRIGHT PROTECTION

There is no such thing as an "international copyright" that will automatically protect an author's writings throughout the entire world. Protection against unauthorized use in a particular country depends, basically, on the national laws of that country. However, most countries do offer protection to foreign works under certain conditions, and these conditions have been greatly simplified by international copyright treaties and conventions. For a list of countries that maintain copyright relations with the United States, request Circular 38a.

The United States belongs to both global, multilateral copyright treaties, the Universal Copyright Convention (UCC) and the Berne Convention for the Protection of Literary and Artistic Works. The United States was a founding member of the UCC, which came into force on September 16, 1955. Generally, a work by a national or domiciliary of a country that is a member of the UCC or a work first published in a UCC country may claim protection under the UCC. If the work bears the notice of copyright in the form and position specified by the UCC, this notice will satisfy and substitute for any other formalities a UCC member country would otherwise impose as a condition of copyright. A UCC notice should consist of the symbol © accompanied by the name of the copyright proprietor and the year of first publication of the work.

By joining the Berne Convention on March 1, 1989, the United States gained protection for its authors in all member nations of the

Berne Union with which the United States formerly had either no copyright relations or had bilateral treaty arrangements. Members of the Berne Union agree to a certain minimum level of copyright protection and agree to treat nationals of other member countries like their own nationals for purposes of copyright. A work first published in the United States or another Berne Union country (or first published in a non-Berne Union country, followed by publication within 30 days in a Berne Union country) is eligible for protection in all Berne Union member countries. There are no special requirements. For information on the legislation implementing the Berne Convention, request Circular 93 from the Copyright Office.

An author who wishes protection for his or her work in a particular country should first find out the extent of protection of foreign works in that country. If possible, this should be done before the work is published anywhere, since protection may often depend on the facts existing at the time of *first* publication.

If the country in which protection is sought is a party to one of the international copyright conventions, the work may generally be protected by complying with the conditions of the convention. Even if the work cannot be brought under an international convention, protection under the specific provisions of the country's national laws may still be possible. Some countries, however, offer little or no copyright protection for foreign works.

COPYRIGHT REGISTRATION

In general, copyright registration is a legal formality intended to make a public record of the basic facts of a particular copyright. However, except in two specific situations,[2] registration is not a

---

[2] Works published with notice of copyright before January 1, 1978, must be registered and renewed during the first 28-year term of copyright to maintain protection.

Under sections 405 and 406 of the Copyright Act, copyright registration may be required to preserve a copyright on a work first published before March 1, 1989, that would otherwise be invalidated because the copyright notice was omitted from the published copies or phono records, or the name or year date was omitted, or certain errors were made in the year date.

condition of copyright protection. Even though registration is not generally a requirement for protection, the copyright law provides several inducements or advantages to encourage copyright owners to make registration. Among these advantages are the following:

- Registration establishes a public record of the copyright claim.

- Before an infringement suit may be filed in court, registration is necessary for works of U.S. origin and for foreign works not originating in a Berne Union country. (For more information on when a work is of U.S. origin, request Circular 93.)

- If made before or within five years of publication, registration will establish prima facie evidence in court of the validity of the copyright and of the facts stated in the certificate.

- If registration is made within three months after publication of the work or prior to an infringement of the work, statutory damages and attorney's fees will be available to the copyright owner in court actions. Otherwise, only an award of actual damages and profits is available to the copyright owner.

- Copyright registration allows the owner of the copyright to record the registration with the U.S. Customs Service for protection against the importation of infringing copies. For additional information, request Publication No. 563 from

  Commissioner of Customs
  ATTN: IPR Branch
  Room 2104
  U.S. Customs Service
  1301 Constitution Avenue, N.W.
  Washington, D.C. 20229.

Registration may be made at any time within the life of the copyright. Unlike the law before 1978, when a work has been registered in unpublished form, it is not necessary to make another registration when the work becomes published (although the copyright owner may register the published edition, if desired).

REGISTRATION PROCEDURES

In General

To register a work, send the following three elements *in the same envelope or package* to the Register of Copyrights, Copyright Office, Library of Congress, Washington, D.C. 20559 (see page 204 for what happens if the elements are sent separately).

1. A properly completed application form
2. A nonrefundable filing fee of $20 for each application.[3]
3. A nonreturnable deposit of the work being registered. The deposit requirements vary in particular situations. The *general* requirements follow. Also note the information under "Special Deposit Requirements" immediately following this section.

- If the work is unpublished, one complete copy or phono record.

- If the work was first published in the United States on or after January 1, 1978, two complete copies or phono records of the best edition.

- If the work was first published in the United States before January 1, 1978, two complete copies or phono records of the work as first published.

- If the work was first published outside the United States, one complete copy or phono record of the work as first published.

---

[3] Copyright fees are adjusted at five-year intervals, based on increases in the Consumer Price Index. The next adjustment is due in 1997. Contact the Copyright Office in January 1997 for the new fee schedule.

For the fee structure for application Form SE/GROUP, see instructions on the form.

To register a renewal, send:

1. A properly completed RE application form, and
2. A nonrefundable filing fee of $12 for each work.

Complete the application form using black ink pen or typewriter. You may photocopy blank application forms; *however*, photocopied forms submitted to the Copyright Office must be clear, legible, on a good grade of 8 1/2-inch by 11-inch white paper suitable for automatic feeding through a photocopier. The forms should be printed preferably in black ink, head-to-head (so that when you turn the sheet over, the top of page 2 is directly behind the top of page 1). *Forms not meeting these requirements will be returned.*

Special Deposit Requirements

Special deposit requirements exist for many types of work. In some instances, only one copy is required for published works, in other instances only identifying material is required, and in still other instances, the deposit requirement may be unique. The following are three prominent examples of exceptions to the general deposit requirements:

- If the work is a motion picture, the deposit requirement is one complete copy of the unpublished or published motion picture *and* a separate written description of its contents, such as a continuity, press book, or synopsis.

- If the work is a literary, dramatic or musical work *published only on phono record*, the deposit requirement is one complete copy of the phono record.

- If the work is an unpublished or published computer program, the deposit requirement is one visually perceptible copy in source code of the *first and last 25 pages* of the program. For a program of fewer than 50 pages, the deposit is a copy of the entire program. (For more information on computer program registration, including deposits for revised programs and provisions for trade secrets, request Circular 61.)

- If the work is in a CD-ROM format, the deposit requirement is one complete copy of the material, that is, the CD-ROM, the operating software, and any manual(s) accompanying it. If the identical work is also available in print or hard copy form, send one complete copy of the print version *and* one complete copy of the CD-ROM version.

- For information about group registration of serials, request Circular 62.

In the case of works reproduced in three-dimensional copies, identifying material such as photographs or drawings is ordinarily required. Other examples of special deposit requirements (but by no means an exhaustive list) include many works of the visual arts, such as greeting cards, toys, fabric, oversized material, video games and other machine-readable audiovisual works, automated databases, and contributions to collective works.

If you are unsure of the deposit requirement for your work, write or call the Copyright Office and describe the work you wish to register.

Unpublished Collections

A work may be registered in unpublished form as a "collection," with one application and one fee, under the following conditions:

- The elements of the collection are assembled in an orderly form.

- The combined elements bear a single title identifying the collection as a whole.

- The copyright claimant in all the elements and in the collection as a whole is the same.

- All of the elements are by the same author, or if they are by different authors, at least one of the authors has contributed copyrightable authorship to each element.

An unpublished collection is indexed in the *Catalog of Copyright Entries* only under the collection title.

CORRECTIONS AND AMPLIFICATIONS OF EXISTING REGISTRATIONS

To correct an error in a copyright registration or to amplify the information given in a registration, file a supplementary registration form (Form CA) with the Copyright Office. The information in a supplementary registration augments but does not supersede that contained in the earlier registration. Note also that a supplementary registration is not a substitute for an original registration, a renewal registration, or recording a transfer of ownership. For further information about supplementary registration, request Circular 8.

MANDATORY DEPOSIT FOR WORKS PUBLISHED IN THE UNITED STATES

Although a copyright registration is not required, the Copyright Act establishes a mandatory deposit requirement for works published in the United States (see definition of "publication" on page 184). In general, the owner of copyright, or the owner of the exclusive right of publication in the work, has a legal obligation to deposit in the Copyright Office, within three months of publication in the United States, two copies (or, in the case of sound recordings, two phono records) for the use of the Library of Congress. Failure to make the deposit can result in fines and other penalties, but does not affect copyright protection.

Certain categories of works are *exempt entirely* from the mandatory deposit requirements, and the obligation is reduced for certain other categories. For further information about mandatory deposit, request Circular 7d.

Note

Library of Congress Catalog Card Numbers

A Library of Congress Catalog Card Number is different from a copyright registration number. The Cataloging in Publication (CIP) Division of the Library of Congress is responsible for assigning LC Catalog Card Numbers and is operationally separate from the Copyright Office. A book may be registered in or deposited with the Copyright Office but not necessarily cataloged and added to the Library's collections. For information about obtaining an LC Catalog Card Number, contact the CIP Division, Library of Congress, Washington, D.C. 20540. For information on International Standard Book Numbering (ISBN), write to ISBN , R.R. Bowker/Martindale-Hubbell, 121 Chanlon Road, New Providence, N.J. 07974. Call (908) 665-6770. For information on International Standard Serial Numbering (ISSN), write to Library of Congress, National Serials Data Program, Washington, D.C. 20540.

USE OF MANDATORY DEPOSIT TO SATISFY REGISTRATION REQUIREMENTS

For works published in the United States, the Copyright Act contains a provision under which a single deposit can be made to satisfy both the deposit requirements for the Library of Congress and the registration requirements. To have this dual effect, the copies or phono records must be accompanied by the prescribed application and filing fee.

WHO MAY FILE AN APPLICATION FORM

The following persons are legally entitled to submit an application form:

- *The author.* This is either the person who actually created the work, or, if the work was made for hire, the employer or other person for whom the work was prepared.

- *The copyright claimant.* The copyright claimant is defined in Copyright Office regulations as either the author of the work or a person or organization that has obtained ownership of all the rights under the copyright initially belonging to the author. This category includes a person or organization who has obtained by contract the right to claim legal title to the copyright in an application for copyright registration.

- *The owner of exclusive right(s).* Under the law, any of the exclusive rights that go to make up a copyright and any subdivision of them can be transferred and owned separately, even though the transfer may be limited in time or place of effect. The term "copyright owner" with respect to any one of the exclusive rights contained in a copyright refers to the owner of that particular right. Any owner of an exclusive right may apply for registration of a claim in the work.

- *The duly authorized agent of such author, other copyright claimant, or owner of exclusive right(s).* Any person authorized to act on behalf of the author, other copyright claimant, or owner of exclusive rights may apply for registration.

There is no requirement that applications be prepared or filed by an attorney.

APPLICATION FORMS

For Original Registration

- *Form TX:* For published and unpublished nondramatic literary works.

- *Form SE:* For serials, works issued or intended to be issued in successive parts bearing numerical or chronological designations and intended to be continued indefinitely (periodicals, newspapers, magazines, newsletters, annuals, journals, etc.).

- *Short Form/SE and Form SE/GROUP:* Specialized SE forms for use when certain requirements are met.

- *Form PA:* For published and unpublished works of the performing arts (musical and dramatic works, pantomimes and choreographic works, motion pictures and other audiovisual works).

- *Form VA:* For published and unpublished works of the visual arts (pictorial, graphic, and sculptural works, including architectural works).

- *Form SR:* For published and unpublished sound recordings.

For a Renewal Registration

- *Form RE:* For claims to renewal copyright in works copyrighted under the law in effect through December 31, 1977 (1909 Copyright Act).

For Corrections and Amplifications

- *Form CA:* For supplementary registration to correct or amplify information given in the Copyright Office record of an earlier registration.

For a Group of Contributions to Periodicals

- *Form GR/CP:* An adjunct application to be used for registration of a group of contributions to periodicals in addition to an application Form TX, PA, or VA.

Free application forms are supplied by the Copyright Office.

MAILING INSTRUCTIONS

All applications and materials related to copyright registration should be addressed to the Register of Copyrights, Copyright Office, Library of Congress, Washington, D.C. 20559.

The application, nonreturnable deposit (copies, phono records, or identifying material), and nonrefundable filing fee should be mailed in the same package.

We suggest that you contact your local post office for information about mailing these materials at lower-cost fourth-class postage rates.

Copyright Office Forms Hotline

Requestors may order application forms and circulars at any time by telephoning (202) 707-9100. Orders will be recorded automatically and filled as quickly as possible. Please specify the kind and number of forms you are requesting.

What Happens If the Three Elements Are Not Received Together

Applications and fees received without appropriate copies, phono records, or identifying material will *not* be processed and will ordinarily be returned. Unpublished deposits without applications or fees will ordinarily be returned also. In most cases, published deposits received without applications and fees can be immediately transferred to the collections of the Library of Congress. This practice is in accordance with section 408 of the law, which provides that the published deposit required for the collections of the Library of Congress may be used for registration only if the deposit is "accompanied by the prescribed application and fee."

After the deposit is received and transferred to another department of the Library for its collections or other disposition, it is no longer available to the Copyright Office. If you wish to register the work, you must deposit additional copies or phono records with your application and fee.

FEES

Do not send cash. A fee sent to the Copyright Office should be in the form of a money order, check, or bank draft payable to the Register of Copyrights, and it should be securely attached to the application. A remittance from outside the United States should be payable in U.S. dollars and should be in the form of an international money order or a draft drawn on a U.S. bank. Do not send a check drawn on a foreign bank.

EFFECTIVE DATE OF REGISTRATION

A copyright registration is effective on the date the copyright office receives all of the required elements in acceptable form, regardless of how long it then takes to process the application and mail the certificate of registration. The time the Copyright Office requires to process an application varies, depending on the amount of material the Office is receiving and the personnel available. Keep in mind that it may take a number of days for mailed material to reach the Copyright Office and for the certificate of registration to reach the recipient after being mailed by the Copyright Office.

If you are filing an application for copyright registration in the Copyright Office, you *will not* receive an acknowledgment that your application has been received, but you can expect the following:

- A letter or telephone call from a Copyright Office staff member if further information is needed.

- A certificate of registration to indicate the work has been registered, or if registration cannot be made, a letter explaining why it has been refused.

Please allow 120 days to receive a letter or certificate of registration.

If you want to know when the Copyright Office receives your material, you should send it by registered or certified mail and request a return receipt from the post office. Allow at least three weeks for the return of your receipt.

INVESTIGATING THE COPYRIGHT STATUS OF A WORK

As a digital scribe who wants to do everything legally, it is important to understand the law as it pertains to the use of other people's work. For example, I have used royalty-free graphics in this book, and the programs on the CD have all been approved for distribution by the authors who own the original copyright. When you choose to use something that you pick up off the Internet, you are taking a chance. It may be subject to copyright law that you may not be aware of. To protect yourself and others, please read the following.

Methods of Approaching a Copyright Investigation

There are several ways to investigate whether a work is under copyright protection and, if so, the facts of the copyright. These are the main ones:

1. Examine a copy of the work (or, if the work is a sound recording, examine the disk, tape cartridge, or cassette in which the recorded sound is fixed, or the album cover, sleeve, or container in which the recording is sold) for such elements as a copyright notice, place and date of publication, author and publisher (for additional information, see page 186, "Copyright Notice").

2. Make a search of the Copyright Office catalogs and other records or have the Copyright Office make a search for you.

A Few Words of Caution about Copyright Investigations

Copyright investigations often involve both methods. Even if you follow both approaches, the results may not be completely conclusive. Moreover, as explained in this circular, the changes brought about under the Copyright Act of 1976 and the Berne Convention Implementation Act of 1988 must be considered when investigating the copyright status of a work.

This section offers some practical guidance on what to look for if you are making a copyright investigation. It is important to realize, however, that this contains only general information and there are a number of exceptions to the principles outlined here. In many cases it is important to consult a copyright attorney before reaching any conclusions regarding the copyright status of a work.

HOW TO SEARCH COPYRIGHT OFFICE CATALOGS AND RECORDS

Catalog of Copyright Entries

The Copyright Office publishes the *Catalog of Copyright Entries* (CCE), which is divided into parts according to the classes of works registered. The present categories include Nondramatic Literary Works, Performing Arts, Motion Pictures and Filmstrips, Sound Recordings, Serials and Periodicals, Visual Arts, Maps, and Renewals. Effective with the Fourth Series, Volume 2, 1979 Catalogs, the CCE has been issued in microfiche form *only;* previously, each part of the catalog was issued at regular intervals in book form. Each CCE segment covers all registrations made during a particular period of time. Renewals made for any class during a particular period can be found in Part 8, "Renewals."

Before 1978, the catalog parts reflected the classes that existed at that time. Renewals for a particular class are found in the back section of the catalog for the class of work renewed (for example, renewal registrations for music made in 1976 appear in the last section of the music catalog for 1976).

A number of libraries throughout the United States maintain copies of the *Catalog*, and this may provide a good starting point if you wish to make a search yourself. There are some cases, however, in which a search of the *Catalog* alone will not be sufficient to provide the needed information. For example;

- Because the *Catalog* does not include entries for assignments or other recorded documents, it cannot be used for searches involving the ownership of rights.

- There is usually a time lag of a year or more before the part of the *Catalog* covering a particular registration is published.

- The *Catalog* entry contains the essential facts concerning a registration, but it is not a verbatim transcript of the registration record.

Individual Searches of Copyright Records

The Copyright Office is located in the Library of Congress James Madison Memorial Building, 101 Independence Ave., S.E., Washington, D.C.

Most records of the Copyright Office are open to public inspection and searching from 8:30 A.M. to 5 P.M. Monday through Friday (except legal holidays). The various records freely available to the public include an extensive card catalog, an automated catalog containing records from 1978 forward, record books, and microfilm records of assignments and related documents. Other records, including correspondence files and deposit copies, are not open to the public for searching. However, they may be inspected on request and payment of a $20 per hour search fee.

If you wish to do your own searching in the Copyright Office files open to the public, you will be given assistance in locating the records you need and in learning searching procedures. If the Copyright Office staff actually makes the search for you, a search fee must be charged. The search will not be done while you wait.

SEARCHING BY THE COPYRIGHT OFFICE

In General

On request, the Copyright Office staff will search its records at the statutory rate of $20 for each hour or fraction of an hour consumed. Based on the information you furnish, we will provide an estimate of the total search fee. If you decide to have the Office staff conduct the search, you should send the estimated amount with your request. The Office will then proceed with the search and send you a typewritten report or, if you prefer, an oral report by telephone. If you request an oral report, please provide a telephone number where you can be reached during normal business hours (8:30 A.M.–5 P.M. Eastern time).

Search reports can be certified on request, for an extra fee of $20. Certified searches are most frequently requested to meet the evidentiary requirements of litigation.

Your request, and any other correspondence, should be addressed to

Reference and Bibliography Section, LM-451
Copyright Office
Library of Congress
Washington, D.C. 20559
(202) 707-6850

What the Fee Does Not Cover

Note that the search fee does *not* include the cost of additional certificates, photocopies of deposits, or copies of other Office records. For information concerning these services, request Circular 6.

Information Needed

The more detailed information you can furnish with your request, the less time consuming and expensive the search will be. Please provide as much of the following information as possible:

- The title of the work, with any possible variants.

- The names of the authors, including possible pseudonyms.

- The name of the probable copyright owner, which may be the publisher or producer.

- The approximate year when the work was published or registered.

- The type of work involved (book, play, musical composition, sound recording, photograph, etc.).

- For a work originally published as a part of a periodical or collection, the title of that publication and any other information, such as the volume or issue number, to help identify it.

- Motion pictures are often based on other works such as books or serialized contributions to periodicals or other composite works. If you desire a search for an underlying work or for music from a motion picture, you must specifically request such a search. You must also identify the underlying works and music and furnish the specific titles, authors, and approximate dates of these works.

- The registration number or any other copyright data.

Searches Involving Assignments and Other Documents Affecting Copyright Ownership

The Copyright Office staff will also, for the standard hourly search fee, search its indexes covering the records of assignments and other recorded documents concerning ownership of copyrights. The reports of searches in these cases will state the facts shown in the Office's indexes of the recorded documents but will offer no interpretation of the content of the documents or their legal effect.

LIMITATIONS ON SEARCHES

In determining whether or not to have a search made, you should keep the following points in mind:

- *No special lists.* The Copyright Office does not maintain any listings of works by subject or any lists of works that are in the public domain.

- *Contributions.* Individual works, such as stories, poems, articles, or musical compositions that were published as contributions to a copyrighted periodical or collection, are usually not listed separately by title in our records.

- *No comparisons.* The Copyright Office does not search or compare copies of works to determine questions of possible infringement or to determine how much two or more versions of a work have in common.

- *Titles and names not copyrightable.* Copyright does not protect names and titles, and our records list many different works identified by the same or similar titles. Some brand names, trade names, slogans, and phrases may be entitled to protection under the general rules of law relating to unfair competition or to registration under the provisions of the trademark laws. Questions about the trademark laws should be addressed to the Commissioner of Patents and Trademarks, Washington, D.C. 20231. Possible protection of names and titles under common law principles of unfair competition is a question of state law.

- *No legal advice.* The Copyright Office cannot express any opinion as to the legal significance or effect of the facts included in a search report.

Some Words of Caution

Searches Are Not Always Conclusive

Searches of the Copyright Office catalogs and records are useful in helping to determine the copyright status of a work, but they cannot be regarded as conclusive in all cases. The complete absence of any information about a work in the office records does not mean that the work is unprotected. The following are examples of cases in which information about a particular work may be incomplete or lacking entirely in the Copyright Office:

- Before 1978, unpublished works were entitled to protection at common law without the need of registration.

- Works published with notice prior to 1978 may be registered at any time within the first 28 year term; to obtain renewal protection, however, the claimant must register and renew such work by the end of the 28th year.

- For works that came under copyright protection after 1978, registration may be made at any time during the term of protection. It is not generally required as a condition of copyright protection (there are, however, certain definite advantages to registration—please call or write for Circular 1, "Copyright Basics").

- Searches are ordinarily limited to registrations that have already been cataloged, so a search report may not cover recent registrations for which catalog records are not yet available.

- The information in the search request may not have been complete or specific enough to identify the work.

- The work may have been registered under a different title or as part of a larger work.

Protection in Foreign Countries

Even if you conclude that a work is in the public domain in the United States, this does not necessarily mean that you are free to use it in other countries. Every nation has its own laws governing the length and scope of copyright protection, and these are applicable to uses of the work within that nation's borders. Therefore, the expiration or loss of copyright protection in the United States may still leave the work fully protected against unauthorized use in other countries.

OTHER CIRCULARS

For further information, request Circulars 15, "Renewal of Copyright"; 15a, "Duration of Copyright"; 15t, "Extension of Copyright Terms"; and 6, "Obtaining Copies of Copyright Office Records and Deposits," from

Publications Section, LM-455
Copyright Office
Library of Congress
Washington, D.C. 20559

Or, you may call (202) 707-9100 at any time, day or night, to leave a request for forms or circulars as a recorded message on the Forms

Hotline. Requests made on the Hotline number are filled and mailed promptly.

THE IMPACT OF THE COPYRIGHT ACT ON COPYRIGHT INVESTIGATIONS

On October 19, 1976, the President signed into law a complete revision of the copyright law of the United States (Title 17 of the United States Code). Most provisions of this statute came into force on January 1, 1978, superseding the previous Copyright Act of 1909 and made significant changes in the copyright law. Other significant changes resulted from the Berne Convention Implementation Act of 1988, which took effect March 1, 1989. If you need more information about the provisions of either law, write or call the Copyright Office. For information about the Berne Law, request Circular 93. Printed information about the 1976 law is available only through the Superintendent of Documents, U.S. Government Printing Office, Washington, D.C. 20402-9325, for $3.75, request stock number 030-002-00168-3. You may order by telephone from the order desk by calling (202) 783-3238. To order via fax machine please call (202) 275-0019.

PUBLIC DOMAIN COPYRIGHT LAW

If you are a computer programmer, you should be aware of the law as it relates to creative property in the public domain. Much work that the digital scribe does is done as part of a team, and certain copyright restrictions apply to each part of an intellectual work. To be certain that you are not losing out on your individual effort, you must be aware of your rights.

There is concern about the copyright status of the programs provided by innovative and diligent members of the CP/M Users

Group to the Group with the understanding, explicitly stated or otherwise, that the programs were contributed to the public domain.

The term *public domain* means, from a legal point of view, a program or other work that does not have copyright protection. The indiscriminate use of the word confuses the copyright issues. A work disclosed to a specific group of people for a limited purpose is not necessarily "public domain" software.

A new federal copyright law went into effect on January 1, 1978, that complicates the following discussion for software written or contributed prior to that date. I will start with a discussion of the law as it applies now and to programs written after January 1, 1978. The new law is Title 17, U.S. Code. Any written material (including computer programs) fixed in a tangible form (written somewhere; i.e. a printout) is considered copyrighted without any additional action on the part of the author. Thus, it is not necessary that a copy of the program be deposited with the Copyright Office in Washington for the program to be protected as copyrighted.

A contribution of a program to the members of the public (CP/M Users Group) for their noncommercial use constitutes a license for that purpose and that purpose only. It does not destroy the programmer's rights in the copyright to the program. *However*, the government does not enforce the programmer's rights. A copyright is a property right, just like the right you have in the house you own. If someone trespasses on your property, the cops may come and put the fellow in jail, but they will not stop him from doing it again nor will they procure compensation for any damage the intruder may have done to your property. You have to do that yourself by going to court. So it is with copyrights. To prevent anyone from selling your program you must ask a court (federal) to stop him or her by an injunction and to give you damages for the injury done to you by selling the program.

Going to court requires that the program be registered with the Copyright Office in Washington, D.C. The fee is $10.

The government will prosecute *criminal* copyright infringements, such as where someone simply copies (as in copying an audio- or videotape) for profit, and when the government can show criminal intent (i.e., knowing violation of the law or fraud in the acts of the copier). This is not done very frequently except in the case of wholesale audio- and videotaping pirates.

The copyright law has a concept known as a *derivative work*. A derivative work is one based on a work already entitled to and protected by copyright. The original author of a work has the sole rights to "derivative" works derived from the work. The author can authorize (license) others to prepare derivative works from the work, as in the case of a programmer of a Users Group program who says "If anyone fixes this for a DCHayes MM-100, let me know."

I suspect that many of the programs contributed to the Group and their modifications fall within this category of license; that is, users have been allowed to prepare derivative works. However, the original author does not lose the original copyright! And all the derivative works made using the original are dependent on the continuation of the license except as to the parts added by the author of the derivative works. A simple explanation might help: A program provides for generating data showing ratios for sales to inventory turnovers (I know the example is silly), and the output is simply a bunch of numbers. The second programmer decides to enhance the program by turning the numbers into some kind of chart or graph. The program that generated the numbers is protected as to the original author. The output formatting *only* is protected as a licensed derivative work to the second programmer.

The restriction placed on the programs in recent years limiting use to individuals on their personal machines and denying use of a program for commercial purposes is probably a valid restriction of the license granted in the CP/M Users Group Library. It constitutes fair warning to all who would lift the program and attempt to convert it to commercial purposes that such use is not licensed. It is not clear that such restriction applies automatically to earlier donations to the

Group, unless something is explicit in the documentation that accompanies the work itself when it is distributed.

In many instances, the programs donated prior to 1978 were not copyrighted (that is, contained no copyright notice and were not registered with the Copyright Office). The status of these programs is not clear, although a case can be made that they were initially distributed only to paid-up members of the CP/M Users Group. My documentation from the Users Group, which is undated but postmarked June 13, 1978, states "The material [donations of programs] is received by the Group with the understanding that the contributor is authorized to make it available to hobbyists for their individual non-commercial use . . . members receiving material are free and encouraged to share it with other hobbyists for their individual non-commercial use." The membership information included a request for any member's knowledge of persons violating the non-commercial restriction on the programs distributed. A membership fee of $4 was charged for 1978 as a prerequisite to receiving material.

This limitation on the prospective use of a program obtained from the Group indicates that the distribution was limited to noncommercial users. Pre-1/1/78 software that was not automatically copyrighted and did not contain a copyright notice could be protected only under state laws in existence at that time. The state laws varied considerably but generally the rule is that, if the work was not distributed willy-nilly to the public without restriction, the state law protected the work even if the federal law niceties were not complied with. The problem is whether the restrictions of the CP/Users Group distribution were sufficient limitations on the "publication" of the program. Publication destroys a state law copyright, making the work free to all. *Publication* here means making it available to the public at large, even though restrictions were placed on the initial disclosure of the program. That is something only the court or jury actually hearing the case can decide and may well turn on facts not available to me. For example, was any real effort made to prevent computer stores from distributing the programs to their customers who were not members of the Group? Were the noncommercial use limitations explained to those customers? To the computer stores?

One other concern has been expressed by some program authors, those authors who did not want to have their programs modified but whose programs nonetheless have been modified. Referring to the preceding discussion about the limitations on use of contributed programs, if the limitation did not authorize anything but "use" of the program, then the modifications constituted "derivative" works that were not authorized.

This, unfortunately, would be a very tricky thing to prove, and it would have to be proven—how did the parties understand the authorization to use the programs; i.e., was modification prevented but noncommercial use allowed? If there was an implied license to modify (for example, because the program was included with other programs in which modifications were explicitly authorized), it might be very difficult to prove infringement under either the state or federal law, depending on which was applicable.

It should be clear from the preceding, however, that modifications of programs entitled to copyright protection are infringements if they are not authorized by the owner of the copyright in the original program. The problem is in the proof of lack of authorization.

Since January 1, 1978, all programs are protected by federal copyright laws without regard to copyright notice or registration with the Copyright Office and the state laws no longer apply. The federal law "preempted" the state laws on that date. But the federal rules apply across the board *only* to works first "fixed" or "written" after that date. However, improvements or modifications in one's own program can qualify for federal copyright protection under the new law and perhaps those interested or affected by the problem should make formal registration of their works as well as including the copyright notice somewhere in the program.

It is obvious that most volunteer programmers lack the finances and time, and inclination for that matter, to pursue a legal remedy in the courts. At the same time, they do not want the software they authored to be used by others for commercial gain without some control over its use.

I suggest that microcomputer software authors nationwide form an organization similar to that of ASCAP or BMI, although on a smaller scale, to monitor improper uses of software donated to the hobbyist for personal use. Only through concentrating the efforts and power of all authors can real protection be obtained. Otherwise, the unscrupulous vendor is going to take a chance that the individual programmer will not or cannot defend his or her copyright.

Such a group might be formed with the support of an active computer group like the NJ Amateur Computer Group or the Homebrew Computer Club in California. Or it could be established independently, if there were sufficient interest and an organizer could be found to do the necessary paperwork, collect the dues needed to provide a war chest, and hire the attorneys and other persons necessary. It wouldn't have to be a full-time job for anyone but it would have to be more than volunteer activity.

I suggest, however, that an early attack, which might include programmers for profit whose programs are slightly modified by fly-by-night vendors without compensation, will establish the principles necessary to deter future invasions of your copyrights.

YOU NEED AN ISSN IF YOU CREATE A MAGAZINE OR "SERIAL"

The ISSN is an internationally recognized identification number for serials. It can be thought of as the "social security number" of the serials world. The ISSN is the serial counterpart of the ISBN (International Standard Book Number). However, the National Serials Data Program (NSDP) does not assign ISBN numbers. ISBNs are assigned by the R. R. Bowker Co. (121 Chanlon Road, New Providence, NJ 07874).

NSDP is the U.S. center of the International Serials Data System (ISDS), the international body that coordinates assignment and use of the ISSN worldwide. NSDP can assign ISSN only to serials published in the United States. ISSN for serials published outside the United States are assigned by ISDS national centers located in the country of publication or by the ISDS International Center located in Paris. Approximately 50 national centers are in the ISDS network. For a referral to the appropriate center, please contact the ISDS International Center (20, rue Bachaumont, 75002 Paris, France).

ISSN can be assigned to serials published in any medium. Different ISSNs are usually required for each physical medium: print, electronic, sound recording, and so on. To be considered a serial all issues (except for volumes in an unnumbered monographic series) must carry unique numerical or chronological designations (e.g., Vol., No., or date) by which individual issues can be identified and distinguished from each other.

The requirement that each serial issues carry a unique designation applies to electronic publications (e.g., CD-ROMs, electronic journals) as well. If an electronic publication is a dynamic database, a bulletin board, or a listserv, it is probably not eligible for an ISSN, but in any case of doubt please contact NSDP.

One major use of the ISSN in the United States is its use by the U.S. Postal Service as an identification number for certain publications mailed at second-class rates. However, it is not necessary to have an ISSN before applying for a second-class mailing permit; the ISSN can be assigned or confirmed as part of the application process. Also, merely printing the ISSN does not automatically confer any special mailing status on a publication. For specific information about obtaining second-class permits, consult your local postmaster.

A growing use of the ISSN is in bar codes. Even though the ISSN is not used in the UPC code (the code seen primarily on trade and mass market titles), it is used in the EAN and SISAC bar codes. In these two codes, the ISSN constitutes the portion of the code that identifies the title of the serial. Other data in various bar codes can represent the number or date of the issue or the price. Bar coding of serials is further speeding the efficiencies in serial processing which can be realized through the use of the ISSN. For information about ISSN in the SISAC bar code, contact the Serials Industry Systems Advisory Committee (160 Fifth Avenue, New York, NY 10010), and for information about ISSN in the EAN code, contact the Uniform Code Council (8163 Old Yankee Road, Dayton, OH 45458).

ISSN can be assigned to serials either before the first issue is published or after publication has begun. ISSN requestors should allow about one month for NSDP to assign the ISSN and send it to them by return mail. There is no charge for an ISSN assignment.

In 1992 an American ISSN friends group, called *AmIS* (as in the French pronunciation) was established to help defray the cost of dues assessed the United States for participation in the International Serials Data System. This dues obligation, one of the several means by which the ISDS International Center is financed, amounted to $100,000 in 1991, of which the Library of Congress could pay only $55,000. AmIS provides the opportunity for those who share in the benefits of the ISSN to help ensure its financial viability. Membership benefits include an annual report containing news from NSDP and ISSN statistics from the previous year, as well as receipt of other ISSN and ISDS information. Subscriptions to AmIS can be arranged through periodical subscription agents such as Faxon or EBSCO or a library's regular agent. Brochures listing categories of membership in AmIS are available from NSDP:

National Serials Data Program
Library of Congress
Washington, DC 20540-4160

SERIALS DEFINED

Serials are print or nonprint publications issued in parts, usually bearing issue numbers or dates. A serial is expected to continue indefinitely. Serials include magazines, newspapers, annuals (such as reports, yearbooks, and directories), journals, memoirs, proceedings, transactions of societies, and monographic series.

INTERNATIONAL STANDARD SERIAL NUMBERING

The various and constant changes to which serials are subject, combined with the large growth in the world's publishing output, prompted the development of a standard (ISO 3297-1975; ANSI Z39.9-1979) for the identification of serials: the International Standard Serial Number (ISSN).

A single ISSN uniquely identifies a title regardless of the language or country in which published, without the burden of a complex bibliographic description. The ISSN itself has no significance other than the unique identification of a serial.

An ISSN is eight digits long, and is always displayed this way: ISSN 1234-5679. The first seven digits serve as the title number and the eighth is a check digit that provides an efficient means for discovering transcription errors. The system used for calculating the check digit sometimes requires a check number of 10, in which case, to prevent a nine digit ISSN, the roman numeral X is substituted.

For each serial with an ISSN there is a corresponding "key title," a commonly acceptable form of the title established at the time of ISSN assignment. The title provides a benchmark to regulate the assignment of ISSN: If the title of a serial changes, a new ISSN must be assigned.

Administration of ISSN

The coordination of the ISSN is international, with registration initiated at the national level, where serials are published. The National Serials Data Program (NSDP) within the Library of Congress is the U.S. Center of the International Serials Data System (ISDS), which coordinates the two-level network with an International Center in Paris. NSDP is responsible for registering and numbering serials published in the United States and for promoting use of and fulfilling requests for ISSN.

Advantages of Use

The ISSN should be as basic a part of a serial as the title. The advantages of using it are abundant, and the more the number is used, the more benefits will accrue.

1. ISSN provides a useful and economical method of communication between publishers and suppliers, making trade distribution systems faster and more efficient.

2. The ISSN results in accurate citing of serials by scholars, researchers, abstracters, and librarians.

3. As a standard numeric identification code, the ISSN is eminently suitable for computer use in fulfilling the need for file update and linkage, retrieval, and transmittal of data.

4. ISSN is used in libraries for identifying titles, ordering and checking in, and claiming serials.

5. ISSN simplifies interlibrary loan systems and union catalog reporting and listing.

6. The U.S. Postal Service uses the ISSN to regulate certain publications mailed at second-class and controlled circulation rates.

7. The ISSN is an integral component of the journal article citation used to monitor payments to the Copyright Clearance Center, Inc.

8. All ISSN registrations are maintained in an international data base and are made available in the *ISDS Register*, a microfiche publication that is scheduled to cease in the near future or in *ISSN Compact*, a newly available CD-ROM.

How to Obtain an ISSN

The assignment of the ISSN is free, and no charge is associated with its use. Publishers are encouraged to allow sufficient time (approximately one month) for the assignment of the ISSN. When publication deadlines are imminent, requests for ISSN may be sent by fax.

Telephone requests can be accepted *only* for prepublication assignments; that is, for ISSN requests for serials that have published *no* issues to date.

When requesting an ISSN for an already published serial, send NSDP a sample issue or copy of the cover, title page, and masthead as appropriate. For prepublication requests, a mock-up or artist's conception of the same identifying parts of the publication should be sent, if possible. In these "vol. 1, no. 1" cases, a follow-up sample issue or surrogate of the actual serial must be sent directly to NSDP after publication has begun.

How to Use the ISSN

To fulfill its purpose, the ISSN should be displayed prominently on every issue, preferably in the top right corner of the cover. It is acceptable, however, for the number to appear elsewhere on the publication (usually in the masthead area). Various user groups, particularly the U.S. Postal Service, have specific printing regulations that must be adhered to.

If the serial has an International Standard Book Number (ISBN) for the individual volumes within a series, in addition to the ISSN for the series as a whole, the two numbers should appear together, each with its own prefix. The ISSN should be printed right after the title of the series, both in books and in advertising pieces.

It is appropriate for both ISBN and ISSN to be assigned to certain other types of publications, most notably annuals and other directories or reference publications. The ISBN identifies the particular year or edition, the ISSN identifies the ongoing serial.

ISSN should appear on publisher's advertisements (both direct mail and space ads) and catalogs, on the serials themselves, and in all other places where details of books and serials normally appear.

Changes Affecting an ISSN

Serials often undergo changes, many of which result in a change of title. When this occurs a new ISSN must be assigned. The earlier ISSN is not discarded, however, because it is a permanent attribute of the serial when it was issued under the earlier title. To avoid printing an incorrect ISSN, publishers must notify NSDP in advance of a pending title change, especially one affecting the cover title (which is often the source for the key title). The notification will be treated as a request for a new ISSN and the procedure is the same as that for the original ISSN request. Other changes to a serial such as those of imprint and frequency do not affect the ISSN assignment.

Display and careful use of the ISSN will help in the worldwide effort to make the number achieve its intended role as a valuable means of identifying serials.

The following is a form for you to use to request a serial number for your publication. It is a necessity, especially if you are getting into professional publishing of your work. The modern digital scribe must be well aware of the law, and this is a good way to protect yourself from any unwanted lawsuits—from the government or from individuals.

Library of Congress
National Serials Data Program
Washington, D.C. 20540-4160

For NSDP Use Only
Date received _____
ISSN:

_____ Req. postpub. issue _____ Call publisher

Instructions: There is no charge for an ISSN assignment. However, a sample issue or photocopy of the cover, title page and masthead is required either at the time of application or after publication of the first issue of a new serial. Furthermore, application for a new ISSN must be made if the title of the serial changes.

1. Complete this form.

2. Attach a sample issue or photocopy. (If available, a mock-up of the requested pages is suggested for prepublication titles.)

3. Return to NSDP at the above address.

If you have any questions, please contact NSDP for assistance.

1. _____ This is a new serial (no issues of this publication have appeared in print under this title). The first issue will appear _____ (expected date of publication) and will carry the following number and/or date designation, e.g., Vol. 1, no. 1, or issue no. 1, or year, etc. _____ .

_____ This is an existing serial which has been published under this title since _____ (date); the first issue under this title had the following number and/or date designation: _____ .

2. TITLE (from the title pages or the cover if there is no title page)

_____

_____

3. VARIANT FORMS OF THE TITLE on the cover, masthead, or other parts of current issues.

_____

_____

4. EARLIER TITLES which this serial continues _____

_____

5. PUBLISHING COMPANY

_____

6. CITY AND STATE OF PUBLISHING COMPANY

_____

7. FORMER PUBLISHING COMPANY (if taking over publication from another publishing

company _____

8. FREQUENCY _____

9. SINGLE ISSUE PRICE _____

10. SUBSCRIPTION ADDRESS _____

_____

11. SUBSCRIPTION PRICE _____

12. ADDITIONAL INFORMATION, COMMENTS, QUESTIONS _____

_____

_____

13. CONTACT PERSON _____

    PHONE _____ FAX _____ DATE _____

14. I WOULD LIKE

    _____ additional application forms

    _____ information on Copyright

    _____ information on ISSN use by U.S. Postal Service

MAIL NOTIFICATION TO:

_____

_____

HAVE YOU:

- Completed all necessary spaces?

- Enclosed a sample issue or mock-up?

- Included the expected date of publication for a new serial?

- Included a daytime telephone number?

INCOMPLETE APPLICATION FORMS OR FORMS WITHOUT REQUIRED SAMPLE ISSUES OR SURROGATES WILL BE RETURNED.

11

Your Rights as a Freelance Author in Cyberspace

This chapter will cover the following:

- The information superhighway as a public access
- What is on-line commerce?
- Various on-line commerce systems
- Which are the best commerce systems?
- Freelancers' rights in cyberspace

Certain issues pertain to writing for electronic media that do not pertain to the print form. The National Writers Union published a position paper that outlines some issues that you should be aware of as a digital scribe. This is particularly important if you plan to write and then attempt to collect money from your clients.

The following text of that position paper is reprinted with permission of the National Writers Union:

Over the past few years, the growth of the Internet has brought with it a remarkable outpouring of self-publishing. The Net now contains a wealth of online newsletters, literary magazines, essays, information services, and other textual material produced by individual writers or informal publishing networks.

Until now, this material has, of necessity, been distributed gratis, since there was no way to collect money online. While many Net publishers will continue to make their material available at no cost, new techniques of digital commerce are emerging that make it possible for those who live off their writing to receive payment—even tiny amounts per user—directly from their online readers. This paper will provide an overview of these new forms of online commerce and analyze how they may be used by writers.

The National Writers Union (NWU) believes that income-producing self-publishing on the Net could be a great boon not only for freelance writers, but for readers as well. The ability to earn a living from online distribution of one's work will encourage a wider range of writers to produce a wider range of materials for a wider range of audiences. This objective is especially important at a time when commercial print publishing continues to grow more concentrated, and corporate publishers are seeking to establish a dominant presence in electronic publishing as well. (In talking about self-publishing, we also mean to refer to electronic publishing activities by small presses, author co-ops, non-profit organizations, etc.)

The NWU's support of commercial self-publishing on the Internet does not mean that we go along with those who seek to commercialize the Net entirely. We continue to believe that the so-called information superhighway should be a public resource and that access to it should be universal. We also oppose commercial abuse of electronic mail and newsgroup discussions. Yet we cannot deny the fact that certain portions of the Internet, particularly the World Wide Web, have become extensively commercialized and will remain that way.

By encouraging online commercial self-publishing, we hope to prevent the complete corporate domination of the Web. The ability of individual writers to make their work available on the commercial part of the Net will create a much-needed diversity of voices. It could also significantly reduce the financial frustration of being a freelance writer.

WHAT IS ONLINE COMMERCE?

In a sense there is nothing new about online electronic transactions. Banks have been transferring huge sums of money this way for years, and many corporations use Electronic Document Interchange to arrange deals with one another—all of which is done through secure private networks. Commercial online services such as CompuServe have for a long time allowed subscribers to shop electronically.

What is new is the emerging ability of consumers to order goods and services from a large number of Internet vendors and pay for them online without openly transmitting a credit card number. Even more significant is the possibility of tiny online transactions that have all the convenience and anonymity of using cash. The more bullish proponents of online commerce believe that Net transactions, along with other forms of electronic money such as smart cards, will eventually displace coins, paper currency, and checks entirely.

The online transaction systems being developed today fall into several categories:

Secure Credit Card Transactions

Given that computer hackers can capture just about any information typed into a computer linked to a network, most people are reluctant to transmit their credit card number to an online vendor. To address this problem, companies such as First Virtual Holdings have begun to set themselves up as online middlemen. Consumers open accounts with these companies by communicating with them offline and giving a credit card number. Online purchases are made using the account number, but the costs are charged to the credit card.

Another approach is being taken by the credit card companies themselves. MasterCard, for instance, has teamed up with Netscape Communications to develop a system that would automatically encrypt credit card numbers transmitted by Net shoppers. This will get around the requirement in systems such as First Virtual's for the buyer to open a special account before making purchases.

Electronic Debit Systems

These are the online equivalents of checks and debit cards. Consumers register with a service such as NetCheque and authorize it to subtract sums from their conventional checking account. Users may then write electronic checks to pay for online purchases. When the vendor deposits the electronic check in its NetCheque account, the amount (minus a service fee) is subtracted from the customer's checking account and deposited in the vendor's account.

Digital Cash

As the term suggests, digital cash is intended to simulate transactions that in the real world are carried out with coins and paper currency. That means convenience and anonymity.

While everyone is in favor of convenience, there is a debate over the merits of anonymity. While companies such as CyberCash Inc. have developed digital cash systems that leave an open electronic trail, other firms such as DigiCash Inc. make it possible for purchasers to shield their identity from vendors.

DigiCash's approach involves the creation of electronic money-tokens that are purchased by a charge to one's checking account or through some other secure transaction. The tokens are given a unique encrypted code to thwart forgery. The tokens can be re-spent or converted back into real currency through a deposit to one's checking account.

NetBank's NetCash is the equivalent of currency notes in various denominations. You purchase NetCash by mailing or faxing a check to NetBank, which sends you by e-mail a series of encrypted serial numbers corresponding to NetCash notes. You can then spend this money by sending an e-mail message to a vendor giving the serial number and denomination of the NetCash notes. The vendor then deposits the amount in its NetBank account by e-mailing the serial numbers, which are then retired.

Digital cash, along with electronic debit systems, would make online transactions available to those without credit cards, either by choice or because they cannot qualify.

HOW IT WOULD WORK FOR WRITERS

Writers could use one or more of these systems to sell their work online. Before doing so they must figure out how their work is going to be publicized to potential customers. Technically sophisticated writers will set up their own World Wide Web sites and spread around their URLs (Web addresses).

The transactions—using one of the methods described above—would take place via e-mail or special Web software. Other writers may wish to take advantage of special online sites set up by the transaction services, which would then also be acting as a kind of online newsstand, bookstore or distributor. See below for an example of such an arrangement.

AN EXAMPLE OF AN ONLINE TRANSACTION SYSTEM AT WORK

Many of the online commerce systems are still at the developmental stage. Among those that are up and running is that of First Virtual Holdings. First Virtual has created a Web site called the Infohaus, on which electronic publishers (including self-publishers) can list materials available for purchase. Sellers pay $10 to establish an account and a modest amount to rent space on the Infohaus server. They also pay a small fee on every transaction and a fee to convert their First Virtual revenues into real money.

Customers with their own First Virtual accounts browse through a catalog of material, and when they see something they want to buy, they transmit an order to the company. The order is verified by e-mail and then the price is charged to the customer's account. Periodically, the customer's account balance is charged to his or her credit card.

Recently there were about 100 sellers offering wares on the Infohaus server. The products included software for learning Japanese ($20), a book about doing business on the Internet ($9.95), short stories ($3.00 each), a brochure on treating the common cold ($2.29), a 1600-word essay on art ($1.85), Christian fundamentalist sermons ($1.50), and recipes for Jewish food ($1.29). About two dozen sellers of erotic material were grouped separately in the "Infohaus of Ill Repute."

[Note: The preceding discussion should not be construed as an NWU endorsement of First Virtual Holdings or any of its services. The same goes for references to other companies and services.]

WHAT DO WRITERS NEED FROM AN ONLINE COMMERCE SYSTEM?

The NWU believes it is too early to embrace a particular method of online commerce, but we do think there are certain features that are necessary for any of these systems to be of use to freelance writers. Now is the time for writers and their organizations to speak up—before certain practices become entrenched.

1. *Low fees.* Until online commerce becomes well developed, the potential income stream for most writers will be modest. This means that selling online will not be feasible unless the costs of doing so are kept low. The NWU urges operators of online transaction systems to keep down initiation fees, rental charges for space on servers, and transaction fees.

2. *The ability to process tiny transactions.* Online sale of information and other textual material will not succeed unless purchase prices are kept very low. Transaction systems should be developed that can accommodate tiny payments, even as low as a few cents for small quantities of material. Keeping prices low will discourage unauthorized reproduction and make it easy for buyers to respect the copyright of the sellers.

3. *Minimal "paperwork."* Writers generally want to spend their time writing, not keeping books. The best online transaction systems for writers will be those that are highly automated and involve a minimum of electronic paperwork.

4. *Copyright notice.* Online transaction systems that include servers such as the Infohaus should display prominent notices that the works available for purchase are protected by copyright law and that the copyrights belong to the sellers. They should also include information on conditions regarding retransmission or reuse of the material by a publisher.

5. *Multiple authors.* Transaction systems should be flexible enough to handle payment of fees for works with multiple authors (even when they may be entitled to different amounts) and for situations in which one work is incorporated into another (as in the case of hypertexts).

6. *Non-exclusivity.* Writers should not be forced to give an online transaction system an exclusive right to distribute their work. The business is simply too new and too uncertain for a writer to be tied to one service. Contracts with the services should also have easy termination provisions.

7. *Absence of censorship or other editorial restrictions.* The transaction systems being discussed here are in effect common carriers rather than publishers, so their owners should play no role in determining the content of what is being sold online. In fact, it will be quite important to distinguish distributors of online materials such as First Virtual from online publishers. The distributors and their transaction systems are merely conduits for materials that are in effect being self-published.

8. *Anonymous transactions.* While all online transactions need not be totally anonymous, the NWU supports the creation of systems that would allow readers the ability to purchase electronic materials in a way that is not traceable. Just as purchasers of certain materials from bookstores and newsstands may choose to use cash and thus leave no record of their transaction, so too should that option be available for online commerce. In another privacy-related issue, it is the NWU's position that owners of online transaction systems should not sell names and addresses of their customers without permission.

ONLINE COMMERCE AND ONLINE PUBLISHERS

There will still be a place for publishers in the online world. While some readers will enjoy the variety and varying quality of self-published material, others will seek out electronic publishing operations that exercise traditional editorial functions and can thereby provide a more predictable and professional product. Commercial online magazines will operate much like their print counterparts, except that no ink will be put on paper, and the techniques of promotion and circulation will be quite different. In fact, the ease with which self-published magazines can be created on the Net means that commercial magazines will have to distinguish themselves primarily by the quality of their editorial work.

In the case of book-length works, online commerce will pose a challenge to the embryonic online book publishing industry that has emerged during the past few years. As the NWU noted in our position paper last year on contract terms between authors and online book publishers, there are two main categories of businesses in this area. First, there are the operations that accept any text submitted on disk, code it, and then insert it in the company's electronic catalog without doing any significant editorial work. Second, there are online book publishers that perform traditional editorial functions and may also add features such as hypertext links to other materials on the Net.

The second category will continue to have a role in online publishing; in fact, many established print publishers will probably migrate into that activity. The first group, however, will have less of a raison d'etre. Why should writers give up half or more of the purchase price of their work to an online operation of that sort when they can sell it through direct online commerce and keep close to 100 percent of the price? In the online world, where production and distribution are vastly simplified, book publishers, like their magazine counterparts, will live or die by their editorial skills.

COLLECTING ROYALTIES FROM COMMERCIAL ONLINE DATABASES

Facilitating electronic self-publishing is not the only way online commerce might assist writers. It could also be a means for writers to collect the royalties that should be paid to them when articles originally published in print publications are later placed on commercial online databases.

Understanding this possibility requires a bit of background: For the past 20 years or so, online database services such as Nexis and Dialog have been selling high-priced electronic information mainly to corporate libraries and other institutional users. In recent years these services have added a great deal of material consisting of the full texts of articles originally published in print periodicals and often written by freelance writers. Some of this material is provided directly by the print publishers; in other cases the print publishers license their text to a database producer such as Information Access Co. that combines content from many different publications into a single electronic database. In either case, the royalties are paid to the print publishers, not to the freelance writers whose work is being redistributed online.

In December 1993 a group of freelance writers including NWU president Jonathan Tasini filed suit in federal court against the New York Times, Nexis, and other publishers and database companies, charging them with copyright infringement for the unauthorized electronic use of their work. The plaintiffs argued that they, as holders of the copyright to their writings, alone had the right to license the electronic reuse of their work and should be the ones to receive the royalties.

The NWU also has launched a project called Operation Magazine Index, which is organizing freelancers to protest the unauthorized use of their work by Information Access Co., the leading compiler of full-text databases.

These disputes remain unresolved, in part because publishers and database services argue that it would not be practical to set up a payment mechanism for the large number of writers involved. Online transaction systems such as those described above could be a solution to the technical aspects of this problem.

Here is how it might work: Freelance writers would arrange to set up an account with one of the online transaction services. Before print publishers transmit the content of their magazines to the database producer or directly to services such as Nexis, each freelance-written article would be coded with the name and online account of the writer. Nexis and the other online services would program their computers to keep track of the royalties earned from access to individual articles, rather than by publication, which is what they say they do now. Those royalties would automatically be transferred to

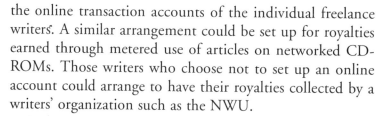

the online transaction accounts of the individual freelance writers. A similar arrangement could be set up for royalties earned through metered use of articles on networked CD-ROMs. Those writers who choose not to set up an online account could arrange to have their royalties collected by a writers' organization such as the NWU.

Such a system of online transactions could also be used by print publishers to make payments to their freelance writers.

CONCLUSION

Online commerce, while still at its earliest stages of development, presents exciting possibilities for freelance writers. The NWU believes that online transaction systems, if structured properly, could help create a vast new world of financially viable self-publishing. It could also be used as an efficient means for writers to receive the income that is rightfully theirs from the electronic uses of their work by corporate-owned online services.

The prospect of online self-publishing, in particular, represents a dramatic development for writers. The absence of significant start-up costs and printing expenses, along with the possibility of easy revenue collection, means that independent publishing would be feasible for a much larger number of writers. For the first time since the days of Ben Franklin, writers—as opposed to publishers, printers, and distributors—would receive the bulk of the money that readers pay for their work, and they would get that money promptly. For a group of people used to being paid too little too late, online commerce could be a godsend.

E-Mail and Web Addresses for the Online Commerce Companies Mentioned in this Position Paper

- First Virtual: info@fv.com or http://www.fv.com

- Netscape: info@mcom.com or http://www.mcom.com

- NetCheque: netcheque@isi.edu or http://nii.isi.edu

- CyberCash: info@cybercash.com or http://www.cybercash.com

- DigiCash: info@digicash.nl or http://www.digicash.com

- NetBank: netbank-info@agents.com or http://www.charm.net/~ibc/ibc2/softw_ag.html

The above-mentioned NWU position paper, which is entitled "Recommended Principles for Contracts Covering Online Book Publishing," is available at ftp://ftp.net-com.com/pub/nw/nwu or via an e-mail request to nwu@net-com.com. Also available at those addresses is a general NWU position paper on new technologies entitled "Authors and the New Information Age: A Working Paper on Electronic Publishing Issues."

Another copy of this paper:

http://www.nlightning.com/e-money.html

ftp://ftp.netcom.com/pub/nw/nwu/press/emoney.txt

National Writers Union (UAW Local 1981)
873 Broadway Suite 203
New York, NY 10003
(212) 254-0279
fax (212) 254-0673
e-mail: nwu@netcom.com

© National Writers Union

These are just a few ways you can get money for the work you publish. Of course, getting a publisher to market your work is advantageous. If it were not for my publisher, AP PROFESSIONAL, I would never have been able to reach the vast audience that they are able to reach with their professional marketing and international connections. There are certainly advantages to having a big publisher behind you, but I do think writer's unions play an important role as well because they prevent the little guy from being squashed by the big boys.

You now have more than enough information to get you started as a professional digital scribe for electronic media. I hope you put it all to good use. However, remember, there is no better way to do things legally (and, in the long run, profitably) than to seek the guidance of a professional lawyer!

The next chapter will begin our journey into the composition process as it pertains to the types of articles and stories that prove successful in electronic media. The modern digital scribe must be aware of the value and interest in these types of writing because they can literally be his or her bread-and-butter at the end of the fiscal year.

I include addresses of e-zines and other publishers on the CD, so you can get to work making money right away! This book is meant to be progressive. First, you learn the basics of creativity; next, you understand the nature of multimedia writing; then, you see what the legalities are; finally, you see how to write the stories that were made for electronic media. Simple, isn't it? Yes, and fun!

Part

IV

I Sing the Story Electric!

12

Stories That Snap, Crackle, and Pop

This chapter will cover the following:

- Where to find an agent on the Net
- How to do research on the Net
- How to write self-help books
- How to write biographies
- How to write travel books
- How to write magazine articles
- How to write sports stories
- How to write current events, features, and editorials
- How to write online multimedia fiction
- Other types of writing for the Net

I have already introduced you to the Net and where you may go to get your work looked at by editors and publishers. This is possibly the best bet, although you may also want to go to an agent.

Figure 12.1 shows the sample home page that will put you in touch with all the on-line literary agents. You can hunt them down by name, by agency, and by specialty. The only warning I want to give you is to make sure you find out if the agent has sold anything recently, and if he or she charges for reading a manuscript. If the latter is true, then I would look elsewhere. Most agents who charge for "reading" are in the business to get fees for their critiques and not to sell your work. If your work is not ready for publication, then you do not need an agent. An agent should only be there to take care of negotiations and to handle your money and royalties. You can get excellent critical feedback from the many newsgroups on-line or from programs like WritePro, which I mentioned earlier. You may also find value in joining a creative writing class at your local college or other location.

As it says on this sample page, the agents' list is just beginning. You may get a more complete list of agents at your local bookstore

![Netscape window showing The Internet Directory of Literary Agents]

The Internet Directory of Literary Agents

Part of WritersNet: The Internet Directory of Published Writers

Note: This Directory is just starting and as such may have very few entries at the beginning. Please be patient while your fellow Internauts help to build this Directory. Thanks!

- **Browse the list of Literary Agents**, sorted by:
  - ☐ Agent's Name
  - ☐ Agency
  - ☐ Area of specialization
  - ☐ Location
- **Search the database**
- **Download the full document**. Can be saved to your own disk by choosing *Save As* from the File menu in Netscape or comparable browser. Then load the text file into your favorite word processor and do searches offline using the word processor search or find command. Sorted by:
  - ☐ Agent's Name

Figure 12.1   Literary agents on the Net

Research on the Net

Before we get too far, I want to give you some suggestions about doing research on the Internet (WWW). Following these suggestions will save you time, money, and hassle. First of all, if you are able, you should take classes at a school, college, or university that has Internet access for its students. You may also be able to join a teacher/student reduced access plan such as the California State University's GINA Core-Plus (Graphical Interface for Network Access) that charges only $60.00 per year for 28.8 modem access, unlimited, and you are only charged for a local phone call—no matter how long you are connected. Both students and faculty are able to get this service in their homes.

Suggestions for Net Researchers

1. Write down your search strategy before you connect with the database. Know exactly what your search terms will be and have second and third choices ready.

2. Narrow the terms. If you're writing a book about abortion, don't search for that word alone. Combine it with other terms that specify what you want, such as *abortion* and *protest* and *clinic*. Or you may want to (if possible) specify by date to get the most recent information.

3. First ask for titles or headlines. Reading entire texts on-line can be costly.

4. Read the rate card. You'll probably find it's cheaper to call at night and on weekends.

5. Learn the commands. It is important to know how to interrupt a search and to cancel a search. Saving is also necessary.

or in the public or college library nearest you. Also, there are other listings on the Net. Do your own search and find out!

Now I will go over the types of writing that you can do on the Net, and I will give you a chance to try your hand at writing some stories as well. The first area of writing I will cover is probably the easiest type to get published and certainly the most profitable. Nonfiction writing often does not appeal to creative writers, but it certainly keeps the wolf from the door much better than the "great American novel."

I will be covering seven categories of on-line writing:

1. Self-help
2. Biography
3. Travel
4. Magazine articles
5. Sports
6. Current events, features, and editorials
7. Fiction

Each of these categories has its own attributes, and I want to teach you how you can cover the information needed in each one. With this in mind, I will give you a "digital scribe's check-off list" for each type that you may use when you write, so that you will be certain to have all the elements necessary to make a sale. This is something that I always wanted when I first began to write, and I know you will put it to good use in your writing career.

SELF-HELP BOOKS

The first type of writing I will be discussing is the so-called self-help book. These are the books that sell into the millions in paperback, and they can be just as successful when they are electronic and on-line. However, they must also be marketed carefully, and you must keep your prose narrowed to a specific audience. For example, you would not want to write about the enjoyment of table wines in

Self-Help Book Check-off Sheet

1. Cluster all the ways you can help your audience overcome its specific problem.

2. Research on the Net and in libraries the main cluster topics (e.g., alcohol recovery, investment strategies, etc.). Collect (save to your disk) all the possible articles, quotations, multimedia files, or any other resources you can collect that relate to your topic and that will make your book different from others.

3. Create a working outline that uses the best topics from step 2. Arrange your content so that it follows a certain organized pattern (e.g., by sequential order, by personal improvement, or by importance of topic).

4. Cluster a cause/effect assortment of "case histories" that you have found from research, from interviews, or from personal experience. Then, tell the reader how each person solved the problem using your "techniques." Use these colorful cases to break up the less interesting but necessary instructional prose.

5. Collect an assortment of graphics, charts, and other visual aids to help your reader better understand the techniques you are explaining. These should be simple and sometimes even humorous.

a self-help book for recovering alcoholics. As a writer, you must show *positive empathy* toward your reader—this is vital to your success as a self-help author. An example of a self-help book is *Men Are from Mars, Women Are from Venus*, which gives an entertaining look at how men and women communicate and how they can help to bridge the gap between their different communication styles. The author has also published a CD-ROM of this book.

In addition, if you do not plan to market the piece yourself, publishers in the nonfiction market will expect you to write what is known as a "query letter," an "outline," and (usually) the first three chapters. The query letter gives the publisher an idea about what you are writing (why it is important and unique), who your audience is, and what you plan to cover. The outline shows what you will cover. The first three chapters give the publisher an idea of how well you write. All three elements are critical to a sale!

What goes into a self-help book? The digital scribe's check-off sheet (see box) may be used to be certain you have all of the elements necessary. After you have completed the check-off sheet, you are ready to create your outline and to write the first three chapters of your text. Make certain you spell-check, go over the work for grammar, punctuation, and spelling mistakes and revise when you think you can improve the meaning.

For your writing assignment, I want you to write a sample outline for a self-help book on a subject of your choosing. Make certain that you research your subject well and that you have an organization plan. Also, if you find that your topic has "sprouted wings," then it is time for you to write the book!

BIOGRAPHIES

Another popular book is the biography. Do not confuse this with the autobiography. An autobiography is your personal story. A biography, on the other hand, is about someone else, usually a famous or noteworthy celebrity. An example is *The Biography of John Lennon.*

Biographies can be classified in two forms: authorized and unauthorized. The authorized biography means that you have personal permission by the subject to write about him or her. The unauthorized biography is not officially approved by the subject.

It is important that you understand a little about libel law when writing unauthorized biographies. A person who is, in the interpretation of the law, "in the public eye" is open to all kinds of investigation, research, and even ridicule. There have been very few cases whereby a publicly known person has been able to successfully sue a writer or publisher for libelous statements against his or her character. Carol Burnett was able to collect from the *National Enquirer* but that is the only case I can remember. Even so, the story was so blatantly defamatory and untrue that no reasonable person (certainly not the jury) would agree with the newspaper. The article said that Ms. Burnett was drunk and rowdy at a restaurant, and she took particular pains to prosecute because both her parents were alcoholic and she did not want her name associated with such behavior.

But, as a rule, you can say just about anything you want if someone is in the public eye; even so, it is the best policy to make certain your sources are as trustworthy as possible before you include them in your biography.

One of the most popular biographers, Margot Peters (Charlotte Brontë, George Bernard Shaw, John Barrymore), says that most of her craft is devoted to research. However, she also says that unless the story is entertaining, biography can become lifeless. All the facts about a person, no matter how gruesome, no matter how personally revealing, must be shown for the reader to make up his or her mind.

The box contains the check-off sheet for writing a biography. Make sure you have accomplished all the elements before committing words to page. Because biography is so research oriented, it is important that you keep a database of your sources. Computers are excellent for this task.

Remember! You can always create your book using the multimedia techniques learned earlier. For example, clickable "hot words" in a biography that allow the reader to go back and forth in someone's history, or film clips that show an actor's major roles, would be an excellent addition to an already fine text!

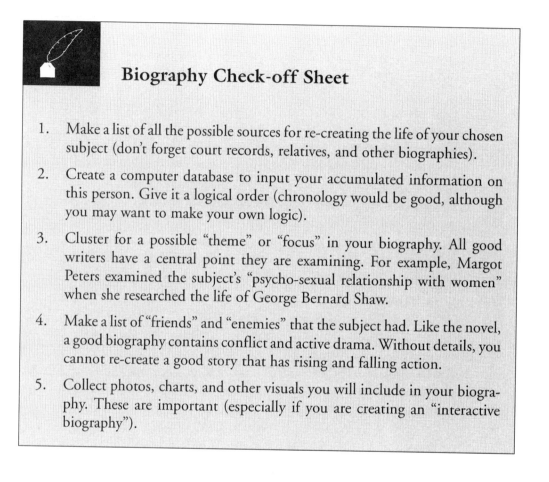

Biography Check-off Sheet

1. Make a list of all the possible sources for re-creating the life of your chosen subject (don't forget court records, relatives, and other biographies).

2. Create a computer database to input your accumulated information on this person. Give it a logical order (chronology would be good, although you may want to make your own logic).

3. Cluster for a possible "theme" or "focus" in your biography. All good writers have a central point they are examining. For example, Margot Peters examined the subject's "psycho-sexual relationship with women" when she researched the life of George Bernard Shaw.

4. Make a list of "friends" and "enemies" that the subject had. Like the novel, a good biography contains conflict and active drama. Without details, you cannot re-create a good story that has rising and falling action.

5. Collect photos, charts, and other visuals you will include in your biography. These are important (especially if you are creating an "interactive biography").

TRAVEL BOOKS

Ever since I saw a movie called *The Accidental Tourist*, I have been intrigued by writers who do travel pieces. What better way to combine wanderlust and writing skill? Naturally, as a travel writer, you have to know how to write just the right combination of "truth" and "fiction." People who read travel books are usually well-seasoned travelers themselves, so if you try to fool them with overly descriptive and theatrical prose that tells little about the practicalities of travel, you will not be a travel writer for very long.

The best travel writers are those scribes who can combine daily cost-saving ideas with entertaining, descriptive, and personably warm prose. You want your reader to enjoy the experience you are creating, but you also want that reader to visit the place (many travel books are paid for by tourist bureaus—a good contact for you to check).

Multimedia lends itself particularly well to the travel book. Imagine all the languages, music, history, and breathtaking photos that can be added to your excellently described content to form a document that comes alive for the reader like no paper book can. In addition, software programs can give topographical, hotel, and road information for the tourist, and these databases can be attached to the multimedia document for easy access!

Here is the check-off sheet for writing a travel book. It is necessary to make certain you have all the details at your fingertips before you begin to write. Also, maps, accommodations, and related costs of travel must be included, along with accompanying photographs.

Travel Book Check-off Sheet

1. Collect all the details about the place: hotels/accommodations, history, people, restaurants, local color, and cost-saving tips.

2. Collect multimedia (if appropriate): photos, maps, databases, music, animation/films.

3. Cluster around the most interesting aspects of this tourist spot. Create images that reflect the local culture and people.

4. Create a working outline that sets your organizational structure (time, value, combination).

5. Determine overall theme of your work. What basic attitude do you want to convey? How do you want to make the reader feel about this place?

MAGAZINE ARTICLES

The world of electronic media has a need for timely, informative articles about a wide range of subjects. As more and more people come on-line, the range of interests and the variety of topics to be covered are growing rapidly. All you have to do is cruise the "e-zine" section of the Net or, better yet, do a search for "magazines" and see how many mainstream and speciality print magazines have come aboard. The cost savings are driving a tremendous number of print media folks to the less expensive and more timely format of electronic communications.

In case you did not know, a war is going on between the print media and the electronic media. All you have to do is pick up the newspaper or read a slick news magazine to read about "porno-peddlers on the Web," or "12-year-old girl gets seduced by pervert hacker!" It is almost as bad as our elections! However, if you watch the Internet, people go about their business, making progress, and making people-to-people communications a real force to be reckoned with. This is, in my opinion, one of the last gasps of print media in the 20th century. With the new millennium, we will be increasing our on-line coverage and multiplying the number of magazines, newspapers, and even (yes) television programs that will be sent through that fiber optic cable. Televisions and stereophonic (sense-around sound) speakers will bring Americans into the new world of interactive, instantaneous, and cross-communicative publications.

In fact, this book is an attempt at creating one of the first of these types of books. Give me feedback so that I can write a revised edition of this book. It is possible to include all the success stories that I have spawned and all the new applications of multimedia, virtual reality, and other communications technologies will be part of a new and better publication. This is the way the magazines and newspapers of the future will work.

People will verify their sources and report to the publications about local news and any other newsworthy stories or features they can write about. On-line magazines will check out the sources and edit the articles, then pay the contributors based on a standard fee schedule (see the paper by the National Writers Union in Chapter 11). Opportunities for the media writer will grow to new levels.

However, just as the conventions must be adhered to with print media, there are definite conventions to which article writers in cyberspace must adhere. These rules are covered in Chapter 13; unless you follow them, you will remain an unpublished digital scribe.

SPORTS STORIES

Color and personality are key ingredients if you want to have a big readership in any sports writing that you do. One of the best writers in the medium is Bill Murray of the *Los Angeles Times*. Bill is successful for the same reason that the famous announcer of the Dodgers, Vin Scully, is successful in his trade: They both add literary qualities to the games they report. What I mean by *literary* is the frequent use of analogy, metaphor, and simile that these sports guys employ. It adds a certain dignity to the writing of professional sports literature and not since the days of Ring Lardner have there been sports writers who can tell a story so well and who involve the reader emotionally in their stories.

The basic task of the sports story writer is to provide some insight into the game he or she is covering or to give a personality description of some famous athlete. Usually, the best sports stories are fast, hard hitting, and descriptive, leaving the reader with the impression that the writer really understands the sport. If you do not follow sports or if you do not understand the variety of terminologies used in the sport you cover, then you should really stay away from sports writing. Of course, there are exceptions, like the Britisher visiting America who wrote a story about his first experience at a major league baseball game or the now-famous reportage of George Plimpton, who wrote as a civilian intellectual participating in the sport he was covering.

Electronic media and multimedia lends itself to writing some exciting stuff for the Net. Once we get some high-speed modems on-line with the advent of cable modems, we shall see a lot of sports stories being written that include many visuals (in real time). There are already organizations on the Net who cater to the immediacy aspect (Instant Sports is one), and once visuals and full-color graphics can load quickly and without the memory problems that exist now, you will see the profession of sports writer take off like never before.

Some of the applications that you may wish to become involved with are re-creating "short versions" of games for the person who does not have the time to see a whole game; adding multimedia to sports stories (hypertext to statistical databases, historical features, music, or other URL links that would interest the reader; movies or color graphics to supplement the story and show more action than the standard print story; interactivity so that the reader can respond to your story, either immediately or as a survey response as in All-Star Ballots). The improvement will be phenomenal for the viewer who wants fast, edited, and "experiential" stories that put the reader in the action. One interesting idea comes from the NetDay project, from a middle-school student: create virtual trading cards of your school's athletes. Of course, professional-type cards can also be created, but you will have to get permission to use their likenesses (how many thousands of dollars will that cost you?).

How can you write the kind of prose that will go well with multisensory images? Practice. Try the exercise and use the check-list the next time you create a story for the Net. Start your own home page, where the viewer can experience the sport. Such places are already on the Net, but I am sure with the help of the creativity you have learned in this book, you will be able to create an even better one!

Exercise

For your exercise, put together a sports story that uses multimedia. Develop at least three uses for hypertext, graphics, and movies or animations. Make certain that these multimedia add-ons directly increase the "reader participation" of your story. This is necessary especially if you are (for example) re-creating a played game or contest. Do this exercise with the belief that you are doing a writing form that will soon be the norm for all sports enthusiasts. Many computer users on the Net today enjoy following competitive sports as a part of their daily lives. As a digital sports scribe, you can be part of their lives as well.

Sports Writing Check-off Sheet

1. Collect all the statistical, biographical, multimedia, and other information you can retrieve about your topic.

2. Cluster for appropriate metaphors, similes and other images that will make your story "literary."

3. Determine whether you want to create interactive multimedia or a prose-only story.

4. Write an outline of your story that encompasses all the multimedia and other elements that you decide to apply.

5. What other details can you include to make the reader feel like an active part of your story?

News, Features, and Editorials Check-off Sheet

1. Peruse the dailies and determine what types of stories are getting the best coverage. Create a "lead" for your story, feature, or editorial by angling it at the "popularity quotient."

2. Gather or take photos, collect sound bites, and even determine URL links to go with your story. Arrange them to go with the paragraphs in your story. Hypertext links *must* be associated with logical connections in news stories (your credibility is at stake).

3. Make certain your sources are credible and that you have authority for all photos and quotations used.

CURRENT EVENTS, FEATURES, AND EDITORIALS

The digital scribe who writes for the "popular media" relies on daily newspapers, weekly magazines, and other relevant news sources. Just as the entrepreneur must find out what the customer needs, the writer of current events, features, and editorials must find out what stories are being spread all over the front pages. Without keeping up with what is popular with editors, a scribe will never make it in this form of writing. Of course, one can always create your own "Editorial or Current Events Home Page" for the Net and forget about mass consumption. However, most writers want to be read by the widest variety of readers, so they are always careful to peruse the dailies to come up with a lead for a story.

How can multimedia change the way these stories are written? It may come slowly at first (most readers are conservative about news, although "front page" programs are very popular on TV), but I sincerely believe that readers on the Net will soon be demanding the same sensory stimuli they get with other "liberal" types of stories (like sports). For example, the popularity of courtroom dramas developed by authors like John Grisham led to the real-life drama of O.J. on trial. It will not take long for Nethawks to want the same action, camera, and sound in their news stories.

With this in mind, the check-off sheet and exercise for this type of writing can be an exciting endeavor for the digital scribe. The final result could be your cutting-edge entry into news reporting that will last for many years to come! Give it a shot.

ON-LINE MULTIMEDIA FICTION

One of the hottest features of the new media is the rise of interactive and multimedia fiction. I have already mentioned organizations and companies that provide development software and marketing services for the fiction writer who needs it. I have also shown the digital scribe how to create his or her own home page. Fiction can be part of your home page, or you can publish your work on-line for the masses to evaluate. No longer are the pinched, market-conscious publishers the sole determiners of what becomes popular. If your fiction catches on with Net cruisers, then you can make a name for yourself without the help of publishers. In fact, as I mentioned earlier, word of mouth is the best advertising vehicle.

The first fiction to appear on the Net was entire volumes of copyright-expired novels, short stories, and poetry that scholars and teachers could dredge up from their libraries and put "in their sometimes gruesome entirety" on the Net for others to download (putting stress on the servers). However, now that hypertext fiction and multimedia fiction have taken off in popularity, you can become a digital fiction author who can create modern literary documents that will stand the test of time.

I know some old warriors in English departments who are getting quite uneasy at the thought of multimedia novels. However, the size of print novels are decreasing at an alarming rate because the modern readership is turning more to electronic highs for their fiction fixes. What can electronic fiction do that the print medium cannot do? Open the minds of readers, for one thing, and also send them into experientially mind-blowing (yet plot-involving) escapades that no print novel has ever been successful doing.

There are basically two schools of creation right now in the field of electronic fiction: (1) hypertext or multimedia and (2) fiction and interactive or "participatory" fiction.

Imagine the plot of a multimedia work of fiction. Instead of the writer having to weave word pages of descriptive setting, the author can simply place a carefully chosen graphic or photo on the page. This is what the earliest novels used to do. They paid artists to create scenes in the novels to heighten the reality. But you can do better! Imagine that same scene coming to life with animation when the reader clicks on it! Sounds of a bubbling brook, a rainstorm, or even a murder scene will come instantly into the reader's consciousness. Therefore, the digital scribe of multimedia fiction must be constantly aware of the senses of the reader (see my first chapters) because the viewer of this fiction must be stimulated much more than the conventional novel presentation. Of course, if you write well, and you can tell a suspenseful story, then the addition of multimedia will increase their pleasure.

Participatory fiction lets the user "participate" in the action of the novel. This can be simply letting the reader hear and watch movies, animation, or sounds; or it can mean letting the user select a different ending or even a different plot path (this is especially effective in carefully written mysteries).

In fact, only a thin line separates this type of writing and some of the most popular CD games on the market. *Myst* is one example, and *Panic in the Park* is another "game" that is just an interactive novel with full-motion video. Then, of course, there are the plethora of "mystery games," like *San Francisco Police Department,* with a variety of graphics, sounds, and full-motion video. The advent of high-speed, cable modems will give developers of this type of fiction a new market. More people will be able to afford the high-memory applications that this type of development entails.

Cliffhanger serials are a new experience to be developed for the Net. Let the readers experience a science fiction thriller, and keep them in suspense until they pay you to see the next episode! SoftLock Software allows the developer to place "partially locked" documents on the Net. The only way the reader can get the rest of the book is to pay for a one-and-only code (see sample demo on the CD). Net servers like Netscape Commerce Server can give you the same ability, but they are more expensive. With your own Net server, however, you cut out the middlemen like SoftLock. That means, of course, that you get to keep the profits!

The box contains a check-off and assignment sheet for on-line fiction. Be certain to create using the techniques I discussed in the

On-Line Fiction Check-off Sheet

1. Cluster or search the news for your story line. Use a program like Dramatica Pro or WritePro if you feel you need help developing plot or character.

2. Assemble possible interactive plot lines that can take the reader in different directions in the story.

3. Assemble possible multimedia graphics, movies, animation, and sounds that can improve your story line and character development.

4. Write a plot outline and character descriptions. Be sure to incorporate possible multimedia applications and where they will fit into the story.

5. Proof your work for inconsistencies and errors in plot.

first chapters of the book. Unless you can develop a good story with plenty of twists and action, the sophisticated readers on the Net will click you off!

Assignment

Write an on-line fiction story in any genre you choose (science fiction, horror, adventure, literary, mystery, romance). Add applicable multimedia to enhance both the plot and the characters. Create a home page (or submit to one) and see how many "hits" you get from people who read your story. If the interest is high, then you may want to consider publication for money!

OTHER TYPES OF WRITING ON THE NET

Many other types of writing can be very successful and popular on the Internet, depending upon how well they are created and how well they are advertised. I will mention four types that I think will have a future: "Dear Abby" advice columns; psychology, religion, and "New Age" columns; true crime articles; and educational materials.

Advice columns are already in effect under the auspices of "Chat Groups." Inter Relay Chat or IRC servers give users the opportunity to discuss their problems in a variety of settings. The Net has been getting some bad press here because many perverts get into these chat sessions and lure teenagers into some pretty compromising situations. Of course, if someone is not being supervised at home, then whose responsibility is it? The opportunity lies in the possibility for the digital scribe to set up a legitimate advice page for teenagers or some other type of helping hand writing station, where fewer perverts can get away with this type of thing.

The trick, of course, is to make your advice home page as attractive and creative as you possibly can. With the clustering, rhythm, and other natural writing techniques you have learned in this book, you can certainly do your best! Perhaps you could even have sound files that the user could download with friendly musical messages or comedic creations. You could also include hypertext that would define psychological terms, give connections to other help URLs, or refer them to professionals (A.A., N.A., and other help groups are now on-line). In other words, this is your chance to play "Dear Abby." You could even post the best e-mail letters and give your responses for the masses to read and enjoy!

There is software that allows users to log in, read messages, post their own replies, and track on-line conversations similar to a news-group. Contact the following Net sites to download software you can use:

http://www.lundeen.com

http://www.webboard.com

Both are the home pages for software packages for the Web that will allow you to use URLs, graphics, and multimedia in your postings, your replies, and your interface to the discussion groups. Webboard also lets you set up moderated groups, meaning only the modera-tor(s) can approve messages; this would be a great way to manage the signal-to-noise ratio in a "Dear Abby" page (the constant "chat-ter" in chat sessions, for example). I will look for you on the Net, Abby dear!

Psychology, religion, and New Age topics are also popular on the Net. Suppose you teach the Bible as literature, and you set up a home page for users who want to know more about how the stories in the Bible relate to the myths of different cultures and other religions. You could have a "little known secrets of the Bible" icon on the page. When clicking on it the reader would get your favorite items of interest. You could also have connections to other URLs, music files, graphics, and even favorite articles. You might also have a copy of the Oxford Annotated Bible in electronic format, which the reader could research as well. Certainly you are getting the idea. Whatever the specialty or interest, the digital scribe can create the best possible site available.

The true crime genre has been gaining increasing popularity in these days of *Pulp Fiction*. My own novel, *Russian Wolves* (sample on the CD), was written from research I did on the Andrei Chikatilo murders. Any digital scribe who can collect enough facts, pictures, and other information can write realistic home pages where the user can visit true crime at its best and worst. There are already sites on the Net pertaining to the Kennedy assassinations and other conspiracies, and interest is growing in other criminal investigations. The articles you write, however, must put the reader in the action, just like a good novel does. With your ability to create sound, motion, and graphics, this task becomes that much easier. Imagine the realism that can be created when your investigator goes hunting for the killer!

One possible way of combining book components into a Web presentation (see Chapter 4, "Creating Your Own Home Page on the Net") might be as follows:

- **Welcome Page**   Cover, author name with link to more information

- **Information Page**   Preface, Foreword, Acknowledgments, copyright notice

- **Table of Contents Page**   Links to individual chapters, appendices, glossaries, etc.

- **Second-level Pages**   Chapter openings, major subheads in chapters, pages with in-line images

- **Third-level Pages**   Details within subheads and links to downloadable figures, charts, software, etc.

Educational home pages are one of the earliest and best features of the digital scribe's repertoire of skills. Many educators got on the Net and gave birth to some tremendous home pages, where fellow teachers, students, and others could get information, hear lectures, and see "real-time" demonstrations of education at its best. Tutorials can be downloaded from your home page, you can provide all kinds of related URLs, and the user can even respond in a variety of ways.

Byte Magazine published a cover article entitled "New Ways to Learn" in the March 1995 issue. This article pointed out that a new paradigm is growing in our schools (see Table 12.1). With this application of computer learning comes a responsibility to give all students access to this ability. I am adamant about this because of the "new segregation" that is happening. We may be doing away with affirmative action and other old ways of forcing companies to comply with equal opportunity, but racism is fast becoming computerized. The poor schools in the poor districts are not getting on-line, and this means they have few computers. My home state,

Table 12.1 Changing Educational Paradigms

Old Model Implications	New Model	Technology
Classroom lectures	Individual exploration	Networked PCs with access to information
Passive absorption	Apprenticeship	Requires skills development and simulations
Individual work	Team learning	Benefits from collaborative tools and e-mail
Omniscient teacher	Teacher as guide	Relies on access to experts over network
Stable content	Fast-changing content	Requires networks and publishing tools
Homogeneity	Diversity	Requires a variety of access tools and methods

Source: Byte magazine, March 1995, pp. 56–57.

California, is a prime example. It has one of the most dismal student/computer ratios, and (coincidentally?) the SAT scores of our young people have been dropping.

If you are an educator, read the article in *Byte*. And then get on-line to let your students in on some of the best research channels and educational information possible.

That same article goes on to give an account of the "Virtual College" at New York University, where the college has revolutionized post-graduate study by putting the curriculum on-line.

This brings me to you, the educated digital scribe of the new era in technology. You could put a course on your home page and offer credit over the Net. My wife and I are considering doing just that! We plan to make an English as a Second Language teaching site where students can sign on for a variety of teaching modules aimed at improving their English skills, both speaking and writing (see Chapter 4, "Creating Your Own Home Page"). Just imagine all the types of education that you could provide: science, economics, business, computers, and even physical education could be taught via the Net. How? Why, by providing multimedia, of course! Piaget's educational principles have never had it so good as when they were applied on the modern home page, with sound, animation, and movies to excite the learner. The learner can also interact, and this is the most positive demonstration of learning that exists. As teachers, we shall respond to our students individually a lot faster than we could in a conventional classroom. And because of the variety of multimedia lessons planned beforehand, we shall diagnose what the student needs much faster. We can even take a writing sample from the student right off the Net!

Many opportunities are out there for the digital scribe who can creatively make a niche for himself or herself. This book has been an attempt to lead you into the world of Net publication as painlessly as possible, and yet I still want you to understand that my first concern is that you learn how to write creatively. Without the proper use of the English language (or *any* language, for that matter), effective and entertaining communication fails to happen. However, if you conscientiously want to create in this new and exciting medium, then you will apply what you have learned and see for yourself how your creativity can be rewarding.

13

How to Submit Your Work in Cyberspace

This chapter will cover the following:

- How to submit magazine articles
- Ways to sell your ideas
- An electronic submissions mailing list
- A note to writers
- A note to editors
- How to set up your own cyberstation—without a computer!
- Other resources for the digital scribe

MAGAZINE ARTICLES

In all cases it is best to first *query* the publisher with a short description of your article idea or outline of an already-written article. In your query, you should address how your article fits in with the magazine's scope and focus. If you are querying multiple editors, do this for each. Make sure that you are familiar enough with their general magazine content to avoid wasting the editor's time with irrelevant pieces or ones that have just recently been covered. If the magazine has writer's guidelines, ask the editor for those first and adhere to them.

Multiple Submissions

In general, if you want to adhere to the utmost standards of politeness, avoid multiple simultaneous submissions. Particularly with e-mail, you generally receive a very rapid turnaround, so that the necessity of multiple submissions is decreased. If you absolutely must attempt simultaneous submissions, and one editor accepts an article, immediately e-mail to all others that you are withdrawing the article. Explicitly noting the status of your submission as exclusive or simultaneous is a good idea. Do not carbon-copy send a single article with no individual attention to the receiving editors.

If you learned of the e-mail address from this source, please tell the editor that. It will encourage the editor to maintain the capability, spur other editors to set up their own e-mail addresses, and in turn help expand your own list of possible and alternative outlets for your writing.

WAYS TO SELL YOUR IDEAS

There are many marketing professionals located on the Internet. You can simply use a search engine (Yahoo, Web Search, etc.) and check them out for yourself. There are also many marketing books on the shelf that lead you through the process as painlessly as possible.

I am going to share some of the least expensive ideas for marketing on the Internet. Because this book will most likely be used by college students, as well as by professionals, it is nice to know there are places you can go where you can get free Web advertising.

Mr. Jon Pennycook in England can turn you on to the biggest list of free Web sites on the Net. You can reach his interactive home page at

> http://www.serve.com/jpsp1/freeweb/sites.html

His e-mail address is jpspl@leicester.ac.uk.

This is possibly the fastest and easiest way to put your home page on the Net. You can find out more about free marketing by writing to the group to which Jon belongs: info@altmedia.com. This book gives you the creativity to construct a fancy home page and you can place what you create at many of these free sites. This way, you can spend your hard-earned money on more profitable enterprises than paying rent at some Web site that may have a variety of extra charge clauses in its contract.

ELECTRONIC SUBMISSIONS LIST

These magazines are published monthly unless otherwise noted. The *content* category describes the general content and requested writing. *Compensation* describes the remuneration policies (if any). *Rights* describes the rights to the material that are sold to the publisher. *Contact* is the e-mail address of the publisher, editor, or the general submission address. Note: The accuracy of this list is not guaranteed. In particular, the rights involved in a particular "sale" may be variable or negotiable.

Make sure you understand the terms of the arrangement with the publisher. If you are interested in only certain kinds of contracts (such as retaining the copyright, which is the usual case but not guaranteed) be sure to tell the editor.

Alternate Hilarities

Type:	Magazine of humor in speculative fiction
Content:	Humorous pieces from all areas of the speculative fiction field, horror, science fiction and fantasy of

all types. "We're looking for stories ranging in length from 1 to 5K words. We like to work with original stories, but reprints are OK if the author still holds the rights. The main point is to be funny."

Compensation: Payment for first-time publication will be 1 cent a word (and one copy). Payment for reprints is two copies.

Rights: (?)

Comments: "We're more likely to buy something that's consistently funny over something that's acceptable to all audiences." E-mail submissions preferred.

Contact: Talestwiceto@Genie.geis.com (Coeditors: Alexandra Zale and Devon Tavern)

The Blind Spot

Type: Small press 'zine (?)

Content: Duke's fantasy, science fiction, and horror fiction. 10K words or less. Artwork.

Compensation: $10 plus contributors copies.

Rights: (?)

Contact: awhit@acpub.duke.edu (Andy Whitfield)

Circlet Press

Type: Small press 'zine, published anthologies (?)

Content: Erotic science fiction and fantasy. Short stories primarily under 10K words. Anthologies. Other subcategories.

Compensation: Half-cent per word. Royalties for single-author anthologies negotiated on case by case basis.

Rights: One-time anthology rights.

Comments:	Write for guidelines or booklist. Query first.
Contact:	ctan@world.std.com

Claustrophobia

Type:	Small press newsletter
Content:	Social issues, privacy (?)
Compensation:	No money, but "credit, exposure, samples for portfolio."
Rights:	Nonsimultaneous publication.
Contact:	dbruedig@magnus.acs.ohio-state.edu

CONNECT

Type:	Small press magazine
Content:	"Covering the major commercial online services, Internet/Usenet and smaller Bulletin Board System networks, CONNECT focuses on telecommunications from a user-oriented perspective."
Compensation:	"Authors are paid a flat rate of $75 for mini-reviews. Authors are paid between $100 and $300 for feature articles, depending on the length, subject matter and newsworthiness of the article. The longer the article and the more complex the subject matter, typically, the more the payment for the submission."
Rights:	(?)
Comments:	Seeks articles and reviews.
Contact:	pegasus@grex.ann-arbor.mi.US

CYBERSPACE VANGUARD

Type:	Electronic magazine

Content: "News and Views of the Science Fiction and Fantasy Universe carries interviews, feature articles, and lots'o'news on current happenings on the science fiction, fantasy, animation, and comics genres."

Compensation: "Right now we cannot pay our writers, but we are trying to line up a publisher for a paper version, and once that happens we will be attempting to pay people."

Rights: "We 'buy' one-time rights, but the remuneration policy may change at any time."

Comments: "We are seeking articles and interviews from writers who can be fun without being long winded. Write for guidelines, but in the meantime a query is preferred to an article." See etext.archive.umich.edu:/pub/Zines/Cyberspace.Vanguard for past issues.

Contact: Submissions should be sent to xx133@cleveland.freenet.edu. Other correspondence should be sent to cn577@cleveland. freenet.edu.

FringeWare Review

Type: Electronic magazine

Content: "Our centroid (th/m)eme [is] 'Building Community around a Fringe Marketplace';" "sidebars, tutorials, interviews and reviews, with tasty, mind-twisting fiction as synthesis."

Compensation: "We pay up to US $0.03 per word plus byline and two copies of each issue in which you appear. We pay the full amount for work we choose to run which (a) hasn't appeared elsewhere, (b) fits within our issues' themes, (c), and meets word count criteria; also, you must provide an e-mail address for the byline. Otherwise, we'll negotiate. We pay US

$20 per page for artwork and comix, or do trade-outs as mentioned above. In the case of comix, we do not need the work to be first run."

Rights:	(?)
Comments:	"We limit our magazine to 48 pages, at least 35% of which contains catalog, subvertising, editorials, letters and administrivia, so writers only have 25-odd pages, less artwork and comix, in which to express their collective brilliance. We seek terse, opinionated, first-person, active-voice, period."
Contact:	<fringeware@wixer.bga.com>

GRIST

Type:	Electronic magazine
Content:	A magazine of poetry, prose, essays, and articles.
Compensation:	(?)
Rights:	(?)
Comments:	Well-crafted prose, experimental prose, discussions of network prose, interactive/collaborative language, all considered and solicited for publication. FTP or Gopher to

etext.archive.umich.edu/pub/Poetry/Grist

Contact:	Mail subscriptions and work submissions to <fowler@phantom.com>.

Hum—The Government Computer Magazine

Type:	Paper magazine (?)
Content:	Canada's national magazine for public sector computing, for 13,000+ mostly government managers—federal, provincial, and municipal.

Rights:	First serial.
Compensation:	Up to $.10 per word.
Comments:	Stories must be about the use of technology in Canadian government settings.
Contact:	Submit query to Mr. Lee Hunter, Managing Editor, ag071@freenet.carleton.ca

InterText

Type:	Bimonthly electronic fiction magazine
Content:	Short stories, primarily under 15,000 words, although exceptions can be made. Not genre specific—stories from all genres welcome. Write for guidelines if needed.
Compensation:	Publication and exposure to approximately 23,000 subscribers on six continents.
Rights:	One-time publication; all copyrights revert to authors immediately.
Comments:	FTP to network.ucsd.edu (128.54.16.3) in /intertext, or Gopher to ocf.berkeley.edu in OCF On-Line Library -> Fiction, InterText on the World-Wide Web, point your WWW browser to
	file://network.ucsd.edu/intertext/other_formats/ HTML/ITtoc.html
Contact:	<intertxt@network.ucsd.edu> Editor: Jason Snell

Internet Informer

Type:	E-mail newsletter
Content:	Includes news and information from both the material and electronic worlds, particularly the Internet.
Compensation:	"Small fee."

Rights:	(?)
Comments:	Works with regular columnists particularly.
Contact:	Informer@Cris.Com or StevenBaker@Delphi.com.

The Lighthouse

Type:	Monthly magazine, e-mail version
Content:	Focuses on various forms of contemporary Christian music (rock to rap to metal to adult contemporary to alternative to dance). Artist spotlights and album reviews. The ministry of Christian music.
Compensation:	"A *big* thank you."
Rights:	No exclusive rights requested.
Comments:	Write for more details and text-only e-mail version.
Contact:	JWS@SABINE.PSU.EDU

Millenium Magazine, Boston

Type:	Small type, published on real paper, 600 DPI B&W graphics, 30–40 pages, saddle stapled, colored card cover.
Content:	B&W art, fiction under 10 pages, poetry: Gothic, techno, industrial, psychedelic, counterculture, urban.
Compensation:	Free copies and short bio in back with contact information.
Rights:	Writers and artists retain all rights.
Comments:	Please send submissions over two pages in compressed form. Been around over three years. First online issue will come out in December 1994. Interactive and HyperCard based.
Contact:	CountREM@aol.com,Internet

Paladin Science Fiction Group

Type: Anthologies and novels

Content: "Fiction anthologies in science fiction, fantasy, and horror for mature readers; erotic science fiction, fantasy, and horror for adult readers. Length: super-short to novella. Maximum 10K words. Novels in science fiction, fantasy and horror 40K–60K words for general to mature audience."

Compensation: One cent per word, two copies for poetry.

Rights: (?)

Comments: Do not submit without reading guidelines first. Both electronic queries and simultaneous submissions OK. No electronic submissions in North America.

Contact: S. G. Johnson <corsair@camelot.com>

Quanta

Type: Online magazine

Content: "Science fiction by amateur and professional authors around the world and across the net."

Compensation: Publication and exposure to approximately 2,200 subscribers.

Rights: (?)

Comments: ASCII and PostScript versions. See ftp.eff.org:/journals/Quanta.

Contact: Submissions to <quanta@andrew.cmu.edu>.

Sixth Dragon (previously, Mushroom Opera)

Type: Student-run magazine published twice a year at Michigan State University at Lansing.

Content:	Generally science fiction and fantasy.
Compensation:	Contributor's copy.
Rights:	(?)
Contact:	David Scott Martin <martind@student.msu.edu> or <bard@cemvax.msu.edu>

Sound News and Arts

Type:	Local small press 'zine
Content:	"Accept writing of *all* types, mainly about arts, music, and interviews with interesting and innovative people. Also accept poetry, short stories, and artwork. *Sound* is a local publication and is pretty open content-wise. Geared toward the younger, more energetic crowd."
Compensation:	"No payment as of yet (save for a few free issues), planned payment in late '93."
Rights:	(?)
Comments:	uuencoded or FTPed submissions to sunsite.unc.edu in the /pub/multimedia/pictures/OTIS/Incoming directory). Submissions should be in ASCII text format (or TIF, GIF or JPEG for pictures).
Contact:	sound-na@unomaha.edu (or ed@sunsite.unc.edu)

The Trincoll Journal

Type:	Liberal arts multimedia magazine
Content:	A liberal arts multimedia magazine created by students from Trinity College in Hartford, Connecticut. The *Journal* is a weekly publication with its writing and art work created by readers from around the world.
Compensation:	(?)

Rights: (?)

Comments: To view the *Journal* use your favorite WWW browser to open a URL to http://www.trincoll.edu/homepage. html FTP: troy.trincoll.edu /pub/incoming/Trin-collJournal sumex-aim.stanford.edu /info-mac/per

Contact: <journal@trincoll.edu> Peter Adams and Paul Tedesco, editors.

Wilde Oaks

Type: Literary journal

Content: South Bay (San Jose, California) Lesbian and Gay Community Center literary journal. Accepts fiction (less than 6K words preferred), prose, poety, photography, and artwork from gay, lesbian, bisexual, transgender, or supportive people. Erotica is okay, but no pornography. Submission guidelines are available.

Compensation: One contributor copy.

Rights: One-time publication rights.

Contact: jrd@frame.com (Jim Drew)

Writer's Nook News

Type: National quarterly magazine

Content: "Dedicated to giving freelance writers specific information for their immediate practical use in getting published and staying published. It contains news; writing tips; book reviews; legislative/tax updates; conference, contest, and market listing; and various related topics."

Compensation: "The *Nook News* pays 6 cents per word on acceptance for first North American serial rights to short, pithy articles (400 words maximum.) on the writing experience."

Rights:	(?)
Comments:	"Simultaneous submissions will be rejected. Articles must be specific, terse, and contain information my readers can put to immediate, practical use. Avoid third person whenever possible. Include a short bio (25 words or so, not a resume) with your submission."
Contact:	<comprophet@delphi.com> (Eugene Ortiz, Publisher)

WIRED

Type:	Monthly national magazine
Content:	Cutting-edge computer technology, "techno-culture and hardware"(?).
Compensation:	(?)
Rights:	(?)
Comments:	Write for guidelines.
Contact:	Submissions@wired.com, editor@wired.com

A Note to Writers

E-mail submissions have many advantages. In addition to the fast and reliable transmission, the editor may give more rapid turnaround to e-mail inquiries. The opportunity for writer–editor communication and feedback is increased. The ability to find the specific outlet for a particular piece is improved. Also, in comparison to the telephone, people can read their mail whenever they want instead of at random interruptions. They can measure their responses carefully and archive them for future reference. For submissions, the intermediate step of rekeying typewritten text is largely eliminated.

Please treat this capability of e-mail submission with the utmost respect. If you abuse it you may jeopardize your own and other writers' future opportunities. An editor may decide capriciously that only junk comes in electronically and ignore or remove the capability. Or, the editor may pay special attention to all the gems of articles that can be discovered and polished there. Always treat the editor with respect. If an article is rejected, simply resubmit elsewhere, make changes, or abandon it. The e-mail address is *not* a hotline to flame or harass editors.

Whenever you hear of a new address, please inform me of this fact. You gain nothing by withholding it from your fellow writers. Everyone benefits when the list is thorough and complete. A comprehensive list of outlets encourages competition between them for your writing based on rights and remuneration policies, similar to an electronic Yellow Pages.

Also, feel free to approach editors you know about the idea of setting up the service of Internet e-mail submission addresses. Tell them that their competitors have set up the system and that there are many potential benefits, perhaps ultimately eliciting improved reader satisfaction and interest.

A Note to Editors

In the near future, conducting writing transactions over the Internet may become the medium of choice for many markets. Of course, there are disadvantages along with the grand incentives to support this capability. Many editors, however, have found the ability to receive submissions and queries via e-mail to be immensely valuable in cultivating future issues' articles.

In some cases, you may be competing with them directly for knowledgeable and interesting articles and writers. If a writer sees two outlets with similar content but one has more ideal rights or remuneration arrangements, to which will she or he submit?

I strongly encourage editors to support and solicit articles via e-mail. It may allow you to interact and direct your writers more effectively and less stressfully. It may improve the quality of your submissions by expanding the available pool and increasing the target and focus of individual pieces. Ultimately, it may make you more responsive to readers than your competition. Potentially, the writer, editor, and reader all benefit from the dynamic arrangement. All this is written in speculative terms, however, because it is not guaranteed. You may find that irrelevant or useless queries increase, but even so, a wider selection pool may render that unproblematic.

The World Wide Web has grown at a breathtaking pace, in some ways more so than the actual physical growth of the Internet. There appears to be a great "cyberspatial Web rush" as diverse individuals and organizations work to broadcast their signal via home pages, electronic brochures and advertisements, and the like. The age of the cyberspatial printing press has arrived.

The old cliché states that "freedom of speech belongs only to people who own presses." Doesn't this strike you as a kind of oppressive sentiment? Why should freedom of speech have anything to do with money or status? Indeed, the invention of the printing press by Gutenberg broke down entrenched barriers in exactly this realm. And the logical conclusion of this "equality, egalitarianism, and populism" in the ability to disseminate ideas is evident in the Web.

Suddenly the computer and networks, "cyberspace," is engendering the same type of revolution that the printing press did, with a fundamental difference: The press made available cheap *books* for distribution; that is, the burden of the *receiver* was diminished greatly but sophisticated skill and expertise was still required of the *sender*. Today, anyone can set up a "printing press in cyberspace" for a very minimal cost, which is dropping rapidly.

How to Set Up Your Own Cyberstation

Let me give an example of how to set up a cyberspatial broadcasting station for about $20 a month so that you don't even need to own a computer. The Internet provider Netcom provides unlimited Internet access for $20 a month, including an anonymous FTP directory, and many providers provide a similar service. The anonymous FTP is capable of supporting not only the mundane (sometimes tedious and arcane) FTP access but also the seamless, transparent, smooth access of hypertext browsers such as Lynx and Mosaic. Netcom is going through growing pains, but provides the most universal Internet coverage in the United States for the least amount of money, makes FTP setup a snap, and the system is entrenched with many local users creating their own stops. Therefore, I am going to describe this provider here.

The Steps

The steps involved in setting up a cyberspatial broadcasting system to cyberspace are simply these:

1. Contact Netcom, 1-800-353-6600 or info@netcom.com, or telnet to netcom.com as "guest." Set up an account. With a credit card, you can get a login in *hours*.

2. Read their FAQ 119 with the command "faq 119." This tells you how the FTP setup works. Send mail to support@netcom.com saying "I have read faq 119." In a few days they will send you back a message, indicating they have set up an account.

3. Run "lynx" to access the WWW. Type "help." In the menu you will find help on the subject of HTML, the hypertext markup language. HTML is easy to learn. Or, leap to any

site and, while viewing a document hit \, which allows you to see the embedded commands in a file. Then, you can emulate the style and see how different commands are formatted.

4. In the FTP directory, create a file called "home.html" that contains your own billboard in cyberspace. Add files in subdirectories. Link the files to each other. Link to other sites. It's as easy as editing text files. Make sure rights are OK (chmod command) so people can get at them!

5. Test using the command "lynx home.html". You can also make sure rights are correct by going through the ftp interface, lynx ftp://ftp.netcom/pub/[you]/home.html

6. Voilà! You are now ready to unveil your masterpiece to the world. Advertise in a relevant newsgroup. Watch enthusiastic people send you mail.

7. Two people at Netcom provide neat services to help you advertise and monitor the accesses to your files: noring@netcom.com keeps a list of all public pages and short descriptions; report@webcom.com provides a slick service of counting accesses to your files, and who accessed them.

This is all it takes to run your own pseudo-BBS or "broadcasting station"! Imagine being able to bypass and thwart the entire world media monopoly with these simple steps! I claimed earlier that you don't even have to *own* a computer to accomplish all this, and it's true. Many libraries and some copier shops have public access terminals that would allow you to accomplish all these steps. If they have floppy disk drives, you could upload your own data!

Ray Bradbury's science fiction novel about a bleak dystopian future, *Farenheit 451*, was written on a typewriter in a library in about a week, according to his Preface. Will a similar brilliant, fledgling, struggling author dazzle the world with masterpieces in the same way, in cyberspace? I certainly have done my part to encourage you to do so!

One of the fantastic aspects of WWW is that it demonstrates how utterly important is the role of *organizing* and *editing* information.

In a sense, our society is undergoing a fundamental shift from a phase of *generating* massive reams of information to now *organizing* them in cyberspace. And, hidden gold is all over the place, waiting for the patient, methodical, inspired "cyberscholar" to plug it together and revolutionize the world. Even the mere act of compiling your "favorite links" to the world is an immense service to your fellow citizens of cyberspace.

OTHER RESOURCES

Newsgroups

alt.cyberpunk.chatsubo

"Original science fiction in the Cyberpunk/Shadowrun genre posted for review. Accomplished and beginning writers as well as fans. Submissions of stories (any length) or poetry related to Cyberpunk themes will get constructive feedback from other writers in this style. Interactive stories with other authors a possibility" (Jay Brandt, FAQ maintainer).

alt.journalism

Journalists and journalism students.

alt.prose, alt.prose.d

Predecessors to rec.arts.prose, lower distribution. Disscussion in alt.prose.d only.

alt.zines

"Zines" or small, low-circulation, low-cost newsletters of fringe elements.

misc.writing

Accomplished and beginning writers. Submissions, queries, markets, and so forth.

news.answers

Also alt.answers, comp.answers, misc.answers, and so forth. The standard moderated newsgroups for "approved" or "official" Usenet FAQs.

rec.arts.prose

Posted fiction for review. Discussion of posted articles.

rec.arts.poems

Posting and discussion of original poetry.

rec.arts.sf.written

Written science fiction. Great authors. Writing style. (?)

rec.mag

Magazines (?)

rec.mag.fsfnet

Fantasy and science fiction discussion, movies and television.

comp.infosystems.www.users; comp.infosystems.www.providers; comp.infosystems.www.misc

WWW (World Wide Web) information groups.

MAILING LISTS TO SUBSCRIBE TO ON THE NET

MAGAZINE

Topics: "Expert opinion or help from established scholars and professionals. Covering the history, current state and future prospects of the American magazine, and issues related to magazine publishing. Primary focus is journalistic, but also addresses other magazine-publishing matters of economic (management, marketing, circulation, production, research), technological, historical, and social importance."

Subscription: Send JOIN MAGAZINE <YourFirstName> <YourLastName> in message body to <COMSERVE@ VM.ITS.RPI.EDU> or (BITNET) <COMSERVE@ RPITSVM.BITNET>

Moderator: David Abrahamson <ABRAHAMSON@ACFCLUSTER.NYU.EDU>

Small Press Mailing List

Topics: "Concerns of authors and editors involved with the small press, both of books and of magazines. Printers and services, announcements, calls for submissions, bookstores, discussion of acceptance and rejections, book and signing events, readings, 'war stories,' advice for writers, editors, self-publishers."

Subscription: Send your human-readable *request* to join or leave to <small-press-request@world.std.com>. *Posts* to the list go to <small-press@world.std.com>.

Moderator: <ctan@world.std.com> (Cecilia M. Tan).

Writer's Workshop

Topics: "Although started for discussion of writing, submissions, critiques, various mind-joggers, and exercises also are passed among the participants. All postings are archived and available to participants."

Subscription: The workshop is self-service—send e-mail to <listserv@vm1.nodak.edu> (or <listserv@ndsuvm1.bitnet>) with the message SUBSCRIBE WRITERS <yourfirstname> <yourlastname>.

Fiction and Writing Lists

Topics: Fiction writers workshop. Fiction list is for submissions and critiques; writing list is for general discussions, new member introductions, and announcements of various sorts. Tone is professional. Most members actually pursue publication. Usually in science fiction or fantasy genres.

Subscription: Send mail to LISTSERVE@psuvm.psu.edu, "subscribe <listname> <yourfirstname> <yourlastname>" where <listname> is "fiction," "writing," "novels-l." For the nonfiction list send "subscribe nfictn-l <yourfirstname> <yourlastname> to listserve@american.edu.

Posting: FICTION@PSUVM.PSU.EDU, WRITING@PSUVM.PSU.EDU. Also, <NOVELS-L@ PSUVM.PSU.EDU> for novels, and <NFICTNL@ american.edu>nonfiction and poetry.

Poetry List

Topics: "This list is designed to be a forum where original poetry (either complete or in progress) may be posted by members interested in critique-style discussion, examination, and analysis of their work. . . . It is assumed that all members will at some point post an original piece, and not merely assume an exclusively responsive role."

Subscription: Send mail to listserve@gonzaga.edu, "subscribe poetry <yourfirstname> <yourlastname>."

Posting: <POETRY@GONZAGA.EDU>

Screen Writing Discussion List

Topics: "A discussion list of the joy and challenge of screen writing for film and TV. . . . Any topic of interest to writers or potential writers is appropriate (i.e., format, story ideas, dialogue, characters, agents, producers, directors, actors, studios, problems and/or solutions)."

Subscription: Send mail to listserve@tamvm1.bitnet, "subscribe scrnwrit <yourfirstname> <yourlastname>."

Posting: <SCRNWRIT@TAMVM1.BITNET>

Creative Writing Pedagogy for Teachers and Students

Topics: "A place to discuss how and why creative writing is being taught at colleges and universities, including the role it plays in the curriculum, the history of creative writing programs, the shape and flavor of creative writing courses, and the influence it has or should have on students' lives."

Subscription: Send mail to listserve@MIZZOU1.BITNET, "subscribe crewrt-l <yourfirstname> <yourlastname>."

Posting: <CREWRT-L@MIZZOU1.BITNET>

Megabyte University

Topics: "An unarchived list primarily for professors, teachers, graduate students, and administrators involved in teaching composition using computers. Topics of discussion have included software descriptions and comparisons for use in teaching composition, determining real audience for composition students, and announcements of upcoming conferences, both actual and virtual. Many of the members of this list also participate in the MediaMOO weekly online conferences and other activities"

Subscription: Send mail to listserve@TTUVM1.BITNET, "subscribe MBU-L <yourfirstname> <yourlastname>."

Posting: <MBU-L@TTUVM1.BITNET>

Moderator: Fred Kemp

The Composition Digest

Topics: "A weekly newsgroup for the study of computers and writing, specifically writing instruction in computer based classrooms."

Subscription: Send mail to listserve@ULKYVX.BITNET, "subscribe COMPOS01 <yourfirstname> <yourlastname>."

Posting: <COMPOS01@ULKYVX.BITNET>

Purdue Rhetoric

Topics: "Rhetoric, professional writing, and language discussion group—a scholarly forum for discussion of rhetoric and composition, professional writing, and language research."

Subscription: Send mail to listserve@URCCVM.BITNET, "subscribe PURTOPOI <yourfirstname> <yourlastname>."

Posting: <PURTOPOI@PURCCVM.BITNET>

English Forum

Topics: "An archived discussion forum on electronic communication in instruction and research of English, writing, and literature."

Subscription: Send mail to listserve@MIZZOU11.BITNET, "subscribe ENGLMU-L <yourfirstname> <yourlastname>."

Posting: <ENGLMU-L@MIZZOU11.BITNET>

WIOLE

Topics: Writing Intensive Online Learning Environment, an archived list for writing instructors.

Subscription: Send mail to listserve@MIZZOU1.BITNET, "subscribe WIOLE-L <yourfirstname> <yourlastname>."

Posting: <WIOLE-L@MIZZOU1.BITNET>

Writing Center

Topics: "A discussion list for directors of academic writing centers, including evaluating software for writing instruction, use of tutors, and other issues specific to writing centers."

Subscription: Send mail to listserve@TTUVM1.BITNET, "subscribe W-CENTER <yourfirstname> <yourlastname>."

Posting: <W-CENTER@TTUVM1.BITNET>

FTP Sites

A large collection of electronic 'zines and other miscellaneous electronic text files can be found on the University of Michigan archives, etext.archive.umich.edu.

Other writing-related FAQs can be found on rtfm.mit.edu:/pub/usenet/news.answers/writing. The FAQ site is also an outstanding collection of highly refined writing by "amatures" on virtually any topic, highly accessible to both readers and writers.

The FAQ maintainers mailing list is available by request to faq-maintainers-request@mit.edu.

Miscellaneous

A more accurate list of electronic 'zines is posted intermittently to alt.mag, alt.zines, posted by John Labovitz <johnl@netcom.com>.

See netcom.com/pub/johnl/zines/e-zine-list (most recent) or rtfm.mit.edu:/pub/usenet/news.answers/writing/zines.

Electronic Writers' Workshops and Online Education in Creative Writing (Bowers & Butcher, 1993) available from gwuvm.gwu.edu/WRITERS.RESOURC, is a compilation of resources for writers and for writing teachers on the national network services (part 1). Part 2 contains virtual classrooms and tools for collaborative writing projects. Part 3 lists "a new breed of literary magazines that are written, published, and read exclusively by network users . . . finding a readership beyond the best hopes of many professional and academic literary magazines' editors." Part 4 deals with copyrights, what constitutes publication in the electronic realm, and antidotes to "remarkable examples of misinformation."

ELECTRONIC PUBLISHING SERVICES

Publishing services are already on-line to help you. For example, Todd Jacobs's book publishing company offers various electronic publishing services and specializes in producing low-cost electronic versions of paperbacks, for which writers are paid royalties. Contact him at #24, 13929 Castle Blvd., Silver Spring, MD 20904, tel. 202-388-9742. Two other sources of publishing services are Paul Peacock's Floppy-back Publishing, Box 2084, Hoboken, New Jersey 07030, tel. 201-963-3012, and John Galuszka's Serendipity Systems, Box 140, San Simeon, CA 93452.

Box 1 lists sources for some of the software discussed in this book. It is followed by a handy reference of manufacturers' Bulletin Board addresses. This is the best way to get in touch with the people who can give you the most useful assistance if you have trouble with their software. The digital scribe of the new era cannot afford to have programs that do not work, so do not hesitate to call!

Box 1

Addresses of Evaluated Software

1. WordPerfect Corporation, 1555 N. Technology Way, Orem, Utah 84057-2399. Phone: (801) 225-5000, Telex: 820618, Fax: (801) 222-5077.

2. Screenplay Systems Incorporated, 150 E. Olive Avenue, Suite 203, Burbank, CA 91502. Phone: (818) 843-6557, Fax: (818) 843-8364.

3. WritePro, 43 South Highland Avenue, Ossining, New York 10562. Phone: (914) 762-1255, Fax: (914) 762-5871.

4. Asymetrix Corporation, 110 110th Avenue N.E., Suite 700, Bellevue, Washington 98004-5840. Phone: (206) 637-1579, Fax: (206) 637-1650, Internet: lisab@asymetrix.com

5. Macromedia, 600 Townsend, San Francisco, CA 94103. Phone: (415) 252-2111, Fax: (415) 626-0554, Internet: scherneff@macromedia.com, CompuServe: 73244, 705

6. Q/Media Software Corporation, 312 East 5th Avenue, Vancouver, B.C. V5T 1H4. Phone: (1-800-444-9356, 604-879-1190).

7. NeoSoft Corp. 354 NorthEast Greenwood Avenue, Suite 108, Bend, Oregon 97701-4631. Orders: 1-800-545-1392, Fax: (503) 388-8221. Phone: (503) 389-5489, BBS: (503) 383-7195.

8. Catalog On Disk for Windows, Curtis Software Corporation, 2730 Monterey St., Suite 111, Torrance, CA 90503. Phone: (310) 320-2451, Fax: (310) 320-0648.

Manufacturer's Contact Information

3COM	408-492-1790	BBS
Acculogic	714-454-8124	BBS
Acculogic	800-234-7811	General
Acer America	800-833-8241	BBS
Acer Technologies Corp.	408-922-0333	Tech Support
Acumen Computer Systems	800-876-0486	General
Adaptec	408-945-7727	BBS
Adaptec	408-945-8600	General
Adaptec	408-945-2550	Tech Support
ADIC	206-861-1446	BBS
ADIC	206-883-4357	Tech Support
ADIC	800-336-1233	General: Novell DCBs
Alpha Research	512-345-6465	General
Altos Computer Systems	408-258-6787	General
Always Technology	818-597-0275	BBS
Always Technology	818-597-9595	Tech Support
Always Technology	818-597-1400	General/Sales
AMI (Bios)	404-246-8780	BBS
AMI (Bios)	404-263-8181	Tech Support
APCUG (Association of PC User Groups)	408-439-9367	BBS
Apple Computer	800-538-9696	Tech Support
Archive Corp.	714-641-0279	General
Areal Technology	408-436-6800	General
ARCO Electronics	305-961-1666	General
Artisoft Inc.	602-293-6363	General: LANtastic
Ashton-Tate	408-431-2275	BBS
AST Research	714-727-4723	BBS
Atari	408-745-2000	General
AT&T	800-247-1212	Tech Support
AT&T Support	201-769-6397	BBS
ATI Technologies	416-756-4591	BBS

ATI Technologies	416-756-0711	Tech Support
Award (Bios)	408-370-3139	BBS
Award (Bios)	408-370-7979	Tech Support
Bi-Tech Enterprises	516-567-8155	General
Borland	408-439-9096	BBS
Brand Technologies	818-407-4040	General
Brown Bag Software	408-371-7654	BBS
Bus Tek	408-492-1984	BBS
Bus Tek	408-492-9090	General
Byte (magazine)	617-861-9764	BBS
Canon USA	516-488-6528	BBS
Cardinal Technologies	717-293-3074	BBS
Catapult Systems	510-659-0365	General
Central Point Software	503-690-6650	BBS
Central Point Software	503-690-8090	Tech Support: PC Tools
Chicony	714-771-9067	Tech Support
Chips and Technologies	408-436-0600	General
Chipsoft	619-453-5232	BBS
Ciprico	612-559-4258	BBS
Ciprico	612-559-2034	General
Colorado Memory Systems	303-679-0650	BBS
Colorado Memory Systems	800-432-5858	Tech Support
Columbia Data Products	407-862-4742	BBS
Colombia Data Products	407-869-6700	General
Commodore Business Machines	215-431-9100	Tech Support
Compaq	800-345-1518	Tech Support
Compuadd	800-456-3116	Tech Support
CompuServe Information Service	800-848-8199	General
Computer Peripherals, Inc.	805-499-9646	BBS

Computer Peripherals, Inc.	805-499-5751	Tech Support
Conner Peripherals	408-456-3388	Tech Support
Control Data Corp. (CDC)	612-851-4131	General
Core International	407-241-2929	BBS
Core International	407-997-6044	Tech Support
Cornerstone Technology	408-435-8943	BBS
Cornerstone Technology	408-435-8900	Tech Support
Creative Labs	408-428-6660	BBS
Crosstalk Communications	404-641-1803	BBS
Data Technology Corp	408-942-4197	BBS
Data Technology Corp	408-262-7700	Tech Support
Dell Computer	800-624-9896	Tech Support
Delphi Online Service	800-365-4636	BBS
Digiboard Inc.	612-922-5604	BBS
Digiboard Inc.	612-922-8055	Tech Support
Digital Equip. Corp. (DEC)	508-493-5111	General
Digital Research	408-646-6464	Tech Support
Digitrend Systems Corp.	818-772-0190	General
Dilog	408-241-3192	General
Distr. Process Technology	407-830-5522	Tech Support
DPT (Dist. Process Tech.)	407-831-6432	BBS
DPT (Dist. Process Tech.)	407-260-3566	General
DPT (Dist. Process Tech.)	407-830-5522	Tech Support
DTK Computer	818-333-6548	BBS
DTK Computer	818-810-0098	General

DTK (Bios)	818-333-7533	Tech Support
Dysan Corp.	408-988-3472	Tech Support
Emulex Corp.	800-368-5393	General
Epson	213-539-9955	Tech Support
Everex Systems	510-226-9694	BBS
Everex Systems	510-498-4411	Tech Support
Fifth Generation Systems	504-295-3344	BBS
Fifth Generation Systems	800-873-4384	Tech Support: Mace, Fastback
Fujitsu America, Inc.	408-944-9899	BBS
Fujitsu America, Inc.	800-826-6112	Tech Support
Future Domain	714-253-0432	BBS
Future Domain	714-253-0400	Tech Support
Gazelle Systems	800-233-0383	Tech Support: Optune
GEnie Information Service	800-638-8369	BBS
Genoa	408-943-1231	BBS
Genoa	408-432-9090	Tech Support
Gibson Research	714-830-3300	BBS
Gibson Research	714-830-2200	Sales/Tech Support: Spinwrite
Goldstar	408-432-1331	Tech Support
GVC Technologies	201-579-2380	BBS
Hayes Public BBS	404-446-6336	BBS
Headland Technology	415-656-0503	BBS
Headland Technology	800-553-1850	Tech Support
Hercules Computer Tech.	415-540-0621	BBS
Hercules Computer Tech.	415-540-6000	Tech Support
Hewlett-Packard Co.	208-323-2551	Tech Support
Hyundai Electronics	800-234-3553	Tech Support
IBM PC Users Group	404-835-6600	BBS
IBM	800-426-2468	General
Intel	800-538-3373	Tech Support

Intel Support	503-645-6275	BBS
Irwin Magnetics	313-930-9380	BBS
Kalok Corp.	408-747-1315	General
Kaypro	619-481-3900	Tech Support
Keytronics	800-262-6006	Tech Support
Kodiak Technology	800-777-7704	Tech support
Kodiak Technology	408-452-0677	BBS
Kolod Research	708-291-1586	General
Kyocera Unison Inc.	415-848-6680	General
LAN (magazine)	415-267-7640	BBS
Laura Technologies	602-940-9800	General
Logitech	415-795-0408	BBS
Logitech	415-795-8100	Tech Support
Lotus Development	617-577-8500	General
Mace, Paul Software	714-240-7459	BBS
Mace, Paul Software	800-523-0258	Tech Support
Maxtor/Miniscribe	303-678-2222	BBS
Maxtor/Miniscribe	800-356-5333	Tech Support
McAffee Association	408-988-4004	BBS, virus protection software
Micro House	303-443-9957	BBS
Micro House	800-926-8299	General: DrivePro software
Microbotics	214-437-5330	Tech Support
Micronet	714-837-6033	General
Micronics	510-651-6837	BBS
Micropolis Corp.	818-709-3310	BBS
Micropolis Corp.	818-709-3325	Tech Support
Microscience Int'l	408-433-9898	Tech Support
Microsoft	206-637-9009	BBS
Microsoft	206-646-5104	Tech Support: DOS 5, person
Microsoft	206-646-5103	Tech Support: DOS 5, recordings

Microsoft	206-637-7099	Tech Support: Windows Application ?
Microsoft	206-637-7098	Tech Support: Windows Interface
Mitsubishi Inc.	213-324-3092	BBS
Mitsubishi Inc.	213-515-3993	Tech Support
Mountain Computer, Inc	408-438-2665	BBS
Mountain Computer, Inc	408-438-7897	Tech Support
Mouse Systems	415-683-0617	BBS
Mouse Systems	415-656-1117	Tech Support
Multi-Tech Systems	612-785-9875	BBS
Multisoft	800-283-6858	General: PCKwik
Mylex Corp.	510-683-4600	General
National Semiconductor	408-245-0671	BBS
NCR	316-688-8529	Tech Support
NEC	508-635-6328	BBS
NEC Information Systems	800-227-9001	General
New Media Graphics	508-663-7612	
Symantec/Norton	503-465-8410	Tech Support, Utilities
Symantec/Norton	503-465-8420	Tech Support, NDW/ND DOS
Symantec/Norton	503-465-8430	Tech Support, pcAnywhere
Symantec/Norton	503-465-8440	Tech Support, Mac Products
Symantec/Norton	503-465-8450	Tech Support, NAV/NC/NE/NBU
Symantec/Norton	503-465-8484	Tech Support, NNA/NAV NLM
Symantec	503-465-8600	Tech Support, Q&A

Symantec	503-465-8640	Tech Support, TimeLine/Win
Symantec	503-465-8650	Tech Support, TimeLine/DOS
Symantec	503-465-8660	Tech Support, OnTarget
Symantec	503-465-8670	Tech Support, Guideline/Win
Symantec	503-465-8680	Tech Support, Guideline/DOS
Symantec	503-465-8690	Tech Support, Guideline Maker
Symantec/Norton	503-465-8555	NAV Newsline (recorded info)
Symantec/Norton	503-465-8585	SAM Newsline
Symantec/Norton	800-554-4403	Automated FaxBack Service
Norton/Symantec	503-484-6669	BBS 9600
Norton/Symantec	503-484-6699	BBS 2400
Symantec/Norton	800-441-7234	Toll-free Customer Service
Symantec/Norton	503-334-6034	Customer Service
Novell CompuServ BBS, Go NetWire		
Novell	800-638-9273	Tech Support
Okidata	800-283-5474	BBS
Okidata	609-235-2600	Tech Support
Olivetti Office USA	201-526-8200	General
OMTI/Scientific Micro	408-954-1633	Tech Support
Ontrack Computer Systems	612-937-0860	BBS
Ontrack Computer Systems	800-872-2599	Data Recovery
Ontrack Computer Systems	800-752-1333	Sales: Disk Manager, Dosutils

Ontrack Computer Systems	612-937-2121	Tech Support
Orchid Technology	510-683-0327	BBS
Orchid Technology	510-683-0323	Tech Support
Packard Bell	818-773-7207	BBS
Packard Bell	800-733-4411	Tech Support
Panasonic Communication Systems	201-863-7845	BBS
Paradise	415-968-1834	BBS
Paradise	800-832-4778	Tech Support
Perceptive Solutions	214-954-1856	BBS
Perceptive Solutions	800-486-3278	General
Perstore	602-894-4605	BBS
Perstore	602-894-4601	Tech Support
Phoenix (Bios)	617-551-4000	Tech Support
PKWare (PKZip)	414-354-8670	BBS
Plus Development	408-434-1664	BBS
Plus Development	800-826-8022	Tech Support in California
Plus Development	900-740-4433	Tech Support out of California
Priam Systems	408-434-1646	BBS
Priam Systems	408-954-8680	Tech Support
Prime Solutions	619-272-9240	BBS
Prime Solutions	800-847-5000	Tech Support: Disk Technician
Procom	800-800-8600	General: Host Adapters
ProComm Support	314-474-8477	BBS: PCPlus Communications
Procomp USA	216-234-6387	General: Novell DCBs
QMS	205-633-3632	BBS
QMS	205-633-4500	Tech Support
Quantum	408-434-1664	BBS
Quantum	408-894-4000	General

Quarterdeck Office Systems	213-396-3904	BBS
Quarterdeck Office Systems	213-392-9851	Tech Support: Manifest, DeskView
Rancho Technology	714-987-3966	Tech Support
Ricoh Corp.	201-882-2000	General
Rodime Inc.	407-997-0774	General
Samsung Information Systems	408-434-5684	BBS
Samsung Information Systems	800-446-0262	Tech Support
Santa Cruz Operation (SCO)	800-347-4381	Tech Support
Seagate Technology	408-438-8771	BBS USA
Seagate Technology	44-628-478011	BBS UK
Seagate Technology	49-89-140-9331	BBS Germany
Seagate Technology	65-292-6973	BBS Singapore
Seagate Technology	61-2-756-2359	BBS Australia
Seagate Technology	408-438-6550	General, Corporate
Seagate Technology	408-438-8222	Tech Support, SeaFONE
Seagate Technology	408-438-8137	Tech Support Fax
Seagate Technology	408-438-2620	Automated SeaFAX System
Seagate Technology	408-438-8111	Sales, Telemarketing
Seagate Technology	800-468-3472	Customer Service (warranty/repair)
Sharp Electronics	404-962-1788	BBS
Shugart	714-770-1100	Tech Support
Silicon Valley Computers	415-967-8081	BBS
Silicon Valley Computers	415-967-1100	General
Softlogic Solutions	800-272-9900	Tech Support: Disk Optimize
Sony Corp.	408-432-0190	General: Drives

Stac Electronics	619-431-5956	BBS: Stacker
Storage Dimensions	408-395-2688	Tech Support: Speedstor
Sumo Systems	408-453-5744	General
Sun Microsystems	800-USA-4SUN	Tech Support
Syquest	415-226-4000	For ST02 V3.1
Tandon Corp.	805-523-0340	General
Tandy Corp.	817-390-3011	General
Tandy Corp.	817-878-6875	Tech Support
Tatung Co. of America	213-979-7055	Tech Support
Teac America, Inc.	213-726-0303	Tech Support
Tech Data	813-538-7090	BBS
Tech Data	800-553-7977	Tech Support
Telebit Corp.	408-745-3803	BBS
Telebit Corp.	800-835-3248	Tech Support
Telix Support	416-439-9399	BBS
Texas Instruments	512-250-6112	BBS
Texas Instruments	512-250-7407	Tech Support
TOPS Support	415-769-8874	BBS
Toshiba America	714-837-4408	BBS
Toshiba America	800-999-4273	Tech Support
Trantor Systems	510-656-5159	BBS
Trantor Systems	510-770-1400	General
Trident	415-691-1016	BBS
Trident	415-691-9211	Tech Support
Ultrastor	714-581-4100	General
Ultrastor	415-623-8955	Tech Support
USNO Time of Day	202-653-0351	BBS
U.S.Robotics	708-982-5092	BBS
Ven Tel	408-922-0988	BBS
Video Seven	(now Headland Tech.)	
Western Digital	714-753-1234	BBS
Western Digital	800-832-4778	Tech Support
WordPerfect Corp.	801-225-4414	BBS
WordPerfect Corp.	800-541-5096	Tech Support
Wyse Technology	408-922-4400	BBS

Wyse Technology	408-435-2770	Tech Support
Xebex	702-883-4000	General
Xerox Computer Serv.	213-306-4000	General
XTree	805-546-9150	BBS
Y-E Data	714-898-3677	General (C.Itoh, drive support)
Zenith Data Systems	800-888-3058	BBS
Zsoft	404-427-1045	BBS
ZyXEL	714-693-0762	BBS

References

Bush, V. (1945). As we may think. *Atlantic Monthly* 176 (July), 101–108.

Fairchild, K., Meredith, G., and Wexelblat, A. (1988). The tourist artificial reality. *Proceedings of ACM CHI '89 Conference on Human Factors in Computing Systems,* 299–304.

Fisher, S. (1994). *Multimedia Authoring.* Boston: AP PROFESSIONAL.

Fisher, S. (1995). *Creating Interactive CD-ROM for Windows and Macintosh.* Boston: AP PROFESSIONAL.

Furnas, G.W. (1986). Generalized fisheye views. *Proceedings of ACM CHI '89 Conference on Human Factors in Computing Systems,* 16–23.

Haynes, C. (1994). *Paperless Publishing*. New York: Windcrest/McGraw-Hill.

Laurel, B., Oren, T., and Don, A. (1989). Issues in multimedia interface design: media integration and interface agents. *Proceedings of ACM CHI '90 Conference on Human Factors in Computing Systems,* 133–139.

Leo, J. (1995). Decadence, the corporate way. *U.S. News and World Report* (January), 122–124.

National Writers Union. (1995). *Recommended Principles for Contracts Covering Online Book Publishing.* New York: NWU Press.

Nielsen, J. (1990). *Hypertext and Hypermedia*. Boston: AP PROFESSIONAL.

Purves, A.C., Quattrini, A.J., and Sullivan, C.I. (1995). *Creating the Writing Portfolio.* Chicago: NTC Publishing Group.

Rico, G.L. (1983). *Writing the Natural Way*. Los Angeles: J.P. Tarcher, Inc.

Trigg, R.H. (1988). Guided tours and tabletops: tools for communicating in a hypertext environment. *Proceedings of ACM CSCW '88 Conference on Computer-Supported Cooperative Work,* 216–226.

Trigg, R.H. and Irish, P.M. (1987). Hypertext habitats: experiences of writers in NoteCards. *ACM Hypertext '87 Proceedings,* 89–108.

Wimberley, D. and Samsel, J. (1995). *Interactive Writer's Handbook.* Los Angeles: The Carronade Group.

Index

ABOUT THE CD-ROM

Most of the programs included on this CD-ROM are referred to in the book and have been provided for your convenience. If you have difficulty running any of these programs, please contact the company that produced it for assistance.

Contents

PC Partition

dostxt directory	DOS applications and text
labels subdirectory	
agents.doc	Literary agents' mailing labels (Word 1.1 document)
agents.txt	Text version of the literary agents' mailing labels
russwolf subdirectory	Sample Writer's Dream application (dream.exe)
writepro subdirectory	Demo of WritePro Creative Tool
ezines directory	
mcimail.doc	List of MCI magazine addresses (BBSes)
grammar directory	Sample multimedia ToolBook application (Grammar Made Easy)
grameasy subdirectory	
runtime subdirectory	
html_eds directory	HTML editor demos
hotmetal subdirectory	Demo of HoTMeTaL editor
html_np subdirectory	Demo of HTML Notepad editor
webwiz subdirectory	Demo of WebWiz HTML editor
mmdemo directory	Multimedia software demos
catwin subdirectory	Demo of Catalog on Disk for Windows (*Note:* If the install program sets up an empty group in the Program Manager, the program can be run by double-clicking on the .cxt files within File Manager.)
macromedia subdirectory	Demos of various Macromedia programs
save_dis subdirectory	Save-disabled versions of Macromedia applications:
action subdirectory	Action! 3.0 for Windows
authorwr subdirectory	Authorware Professional for Windows
director subdirectory	Director 4.0 for Windows
macromdl subdirectory	MacroModel version 1.5
qmedia subdirectory	Q-Media demo
nscape directory	Netscape 2.0 page samples
htm subdirectory	Home page samples in Netscape 2.0 format
netguide	Netscape pages that contain links to resources on the Internet

shareapp directory	DOS demos of electronic publishing shareware
softlock subdirectory	
!ares.exe	Ares, a hypertext miniviewer
!dart.exe	Dart, a hypertext browser
!iris.exe	Iris, a virtual book processor
!epub.exe	Epub, an electronic publishing press kit
storybrd directory	
interact.wpd	Sample interactive storyboard module (WordPerfect document)
toolbook directory	Multimedia ToolBook applications
mmw3 subdirectory	Multimedia World Wide Web: play ToolBook applications on the Web
vrxplore subdirectory	VRXplore: create and play virtual reality files on the Web
w3kiosk subdirectory	World Wide Web Kiosk: play kiosk applications on the Web
vrml_ed1 directory	VRML software demos
hsbuild1 subdirectory	Home Space Builder (vhsb.exe)
hsbuild2 subdirectory	Home Space Builder demo, church interior (vhsbview.exe)
vrml_ed2 directory	VRML software demos
virtuswt subdirectory	Virtus WalkThrough Pro demo (vprosd.exe)
voyager subdirectory	Virtus Voyager VRML browser demo (*Note:* This is a 32-bit application; Windows 3.x users will need to install the Winsock utility—found in the win32s subdirectory—in order to run the program.)

Mac Partition

Addresses folder	
Agents	Literary agents' mailing labels (Word document)
MCIMAIL	List of MCI magazine addresses (BBSes)
HTML Editors folder	Demos of HTML editors
Storyboard Sample folder	
Interact	Sample interactive storyboard module (Word document)
Virtual Walk-Through folder	VRML software demos
Player 1.0.1 Installer	Installation application for Virtus Player, a freeware utility for 3D design publication (Macs and Power Macs)
Pro 2.0.1 68k Demo	Virtus WalkThrough Pro demo for Mac 68K
voyager_a145_68k	Virtus Voyager browser for Mac 68K

System Requirements

Windows 3.1 or higher, or a Macintosh with System 7.0 or higher running on at least a 68020 processor or Power Macintosh. All systems should have at least 4 MB or RAM (preferably 8). Sound card and multimedia functionality required for most programs.